W9-APL-907

华裔大学生一年级中文教材

First-Year Mandarin for Heritage Speakers

简繁体对照

我和中國

ME AND CHINA

贺谦 Qian He　吴燕娜 Yenna Wu　杨颖 Ying Petersen

ME AND CHINA, FIRST EDITION

Published by McGraw-Hill, an imprint of The McGraw-Hill Companies, Inc., 1221 Avenue of the Americas, New York, NY 10020. Copyright © 2008 McGraw-Hill Companies, Inc. and Foreign Language Teaching and Research Press.

All rights reserved. No part of this publication may be reproduced or distributed in any form or by any means, or stored in a database or retrieval system, without the prior written consent of the publisher, including, but not limited to, in any network or other electronic storage or transmission, or broadcast for distance learning.

The production of these materials was funded by a grant from the University of California Consortium for Language Learning & Teaching.

ISBN 0-07-338578-6 Me and China
ISBN 0-07-333252-6 Me and China Student Audio CDs

McGraw-Hill:
Editor in Chief: Emily Barrosse
Publisher: William R. Glass
Executive Marketing Manager: Nick Agnew
Sponsoring Editor: Katherine K. Crouch

FLTRP:
Publisher: Li Pengyi
Editor in Chief: Cai Jianfeng
Editorial Director: Peng Donglin
Project Editor: Guan Lei
Cover Designer: Zhang Feng, Cai Ying

Boston Burr Ridge, IL Dubuque, IA Madison, WI New York San Francisco
St. Louis Bangkok Bogotá Caracas Kuala Lumpur Lisbon
London Madrid Mexico City Milan Montreal New Delhi
Santiago Seoul Singapore Sydney Taipei Toronto

www.mhhe.com
Printed in China

编写说明

近年来，在美国各大学选修中文课的学生中，具有普通话背景的越来越多。把他们与没有普通话背景的学生分班教学，编写适合他们特点的中文教材，这在中文教学界已经形成共识。《我和中国》就是顺应这种形势，为听说能力已经达到了能进行一般日常交流的水平，但读写能力仍处在起点的大学生编写的一套一年级中文教材。

在编写教材前，我们曾以问卷和个别面谈的形式对该类学生的需求和愿望做了大量的调查。结果表明，这类学生学习中文有以下四个目的：

1. 希望能用中文得体地表达自己的思想；

2. 有寻根的愿望；

3. 打算到中国去看看；

4. 以前去中国时曾产生过一些困惑和疑问，希望通过学习中文寻找到答案。

根据学生的这些要求和愿望，我们设计编写了这套《我和中国》。

教材内容

1.《我和中国》共分四个部分：导言、第一单元、第二单元和第三单元。

导言包括汉语拼音、相关的拼写规则以及汉语拼音表；汉字的偏旁部首；汉字的笔画笔顺；繁体字和简体字。

第一单元有五课，课文的内容主要是围绕学生自己以及他们身边的事，如介绍自己、介绍家庭、介绍祖父母和大学生活等。

第二单元有五课，课文的内容主要是一些关于中国文化方面的知识，如中国的人口、面积、民族、汉字和百家姓等。

第三单元有六课，课文的内容主要是中国人的行为文化以及与这些行为有关的文化心理，如中国人“吃”的文化、中国人怎么打招呼、中国人的称谓以及中国人的谦虚等。

2. 每一课都包括课文、生词表、汉字的笔画笔顺（从第一课到第十课）、语法简注，还有阅读和练习。全书都是简体字和繁体字对照的。

3. 全书的最后附有按字母顺序排列的汉英对照的生词索引。

4. 每课简体和繁体相同的生字，我们都给出了笔画和笔顺，而简体和繁体不同的字以及一些比较难的字则都标出了书写顺序的序号。

5. 教材配有光盘，有课文、生词和阅读的录音。

新的尝试

1. 语言、文化融为一体

《我和中国》共有16篇课文和16篇阅读。在每一篇课文和阅读里，我们不但为学生提供新的语法现象和词汇，而且把中国文化融入其中。这就是说，每一篇课文和阅读都是语言和文化的融合体。语言和文化密不可分。语言只有融入了文化内涵，才显得更有价值、更有生命力。特别是对这些有普通话背景的学生来说，中国文化是他们成长和赖以生存的极其重要的文化心理支撑点。因此，只有在他们学习的语言中注入了中国文化的乳汁，才能从深层触动他们，启发和调动他们的学习热忱。

2. 一切以学生为中心

从每一课题目的确立到课文内容的编写，以及练习项目、练习形式的设计等，我们都始终把学生的需求、愿望和兴趣放在首位考虑。现在教材所选的题目和内容基本上是我们多次征求学生的意见，然后将这些意见进行集中、筛选、归类的结果。例如，课文内容是以这类学生的缩影——“宋宜凡”为中心，逐渐扩大到其家庭、学校，然后再扩大到中国社会，最后深入到中国人的行为以及与这些行为有关的文化心理基础。这一切都是把学生作为中心，围绕着学生的过去、现在和将来而进行的。

3. 开放性

在设计教材的结构特别是练习形式的时候，我们非常注重教材的开放性。老师在引导学生学习教材现有内容的基础上，还可以根据自己的实际情况进行扩展和发挥。以第一课为例，课文的内容主要是宋宜凡与母亲围绕起床和宜凡到底算中国人还是算美国人的对话，阅读是一篇“自我介绍”，练习部分扩展到如何在各种不同的场合介绍自己和他人。这就为老师提供了发挥的空间和可能。

4. 参与性

《我和中国》每一课后面都有十一二项练习。其中有传统的翻译、填空、重组、改错、改写等，同时也有一些新的尝试，如课上活动、课外活动、上网查资料等。如果说传统的练习方式是帮助学生学习语言本身的话，那么，我们设计的课上活动和课外活动则给学生提供了参与的机会，如编写“家谱”、设计“学生俱乐部广告”、介绍自己“记汉字的办法”、查自己的姓在《百家姓》中的排名，等等。为了完成这些活动，学生要与家人、朋友联系，要上网查资料，要进行采访，要与他人合作。学生的语言水平在参与中得到提高，学习中文的主动性在参与中得到增强，学习的潜力在参与中逐渐被发掘出来。

5. 力求语言的真实性

本教材力求使用真实的语言，而避免使用“造句”式的语言。这样做虽然在一定程度上增加了课文的难度，但这对具有普通话背景的学生却是极好的挑战。另外，我们的课文大部分采用的是“叙述体”而不是“对话体”，这也是由于具有普通话背景的学生已经不需要学习在特定环境下如何与他人进行交流。

6. **有针对性的语法简注**

具有普通话背景的学生已经具备了进行一般日常交流的听说能力。这就是说，他们在选学中文课以前已经从父母那里获得了中文语法结构的一些基本框架。因此我们没有像为"母语为非汉语"的学生编写教材那样，把语法点从简到难，逐条加以详细解释，而是根据我们多年的教学经验，把他们容易犯的语法错误以及用得不规范的部分挑选出来，简单地加以说明。同时，语法点注释的先后顺序也是随课文内容而定的，即先出现的先注释，后出现的就后注释。语法注释的内容和范围也是就语法点出现的那一课而论的。

编写人员

贺谦老师，来自美国加州大学圣迭戈分校，负责本书的策划、设计和组织工作，撰写了课文、阅读和语音部分，参与了语法和练习的编写。

吴燕娜教授，来自美国加州大学里弗赛德分校，负责撰写导言和生词表，编写了语法简注、汉字的笔画笔顺和练习。

杨颖老师，来自美国加州大学伊耳文分校，负责编写练习。

特别鸣谢

从教材的酝酿到诞生，美国加州大学圣迭戈分校的胡张苹老师、美国加州大学戴维斯分校的储诚志教授在各个方面都给予了无微不至的关怀、帮助和支持。

教材的顾问，北京语言大学的刘珣教授和崔永华教授、美国俄亥俄州立大学的吴伟克（Galal Walker）教授，都在该教材的整体设计思想、编写原则以及具体内容安排等重大问题上给予了很多方向性的指导和帮助。

美国加州大学圣迭戈分校的几个在校博士生、硕士研究生和加州大学里弗赛德分校的电脑工作者James Lin也为该教材做了大量的工作。

另外，美国加州大学洛杉矶分校的Michelle Fu老师和加州大学伯克利分校的刘莉老师曾参与过教材编写初期的讨论活动。

在此我们一一表示感谢。

编者 贺谦

編寫説明

近年來,在美國各大學選修中文課的學生中,具有普通話背景的越來越多。把他們與沒有普通話背景的學生分班教學，編寫適合他們特點的中文教材，這在中文教學界已經形成共識。《我和中國》就是順應這種形勢，爲聽説能力已經達到了能進行一般日常交流的水平，但讀寫能力仍處在起點的大學生編寫的一套一年級中文教材。

在編寫教材前，我們曾以問卷和個别面談的形式對該類學生的需求和願望做了大量的調查。結果表明，這類學生學習中文有以下四個目的：

1. 希望能用中文得體地表達自己的思想；
2. 有尋根的願望；
3. 打算到中國去看看；
4. 以前去中國時曾産生過一些困惑和疑問，希望通過學習中文尋找到答案。

根據學生的這些要求和願望，我們設計編寫了這套《我和中國》。

教材内容

1.《我和中國》共分四個部分：導言、第一單元、第二單元和第三單元。

導言包括漢語拼音、相關的拼寫規則以及漢語拼音表；漢字的偏旁部首；漢字的筆畫筆順；繁體字和簡體字。

第一單元有五課，課文的内容主要是圍繞學生自己以及他們身邊的事，如介紹自己、介紹家庭、介紹祖父母和大學生活等。

第二單元有五課，課文的内容主要是一些關於中國文化方面的知識，如中國的人口、面積、民族、漢字和百家姓等。

第三單元有六課，課文的内容主要是中國人的行爲文化以及與這些行爲有關的文化心理，如中國人“吃”的文化、中國人怎麽打招呼、中國人的稱謂以及中國人的謙虛等。

2. 每一課都包括課文、生詞表、漢字的筆畫筆順（從第一課到第十課）、語法簡注，還有閱讀和練習。全書都是簡體字和繁體字對照的。

3. 全書的最後附有按字母順序排列的漢英對照的生詞索引。

4. 每課簡體和繁體相同的生字，我們都給出了筆畫和筆順，而簡體和繁體不同的字以及一些比較難的字則都標出了書寫順序的序號。

5. 教材配有光盤，有課文、生詞和閱讀的録音。

新的嘗試

1. 語言、文化融爲一體

《我和中國》共有16篇課文和16篇閱讀。在每一篇課文和閱讀裏，我們不但爲學生提供新的語法現象和詞彙，而且把中國文化融入其中。這就是説，每一篇課文和閱讀都是語言和文化的融合體。語言和文化密不可分。語言只有融入了文化内涵，才顯得更有價值、更有生命力。特别是對這些有普通話背景的學生來説，中國文化是他們成長和賴以生存的極其重要的文化心理支撑點。因此，只有在他們學習的語言中注入了中國文化的乳汁，才能從深層觸動他們，啓發和調動他們的學習熱忱。

2. 一切以學生爲中心

從每一課題目的確立到課文内容的編寫，以及練習項目、練習形式的設計等，我們都始終把學生的需求、願望和興趣放在首位考慮。現在教材所選的題目和内容基本上是我們多次徵求學生的意見，然後將這些意見進行集中、篩選、歸類的結果。例如，課文内容是以這類學生的縮影——“宋宜凡”爲中心，逐漸擴大到其家庭、學校，然後再擴大到中國社會，最後深入到中國人的行爲以及與這些行爲有關的文化心理基礎。這一切都是把學生作爲中心，圍繞着學生的過去、現在和將來而進行的。

3. 開放性

在設計教材的結構特别是練習形式的時候，我們非常注重教材的開放性。老師在引導學生學習教材現有内容的基礎上，還可以根據自己的實際情況進行擴展和發揮。以第一課爲例，課文的内容主要是宋宜凡與母親圍繞起床和宜凡到底算中國人還是算美國人的對話，閱讀是一篇“自我介紹”，練習部分擴展到如何在各種不同的場合介紹自己和他人。這就爲老師提供了發揮的空間和可能。

4. 參與性

《我和中國》每一課後面都有十一二項練習。其中有傳統的翻譯、填空、重組、改錯、改寫等，同時也有一些新的嘗試，如課上活動、課外活動、上網查資料等。如果説傳統的練習方式是幫助學生學習語言本身的話，那麽，我們設計的課上活動和課外活動則給學生提供了參與的機會，如編寫“家譜”、設計“學生俱樂部廣告”、介紹自己“記漢字的辦法”、查自己的姓在《百家姓》中的排名，等等。爲了完成這些活動，學生要與家人、朋友聯繫，要上網查資料，要進行采訪，要與他人合作。學生的語言水平在參與中得到提高，學習中文的主動性在參與中得到增强，學習的潛力在參與中逐漸被發掘出來。

5. 力求語言的真實性

本教材力求使用真實的語言，而避免使用“造句”式的語言。這樣做雖然在一定程度上增加了課文的難度，但這對具有普通話背景的學生却是極好的挑戰。另外，我們的課文大部分采用的是“叙述體”而不是“對話體”，這也是由於具有普通話背景的學生已經不需要學習在特定環境下如何與他人進行交流。

6. 有針對性的語法簡注

具有普通話背景的學生已經具備了進行一般日常交流的聽説能力。這就是説，他們在選學中文課以前已經從父母那裏獲得了中文語法結構的一些基本框架。因此我們没有像爲“母語爲非漢語”的學生編寫教材那樣，把語法點從簡到難，逐條加以詳細解釋，而是根據我們多年的教學經驗，把他們容易犯的語法錯誤以及用得不規範的部分挑選出來，簡單地加以説明。同時，語法點注釋的先後順序也是隨課文内容而定的，即先出現的先注釋，後出現的就後注釋。語法注釋的内容和範圍也是就語法點出現的那一課而論的。

編寫人員

賀巍老師，來自美國加州大學聖達戈分校，負責本書的策劃、設計和組織工作，撰寫了課文、閱讀和語音部分，參與了語法和練習的編寫。

吴燕娜教授，來自美國加州大學里弗賽德分校，負責撰寫導言和生詞表，編寫了語法簡注、漢字的筆畫筆順和練習。

楊穎老師，來自美國加州大學伊耳文分校，負責編寫練習。

特別鳴謝

從教材的醞釀到誕生，美國加州大學聖達戈分校的胡張蘋老師、美國加州大學戴維斯分校的儲誠志教授在各個方面都給予了無微不至的關懷、幫助和支持。

教材的顧問，北京語言大學的劉珣教授和崔永華教授、美國俄亥俄州立大學的吴偉克（Galal Walker）教授，都在該教材的整體設計思想、編寫原則以及具體内容安排等重大問題上給予了很多方向性的指導和幫助。

美國加州大學聖達戈分校的幾個在校博士生、碩士研究生和加州大學里弗賽德分校的電腦工作者James Lin也爲該教材做了大量的工作。

另外，美國加州大學洛杉磯分校的Michelle Fu老師和加州大學伯克利分校的劉莉老師曾參與過教材編寫初期的討論活動。

在此我們一一表示感謝。

編者 賀巍

Preface

In recent years, more and more American university students who choose to study Chinese have already had some Mandarin background. It is agreed in Chinese-teaching circles that students with Mandarin background should be taught separately from those otherwise, and a textbook suitable for the former group should be compiled accordingly. *Me and China* is designed to meet this purpose; it is a first-year Chinese textbook for the university students who have listening and speaking skills to conduct everyday conversations in Mandarin while the reading and writing ability is still at the beginning level.

Before compiling this textbook, we had made a lot of investigations on the students' demands and expectations in the form of questionnaires and individual interviews. According to our investigations, they study Chinese mainly for four purposes,

1. To appropriately express their ideas in Chinese.
2. To seek their Chinese roots.
3. To visit China.
4. To find answers to questions and confusions during their previous visit to China through studying Chinese.

According to their demands and expectations, we compiled *Me and China.*

Contents

1. The textbook consists of four parts, Introduction, Unit One, Unit Two and Unit Three.

The Introduction consists of Pinyin, relevant Pinyin spelling rules and a Pinyin Chart, basic components and radicals of Chinese characters, the strokes and stroke-order of Chinese characters, the comparison between traditional and simplified characters.

Unit One has five lessons, which are mostly focused on the students themselves and their life, such as introducing oneself, one's family, one's grandparents and university life.

Unit Two also has five lessons, which mostly concern Chinese culture, such as Chinese population, surface area, ethnic groups, Chinese characters and family names.

Unit Three has six lessons, regarding Chinese behavioral culture and related cultural psychology, such as the gastronomic culture, how the Chinese address one another, terms of address used by Chinese people, and Chinese modesty, etc.

2. Each lesson includes a text, a vocabulary, strokes and stroke-order of Chinese characters (from Lesson 1 to Lesson 10), grammar notes, a reading passage and exercises. This textbook comes in both traditional and simplified characters.

3. At the end of the textbook, there is a Chinese-English vocabulary index in alphabetical order.

4. We show the strokes and stroke-order for the new words whose traditional form and simplified form are the same. The new words whose traditional and simplified forms are different and certain difficult characters are marked with the serial numbers of writing order.

5. There is a CD attached to the book, including the texts, new words and reading passages.

New Attempts

1. Harmonious blend of language and culture

There are sixteen texts and reading passages in *Me and China*. In every text and reading passage, we not only provide new grammar points and a vocabulary, but also blend Chinese culture into them. That is to say, the text and reading passage are the blend of language and culture. Language and culture is inseparable. Language is of more value and vitality only if blended with cultural connotation. Especially to those students with Mandarin background, Chinese culture is an important cultural and psychological basis. The textbook can deeply touch those students with Mandarin background and arouse their study enthusiasm if we merge culture into the language they study.

2. Student-centered

From deciding on the title of every text to designing the contents and exercises, we give priority to the student's interest, needs and expectation. Therefore, the topics and contents of this textbook are the final results of consulting, selecting and grouping the opinions of the students. For example, the text takes Song Yifan—a miniature of these students as the center, then gradually expands to her family, her school, the society of China, and then deepens to the behaviors of Chinese people and the psychology of these behaviors. All of these focus on the students and their past, present and future.

3. Open teaching

When designing the structure of this textbook and the exercises, we attach great importance to the feature of open teaching. The teacher can expand the content of the lesson according to actual needs on the basis of instructing students to study the basic content. For example, the first lesson is a dialog between Song Yifan and her mother about "getting up" and "whether on earth Song Yifan is American or Chinese". The reading passage is a self-introduction. The exercises are how to introduce oneself and others in different circumstances. All of these make possibility and room for the teacher to develop.

4. Involvement

For every lesson, we design eleven or twelve exercises. There are traditional exercises such as translation, filling in blanks, word order, correcting mistakes and rewriting, as well as some new attempts, such as in-class activity, after-class activity and going online, etc. The traditional exercises help students study language and the in-class or after-class activities provide opportunities for students to be actively involved, such as drawing the family tree, designing an advertisement of the students' club, introducing the methods to memorize Chinese characters, and finding one's own family name in the *Book of China's Family Names*. In order to participate in these activities, students are supposed to contact their family and friends, go online for information, interview someone, and cooperate with others. The students' language will be improved during participation and their initiation of studying Chinese will be enhanced and their potential of study will be probed gradually.

5. Searching for authentic Chinese

In the textbook, we use authentic Chinese and avoid strained Chinese. To some extent, this increases the difficulty of compilation. But this is a good challenge for the students with Mandarin background. Moreover, the language of some texts is narrative rather than dialogic because we believe that there is no need for the students with Mandarin background to learn how to communicate with others in specific everyday situations.

6. Grammar notes tailored to students' needs

The students with Mandarin background have already acquired certain ability of listening and speaking in everyday conversations. That is to say, they have already learnt basic structures of Chinese grammar from their parents. Therefore, we do not explain grammatical points from easy ones to difficult ones, as in textbooks designed for students whose native language is not Chinese. Instead, based on our long-time teaching experiences, we single out and briefly explain grammatical mistakes that these students are liable to make as well as the non-standard expressions in their Chinese language. The sequence of grammatical points is determined by the contents of the texts, that is, the grammatical points which appear earlier are first explained, and those that appear later are later explained. The explanations of grammatical points are limited to their usage in the respective lessons.

The Editors

Qian He (UCSD) planned and designed this book, and organized the compilation. She wrote texts, reading passages and the introduction to phonetics. She also took part in the compilation of grammar and exercises.

Yenna Wu (UCR) wrote the introduction, vocabulary, grammar notes, stroke-order of Chinese characters and exercises.

Ying Petersen (UCI) compiled the exercises.

Acknowledgements

From the preparation to the birth of this book, Ping Chang Hu of UCSD and Chengzhi Chu of UC Davis had given us invaluable support and help.

The consultants, Professor Xun Liu and Professor Yonghua Cui of Beijing Language and Culture University, and Galal Walker of the Ohio State University, had given support and help in such important issues as the whole designing concept, the compilation principles and the contents.

Some current graduate students in UCSD and computer workers James Lin in UCR have done a lot of work for the textbook.

Michelle Fu in UCLA and Li Liu in UC Berkeley took part in the discussion over this book's compilation in the early stage.

We are very grateful to all these people for their work.

Compiler Qian He

目录 / 目錄
Table of Contents

第三单元 / 第三單元 **走进中国 / 走進中國**
Unit Three Approaching China

语法术语缩写表
ABBREVIATIONS OF GRAMMATICAL TERMS
語法術語縮寫表

adj	adjective
adv	adverb
aux	auxiliary verb
conj	conjunction
prep	preposition
idiom	idiom
int	interjection
m	measure word
n	noun
nu	number
obj	object
particle	particle
pn	proper noun
pron	pronoun
pref	prefix
subj	subject
suf	suffix
v	verb
vc	verb-complement
vo	verb-object

导言 / 導言
Introduction

I. Pinyin

A Chinese syllable is usually made up of three parts, an initial, a final and a tone. For example, the syllable "hàn" consists of the initial "h", the final "an" and the fourth tone " ˋ ".

1. Initials

There are a total of twenty-one initials in Chinese Pinyin.

Labial	b	p	m	f
Blade-alveolar	d	t	n	l
Velar	g	k	h	
Coronal	j	q	x	
Blade-palatal	zh	ch	sh	r
Dental	z	c	s	

Of the twenty-one initials, six pairs are distinguished by whether they are aspirated or unaspirated.

Unaspirated—Aspirated	**Example**
b—p	ba—pa
d—t	de—te
g—k	ge—ke
j—q	ji—qi
z—c	ze—ce
zh—ch	zhe—che

Three other pairs are distinguished by whether they are twisting or flat tongue.

Retroflex—Unretroflex	**Example**
zh—z	zhi—zi
ch—c	chi—ci
sh—s	shi—si

2. Finals

There are thirty-six finals in Chinese Pinyin.

	i	u	ü
a	ia	ua	
o		uo	
e(ê)	ie		üe
ai		uai	
ei		uei	
ao	iao		
ou	iou		
an	ian	uan	üan

拼音与注音符号对照表 / 拼音與注音符號對照表

Table of the Pinyin and Phonetic Notation

		ㄚ	ㄛ	ㄜ	ㄭ	ㄦ	ㄞ	ㄟ	ㄠ	ㄡ	ㄢ	ㄣ	ㄤ	ㄥ	ㄨㄥ
		a	o	e	-i	er	ai	ei	ao	ou	an	en	ang	eng	ong
						er									
ㄅ	b	ba	bo				bai	bei	bao		ban	ben	bang	beng	
ㄆ	p	pa	po				pai	pei	pao	pou	pan	pen	pang	peng	
ㄇ	m	ma	mo	me			mai	mei	mao	mou	man	men	mang	meng	
ㄈ	f	fa	fo					fei		fou	fan	fen	fang	feng	
ㄉ	d	da		de			dai	dei	dao	dou	dan	den	dang	deng	dong
ㄊ	t	ta		te			tai		tao	tou	tan		tang	teng	tong
ㄋ	n	na		ne			nai	nei	nao	nou	nan	nen	nang	neng	nong
ㄌ	l	la		le			lai	lei	lao	lou	lan		lang	leng	long
ㄗ	z	za		ze	zi		zai	zei	zao	zou	zan	zen	zang	zeng	zong
ㄘ	c	ca		ce	ci		cai		cao	cou	can	cen	cang	ceng	cong
ㄙ	s	sa		se	si		sai		sao	sou	san	sen	sang	seng	song
ㄓ	zh	zha		zhe	zhi		zhai	zhei	zhao	zhou	zhan	zhen	zhang	zheng	zhong
ㄔ	ch	cha		che	chi		chai		chao	chou	chan	chen	chang	cheng	chong
ㄕ	sh	sha		she	shi		shai	shei	shao	shou	shan	shen	shang	sheng	
ㄖ	r			re	ri				rao	rou	ran	ren	rang	reng	rong
ㄐ	j														
ㄑ	q														
ㄒ	x														
ㄍ	g	ga		ge			gai	gei	gao	gou	gan	gen	gang	geng	gong
ㄎ	k	ka		ke			kai	kei	kao	kou	kan	ken	kang	keng	kong
ㄏ	h	ha		he			hai	hei	hao	hou	han	hen	hang	heng	hong

		ㄧ	ㄧㄚ	ㄧㄝ	ㄧㄠ	ㄧㄡ	ㄧㄢ	ㄧㄣ	ㄧㄥ	ㄧㄤ	ㄩㄥ
		i	ia	ie	iao	iu	ian	in	ing	iang	iong
		yi	ya	ye	yao	you	yan	yin	ying	yang	yong
ㄅㄧ	b	bi		bie	biao		bian	bin	bing		
ㄆㄧ	p	pi		pie	piao		pian	pin	ping		
ㄇㄧ	m	mi		mie	miao	miu	mian	min	ming		
	f										
ㄉㄧ	d	di		die	diao	diu	dian		ding		
ㄊㄧ	t	ti		tie	tiao		tian		ting		
ㄋㄧ	n	ni		nie	niao	niu	nian	nin	ning	niang	
ㄌㄧ	l	li	lia	lie	liao	liu	lian	lin	ling	liang	
	z										
	c										
	s										
	zh										
	ch										
	sh										
	r										
ㄐㄧ	j	ji	jia	jie	jiao	jiu	jian	jin	jing	jiang	jiong
ㄑㄧ	q	qi	qia	qie	qiao	qiu	qian	qin	qing	qiang	qiong
ㄒㄧ	x	xi	xia	xie	xiao	xiu	xian	xin	xing	xiang	xiong
	g										
	k										
	h										

		ㄨ	ㄨㄚ	ㄨㄛ	ㄨㄞ	ㄨㄟ	ㄨㄢ	ㄨㄣ	ㄨㄤ	ㄨㄥ
		u	ua	uo	uai	ui	uan	un	uang	ueng
		wu	wa	wo	wai	wei	wan	wen	wang	weng
ㄅㄨ	b	bu								
ㄆㄨ	p	pu								
ㄇㄨ	m	mu								
ㄈㄨ	f	fu								
ㄉㄨ	d	du		duo		dui	duan	dun		
ㄊㄨ	t	tu		tuo		tui	tuan	tun		
ㄋㄨ	n	nu		nuo			nuan			
ㄌㄨ	l	lu		luo			luan	lun		
ㄗㄨ	z	zu		zuo		zui	zuan	zun		
ㄘㄨ	c	cu		cuo		cui	cuan	cun		
ㄙㄨ	s	su		suo		sui	suan	sun		
ㄓㄨ	zh	zhu	zhua	zhuo	zhuai	zhui	zhuan	zhun	zhuang	
ㄔㄨ	ch	chu	chua	chuo	chuai	chui	chuan	chun	chuang	
ㄕㄨ	sh	shu	shua	shuo	shuai	shui	shuan	shun	shuang	
ㄖㄨ	r	ru		ruo		rui	ruan	run		
	j									
	q									
	x									
ㄍㄨ	g	gu	gua	guo	guai	gui	guan	gun	guang	
ㄎㄨ	k	ku	kua	kuo	kuai	kui	kuan	kun	kuang	
ㄏㄨ	h	hu	hua	huo	huai	hui	huan	hun	huang	

	ㄩ	ㄩㄝ	ㄩㄢ	ㄩㄣ
	ü	üe	üan	ün
	yu	yue	yuan	yun
ㄋㄩ	nü	nüe		
ㄌㄩ	lü	lüe		
ㄐㄩ	ju	jue	juan	xun
ㄑㄩ	qu	que	quan	qun
ㄒㄩ	xu	xue	xuan	xun

en	in	uen	ün
ang	iang	uang	
eng	ing	ueng	
		ong	iong

And there is a special final "er" which is never used together with initials.

3. A Table of Pinyin

There are over four hundred meaningful syllables in Chinese. Together with the tones, they can make over twelve hundred syllables. Please refer to the Table of the Pinyin and Phonetic Notation (also the insert).

4. Four Tones

There are four tones in Chinese. The first tone shows as "ˉ", the second "ˊ", the third "ˇ" and the fourth "ˋ". Tones are used to differentiate meanings, which mean that if the tones are different, the meanings of syllables are different. Such as,

tāng 汤 soup
táng 糖 sugar
tǎng 躺 to lie down
tàng 烫 to scald

5. Neutral Tones

Apart from four basic tones, some syllables are pronounced short and weak, often losing the original tone. These syllables are called neutral tones. No symbol is used to represent neutral tone. Such as,

māma 妈妈 mother　　Máng ma? 忙吗？ Busy?
Xièxie. 谢谢。Thanks.　　Nǐ ne? 你呢？ How about you?
Lái le. 来了。 It's coming.　　Hǎo ba. 好吧。 OK!

6. Retroflex Final

There is also a retroflex final in some Chinese syllables. In written form, we usually add "r" at the end of the syllables. Such as,

liáotiānr 聊天儿 chat　　fànguǎnr 饭馆儿 restaurant　　huār 花儿 flower

7. Third-tone Sandhi

When a third tone is followed by another third tone, the first third tone is pronounced as a second tone. Such as,

Ní zǎo. 你早。Good morning.　　Ní hǎo. 你好。How are you?　　Wó hén hǎo. 我很好。I am fine.

When a third tone is before a first tone, second tone, fourth tone or other non-third tone, the third tone is pronounced as a half third tone. Such as,

hěn hēi 很黑 very dark　　nǐ lái 你来 come here　　wǒ huì 我会 I can do

8. Tone Sandhi of " 一 "

" 一 " is pronounced as a first tone, but when it is before a fourth tone, it is pronounced as a second tone. Such as,

yící 一次 once　　yíhuìr 一会儿 a little while　　yízài 一再 time and again

When " 一 " is before a first tone, second tone, or third tone, it is pronounced as a fourth tone. Such as,

yì tiān 一天 one day　　yì bēi 一杯 one glass of　　yìbān 一般 general
yìlián 一连 in succession　　yìzhí 一直 always　　yìpáng 一旁 one side
yìqǐ 一起 together　　yìzǎo 一早 early morning　　yìdiǎnr 一点儿 a little

9. Tone Sandhi of " 不 "

The basic tone of " 不 " is a fourth tone. If it is before a first tone, second tone or third tone, it is still pronounced as a fourth tone. Such as,

bù gāo 不高 not tall　　bù lái 不来 not come　　bù hǎo 不好 not good

But, " 不 " is pronounced as a second tone when it is before a fourth tone. Such as:

bú ài 不爱 not love　　bú qù 不去 not go　　bú zài 不在 not here

II. Basic Components and Radicals of Chinese Characters

The earliest Chinese language writings date back to the Shang Dynasty from around the 16th century BC to the 11th century BC. Most of the writings of that time were found on oracle bones—tortoise shells and cattle's shoulder blades used for divination purposes. Since its invention, the Chinese writing system has undergone many stages of change and development. What remains unchanged, however, is that each character is monosyllabic and uninflected. Unlike western scripts, Chinese characters are unique, graphic, and aesthetically appealing.

In modern Mandarin Chinese many characters are homonyms. While the largest Chinese dictionary contains over eighty thousand characters, most of them are archaic or variant forms no longer in use. Well-educated Chinese may know four or five thousand characters, yet orally fluent learners who have mastered about one thousand commonly-used characters, or even just five hundred of the highest-frequency characters, would already be able to read a newspaper with the aid of a dictionary.

Only an extremely small percentage of Chinese characters can be considered pictographs or ideographs. Pictographs such as 日 (rì, sun), 月 (yuè, moon), and 木 (mù, wood) used to be written like pictures that resemble the sun, the moon, and wood. Ideographs such as 上 (shàng, above) and 下 (xià, below) clearly indicate being "above" or "below" by their very forms.

Nonetheless, the overwhelming majority of Chinese characters are complex characters consisting of both a phonetic element that suggests the real or approximate pronunciation and a semantic element that hints at the meaning. The semantic elements are commonly referred to as radicals and sometimes as classifiers or index glyphs, which classify characters into different groups. The phonetic elements and semantic elements are usually existing characters or derived from characters already in existence. For example, the character 姑 (gū, aunt) is made up of the semantic element 女 (nǚ, woman), which hints the meaning (classified under the category of "woman"), and the phonetic element 古 (gǔ, ancient), which suggests the pronunciation. Both 女 and 古 are characters already in existence. The character 妈 (mā, mother) consists of the same semantic element 女 (nǚ, woman) and the phonetic element 马 (mǎ, horse). The character 马 (mǎ, horse) combines with a smaller version of 口 (kǒu, mouth), which serves as the semantic element, to form the question particle 吗 (ma). The character 金 (jīn, metal or gold), serving as the semantic element, combines with the character 令 (lìng, order or command) to form a new character 铃 (líng, bell). Since a good number of characters serve as phonetic elements and combine with semantic elements to form more complex characters, sometimes you can guess the approximate pronunciation or even the basic meaning of a character that you have never seen before.

Although each character is monosyllabic, characters in modern Chinese usually do not exist alone as individual characters and syllables, but rather combine with other characters to form compounds. Most compounds consist of two characters, that is, two syllables. For example, 姑妈 (gūmā, aunt) and 早上 (zǎoshang, morning).

In writing Chinese characters, you need to pay attention to the fact that all the characters should fit into squares of the same size. Each individual character should be spaced apart from other characters. When writing complex characters such as 姑 , you need to make sure that each component appears thinner than when it exists alone as a character, and both components in this complex character should be very close to each other so as to form an entity, rather than remaining as separate entities.

III. The Strokes and Stroke-Order of Chinese Characters

All Chinese characters consist of strokes. It is important to learn the basic strokes. The character 永 (yǒng, forever) is often used to demonstrate eight essential types of strokes, though its number of strokes is only five. There are twenty-five different strokes in all. The following are fourteen basic strokes,

dot:	丶	Ex: 文
horizontal:	一	Ex: 三
vertical:	丨	Ex: 十
left-falling:	丿	Ex: 人
right-falling:	㇏	Ex: 大
rising:	㇀	Ex: 打
vertical+rising:	㇙	Ex: 辰
level right-falling:	㇏	Ex: 这
left-falling+dot:	㇛	Ex: 好
horizontal hook:	㇖	Ex: 家
slanting hook:	㇂	Ex: 弋
vertical+hook:	亅	Ex: 到
vertical+turning+hook:	㇟	Ex: 己
horizontal+turning+hook:	㇆	Ex: 那

When you can recognize the basic types of strokes, you will be able to count how many strokes there are in each Chinese character. Any given character may be made up of only one single stroke or as many as sixty-four strokes. Fortunately for learners, most commonly-used characters consist of no more than twenty strokes, and many of them have less than ten strokes.

There is a fairly well-established order for writing the strokes of every character, though there may be occasional variations in the stroke order of a few characters. In general, if the stroke order is wrong, the character will seldom appear normal in shape or well-proportioned. Students are urged to conscientiously learn the correct stroke order for each character from the very beginning, and to practise writing new characters repeatedly. If you use the same standard stroke order each time, you will be more likely to write well-proportioned characters and to learn and memorize new characters quickly.

Some useful principles for stroke order are as follows,

1. From top to bottom. Ex: 三，上
2. From left to right. Ex: 你，叫
3. Middle before sides. Ex: 小，少
4. Horizontal before vertical strokes. Ex: 十，下
5. Left-falling before right-falling. Ex: 人，文
6. Boxes before strokes that cut through. Ex: 中，申
7. From outer strokes to inside ones. Ex: 同，用
8. Outer strokes before inside ones, and then the sealing stroke. Ex: 回，田
9. Enclosed strokes before enclosing strokes on the left and the bottom. Ex: 这，建

IV. Comparing and Contrasting Traditional Characters with Simplified Characters

Currently, there are two main versions of Chinese, simplified Chinese characters and traditional Chinese characters. Traditional characters are also referred to as complicated characters or long-form characters. The modern-day appearance of traditional characters has been in existence for about two thousand years, though the writing system was established as early as the Shang Dynasty, around three and a half millennia ago.

In the early 1950s, the government of the People's Republic of China began publishing official lists of simplified characters and formally adopting the characters in various publications. There are apparent advantages in this move, since simplified characters with less strokes are easier to learn and would therefore enable more people to become literate sooner. Nowadays all the publications and writings by the PRC are in simplified characters.

By contrast, the people in Taiwan Province of PRC continue to use only traditional characters so far, though they may have simplified a few characters informally and in their own way. Many overseas Chinese still use traditional characters in their writing, publications, and newspapers. Practically all publications before the 1950s were printed in traditional characters.

Suffice it to say that there are advantages in learning simplified characters, since they are used by numerous people in the PRC. However, being able to recognize traditional characters enables you to delve more deeply into China's rich culture, history, and literature. Students are encouraged to learn to recognize both traditional and simplified forms and write either of these two forms. It may be easier to begin with learning the traditional forms and then move on to the simplified forms.

It is important to note that a large number of characters have not been simplified, and there are rules to follow in simplifying certain characters as well as certain semantic and phonetic elements in characters.

Examples of some commonly-used characters whose traditional and simplified characters are the same,

你，我，他，她， 的，信心，不，是，新，朋友

Examples of traditional and simplified characters,

Traditional Characters	見	們	國	話	紙	這	嗎	鈴	麼	飯	魚
Simplified Characters	见	们	国	话	纸	这	吗	铃	么	饭	鱼

Traditionally Chinese texts were written from right to left, and often vertically—from top to bottom. However, Chinese publications in the PRC since the 1950s have adopted a westernized format, the texts running horizontally from left to right. This format allows the texts to be easily combined with Roman script, other western scripts such as English, as well as Arabic numbers.

宋宜凡的一家

第一单元 第一單元

我 家庭 学校 我 家庭 學校

Unit One My Family, My School, and Me

LESSON 1

第一课

我

“凡凡，起床了！”

星期天早上才八点多，妈妈就叫我起床。

“凡凡，你是中国人，不要学你那些美国朋友，晚上不睡、早上不起。”

“妈，我是在美国出生、美国长大的，我就是美国人。”

“真没办法，已经是大学生了，还不清楚自己是不是中国人！”

“我很清楚自己是不是中国人，是您老觉得我不清楚。”

“好了，好了。再过一个多月，爷爷、奶奶就要来美国了。从今天起，你得多说中文了！”

LESSON 1

第一課

我

“凡凡，起床了！”

星期天早上纔八點多，媽媽就叫我起床。

“凡凡，你是中國人，不要學你那些美國朋友，晚上不睡、早上不起。”

“媽，我是在美國出生、美國長大的，我就是美國人。”

“真沒辦法，已經是大學生了，還不清楚自己是不是中國人！”

“我很清楚自己是不是中國人，是您老覺得我不清楚。”

“好了，好了。再過一個多月，爺爺、奶奶就要來美國了。從今天起，你得多說中文了！”

New Words
生词表/生詞表

第		dì	*pref*	(a prefix for ordinal number)
第一		dì-yī		the first
一		yī	*nu*	one
课	課	kè	*n*	lesson
我		wǒ	*pron*	I; me
凡凡		Fánfan	*pn*	(a given name)
起床		qǐchuáng	*vo*	get up; get out of bed
了		le	*particle*	(often used to indicate change of situation)
星期		xīngqī	*n*	week
星期天		xīngqītiān	*n*	Sunday
早上		zǎoshang	*n*	morning
才	纔	cái	*adv*	only; just
八点	八點	bādiǎn	*nu*	eight o'clock
多		duō	*adj*	many; much; more
妈妈	媽媽	māma	*n*	mom; ma
就		jiù	*adv*	as early as; already; at once; in a moment
叫		jiào	*v*	ask; order
你		nǐ	*pron*	you
是		shì	*v*	be
中国	中國	Zhōngguó	*pn*	China
中国人	中國人	Zhōngguórén	*pn*	Chinese
不		bù	*adv*	not; no
要		yào	*v/aux*	want; wish; be about; going to
学	學	xué	*v*	imitate; learn; study
那些		nàxiē	*pron*	those
美国	美國	Měiguó	*pn*	United States of America (USA)
美国人	美國人	Měiguórén	*pn*	American
朋友		péngyou	*n*	friend
晚上		wǎnshang	*n*	evening; night
睡		shuì	*v*	sleep
起		qǐ	*v*	rise; get up; start (used before a noun of time or place preceded by 从 or 由)
在		zài	*v/prep*	be (in a place); in; on; at
出生		chūshēng	*v*	be born

长大	長大	zhǎng dà		grow up
的		de	*particle*	(a particle indicating possession or modification)
真		zhēn	*adv/adj*	really; truly; indeed; real
没		méi	*adv*	not have; be without
办法	辦法	bànfǎ	*n*	way; means
已经	已經	yǐjing	*adv*	already
大学	大學	dàxué	*n*	college; university
大学生	大學生	dàxuéshēng	*n*	college or university student
还	還	hái	*adv*	still
清楚		qīngchu	*v*	know; be aware of
自己		zìjǐ	*pron*	self; oneself
很		hěn	*adv*	very; quite
您		nín	*pron*	you (polite singular)
老		lǎo	*adv/adj*	always; old; aged
觉得	覺得	juéde	*v*	think; feel
好		hǎo	*adj*	good; fine; nice; (used to express approval, conclusion, discontent, etc.)
再		zài	*adv*	once more; again
过	過	guò	*v*	spend (time); cross; pass
个	個	gè	*m*	(a generic measure word)
月		yuè	*n*	month
爷爷	爺爺	yéye	*n*	paternal grandpa
奶奶		nǎinai	*n*	paternal grandma
来	來	lái	*v*	come; arrive
从	從	cóng	*prep*	from
今天		jīntiān	*n*	today
得		děi	*aux*	must; have to
说	說	shuō	*v*	speak; say
中文		Zhōngwén	*pn*	Chinese language

Chinese Characters
汉字一/漢字一

㇇ 了 (2)											
了	了	了	了								
ノ 人 (2)											
人	人	人	人								
一 ナ 大 (3)											
大	大	大	大								
一 二 チ 天 (4)											
天	天	天	天								
丨 卜 上 (3)											
上	上	上	上								
一 ㇇ 不 不 (4)											
不	不	不	不								
丶 亠 ナ 文 (4)											
文	文	文	文								
丶 冫 氵 氵 汁 注 法 法 (8)											
法	法	法	法								
ノ 人 亼 今 (4)											
今	今	今	今								
㇆ コ 己 (3)											
己	己	己	己								

Chinese Characters
汉字二/漢字二

丨 冂 口 中 (4)
中 中 中 中
一 ナ 𠂇 𠂇 存 在 (6)
在 在 在 在
丿 刀 月 月 月 朋 朋 朋 (8)
朋 朋 朋 朋
一 ナ 方 友 (4)
友 友 友 友
′ 亻 白 白 自 自 (6)
自 自 自 自
′ ク 夕 夕 多 多 (6)
多 多 多 多
ㄑ 女 女 女′ 好 好 (6)
好 好 好 好
丨 冂 日 日 旦 早 (6)
早 早 早 早
′ 二 于 手 我 我 我 (7)
我 我 我 我
′ 亻 白 白 白 白′ 的 的 (8)
的 的 的 的

Chinese Characters
汉字三/漢字三

課	课	纔	才
國	国	長	长
媽	妈	辦	办
學	学	經	经
過	过	個	个

Chinese Characters
汉字四/漢字四

還	还	說	说
來	来	覺	觉
從	从	點	点
很	些	沒	就
起	是	睡	晚

Grammar Notes
语法简注/語法簡注

1. 才……，就……/纔……，就……：(only/only then)…, as early as…

   就 here indicates that something happens "earlier than expected".

📖 星期天早上才八点，妈妈就叫我起床。

星期天早上纔八點，媽媽就叫我起床。

It's only 8 o'clock on Sunday morning, and Mom has already tried to wake me up.

▶ 早上才五点，我就起床了。

早上纔五點，我就起床了。

It's only 5 o'clock in the morning and I've already got up.

▶ 晚上才八点，她 [tā] 就睡了。

晚上纔八點，她 [tā] 就睡了。

It's only 8 o'clock in the evening and she has already gone to bed.

2. 是……的：it is … that …

subject + 是 + time/place/manner/purpose + verb + (object) + 的

This pattern emphasizes the place, the time, the purpose, or how an action took place in the past.

📖 我是在美国出生的。

我是在美國出生的。

I was born in the US.

▶ 奶奶来美国了，她是上星期天来的。

奶奶來美國了，她是上星期天來的。

Grandma came to the US. It was last Sunday that she came.

▶ 哥哥[gēge]来了，他[tā]是来看爷爷的。

哥哥[gēge]來了，他[tā]是來看爺爺的。

Elder Brother came. He came here to visit Grandpa.

3. 是不是：whether or not

   是不是is not a question here, but a declaration in question form.

📖 我很清楚自己是不是中国人。

我很清楚自己是不是中國人。

I am very clear about whether I am a Chinese or not.

▶ 我不清楚他是不是学生。

我不清楚他是不是學生。

I am not clear about whether he is a student or not.

▶ 我很清楚今天是不是星期天。

I am very clear about whether today is Sunday or not.

4. 就要……了：about to; going to

📖 爷爷、奶奶就要来美国了。

爺爺、奶奶就要來美國了。

Grandpa and Grandma are coming to the US soon.

▶ 妈妈就要起床了。

媽媽就要起床了。

Mom is about to get up.

▶ 我就要去睡了。

I am going to sleep soon.

5. 从……起/從……起：starting from; from…on

📖 从今天起，你得多说中文了！

從今天起，你得多說中文了！

Starting from today, you must speak Chinese more!

▶ 从今天起，我就是大学生了。

從今天起，我就是大學生了。

From today on I will be a college student.

▶ 从下个月起，你得学中文了。

從下個月起，你得學中文了。

You'll have to learn Chinese starting from next month.

自我介绍

中国人在做“自我介绍”的时候，一般会介绍自己姓什么，叫什么，做什么工作。有时候还会介绍自己有什么爱好等等。下面是宋宜凡的自我介绍：

我姓宋，叫宋宜凡。英文名字是Yvonne。我是在美国出生、美国长大的，今年十八岁，是大学一年级新生。我喜欢听音乐、跑步，周末喜欢睡懒觉。

自我介紹

中國人在做“自我介紹”的時候，一般會介紹自己姓什麼，叫什麼，做什麼工作。有時候還會介紹自己有什麼愛好等等。下面是宋宜凡的自我介紹：

我姓宋，叫宋宜凡。英文名字是Yvonne。我是在美國出生、美國長大的，今年十八歲，是大學一年級新生。我喜歡聽音樂、跑步，周末喜歡睡懶覺。

自我介绍	自我介紹	zìwǒ jièshào	self-introduction
一般		yībān	general; generally
工作		gōngzuò	work; job
爱好	愛好	àihào	hobby
喜欢	喜歡	xǐhuan	like
听音乐	聽音樂	tīng yīnyuè	listen to music
跑步		pǎobù	run
周末		zhōumò	weekend
睡懒觉	睡懶覺	shuì lǎnjiào	sleep in

判断正误/判斷正誤

Identify the following statements as true or false based on the reading passage.

1. _______ 宋宜凡是在美国出生的中国人，也叫ABC。
2. _______ 宋宜凡才上大学。
3. _______ 宋宜凡觉得她是美国人。
4. _______ 宋宜凡常常听音乐。
5. _______ 宋宜凡周末起床起得很晚。

1. _______ 宋宜凡是在美國出生的中國人，也叫ABC。

2. _______ 宋宜凡纔上大學。

3. _______ 宋宜凡覺得她是美國人。

4. _______ 宋宜凡常常聽音樂。

5. _______ 宋宜凡周末起床起得很晚。

一、辨音练习/辨音練習

Distinguish between the following pairs of sounds.

1. pàntú	叛徒	bàntú	半途	2. pàibié	派别	bàibié	拜别
3. mínxīn	民心	míngxīng	明星	4. mínsú	民俗	mínzú	民族
5. mùcái	木材	mùchái	木柴	6. fāchóu	发愁	fā qiú	发球
7. tùzi	兔子	dùzi	肚子	8. nèi qiáng	内墙	nèixiáng	内详
9. liúliàn	留恋	liúniàn	留念	10. nǚhuáng	女皇	nǚwáng	女王
1. pàntú	叛徒	bàntú	半途	2. pàibié	派別	bàibié	拜別
3. mínxīn	民心	míngxīng	明星	4. mínsú	民俗	mínzú	民族
5. mùcái	木材	mùchái	木柴	6. fāchóu	發愁	fā qiú	發球
7. tùzi	兔子	dùzi	肚子	8. nèi qiáng	內墻	nèixiáng	內詳
9. liúliàn	留戀	liúniàn	留念	10. nǚhuáng	女皇	nǚwáng	女王

二、标声调/標聲調

Mark the tones.

Mark the tone for the first syllable.

A. 3rd tone + 3rd tone.

1. ni hǎo　　2. wo hǎo　　3. hen hǎo

4. wo hen hǎo　　5. hen xiǎo　　6. wo hen zǎo

B. 3rd tone + 1st /2nd / 4th tone.

	3rd + 1st	3rd + 2nd	3rd + 4th
1	ni shuō	ni máng	ni duì
2	hen duō	qichuáng	wo pà
3	lao Dīng	wo máng	hen chòu

三、根据拼音写汉字／根據拼音寫漢字

Write the Chinese characters equivalent of the following Pinyin.

1. qǐchuáng
2. péngyou
3. chūshēng
4. zhǎngdà
5. Zhōngwén
6. dàxuéshēng
7. zǎoshang
8. qīngchu
9. xīngqītiān
10. zìjǐ
11. Zhōngguórén
12. jīntiān

四、根据课文回答问题／根據課文回答問題

Answer the following questions by using complete sentences based on information in the text.

1. 凡凡的妈妈星期天早上几[jǐ]点叫她起床？
2. 凡凡的妈妈为什么[wèishénme]星期天早上八点叫她起床？
3. 凡凡觉得自己是中国人还是[háishi]美国人？为什么？
4. 凡凡的妈妈为什么说“从今天起，你得多说中文了”？
5. 你觉得自己是中国人还是美国人？为什么？

1. 凡凡的媽媽星期天早上幾[jǐ]點叫她起床？
2. 凡凡的媽媽爲什麼[wèishénme]星期天早上八點叫她起床？
3. 凡凡覺得自己是中國人還是[háishi]美國人？爲什麼？
4. 凡凡的媽媽爲什麼說“從今天起，你得多說中文了”？
5. 你覺得自己是中國人還是美國人？爲什麼？

五、填空

Fill in the blanks.

A. Fill in the blanks based on the text.

1. 星期天早上才______点，妈妈就叫我______ ______。
2. 我的朋友，晚上不______、早上不______。
3. 我是在美国______ ______、美国______ ______的，我就是美国人。
4. 我很______ ______自己是不是中国人。
5. 再过一个多月，爷______、奶______就要来______ ______了。
6. 从______ ______起，我得______说中文了！

1. 星期天早上纔______點，媽媽就叫我______ ______。
2. 我的朋友，晚上不 ______、早上不______。
3. 我是在美國______ ______、美國______ ______的，我就是美國人。
4. 我很______ ______ 自己是不是中國人。
5. 再過一個多月，爺______、奶______就要來______ ______了。
6. 從______ ______起，我得______説中文了！

B. Fill in each of the following blanks with “就” or “才/纔”.

1. 妈妈星期天早上六点______起床了，可是我十一点______起。
2. 再过一个多月，我______是大学生了。
3. 她晚上很早______睡了，可是早上很晚______起床。
4. 再过一个月，爷爷、奶奶______要来美国了。

1. 媽媽星期天早上六點______起床了，可是我十一點______起。
2. 再過一個多月，我______是大學生了。
3. 她晚上很早______睡了，可是早上很晚______起床。
4. 再過一個月，爺爺、奶奶______要來美國了。

六、重组/重組

Word order.

1. 早上/奶奶/来了/星期天/就要

   早上/奶奶/來了/星期天/就要

   Grandma is coming on Sunday morning.

2. 中文了／多说／爷爷／我得／来了

中文了／多說／爺爺／我得／來了

I have to speak more Chinese after Grandpa comes.

3. 长大的／我朋友／是／出生／在美国

長大的／我朋友／是／出生／在美國

It was in the US that my friend was born and raised.

4. 很清楚／是／凡凡／中国人／不是／自己

很清楚／是／凡凡／中國人／不是／自己

Fanfan is very clear about whether she is Chinese or not.

5. 八点多了／起床／那些／已经／还不／大学生

八點多了／起床／那些／已經／還不／大學生

It's already over eight o'clock. Those college students haven't gotten up yet.

七、翻译／翻譯

Translate the following sentences into Chinese.

1. I was born and raised in the US.
2. Mom always wakes me up very early in the morning.
3. My mom always says, " Don't go to bed late and get up late."
4. I don't speak Chinese. I want to learn more Chinese.
5. In about a month, my friend will come.

八、改错／改錯

Correct mistakes.

1. 我名字姓宋宜凡。
2. 在过一个多月，爷爷、奶奶就要来美国。
3. 从今天起，我得说多中文。
4. 我不觉得我是中国人。
5. 我是在美国出生、长大。

1. 我名字姓宋宜凡。
2. 在過一個多月，爺爺、奶奶就要來美國。
3. 從今天起，我得說多中文。

4. 我不覺得我是中國人。

5. 我是在美國出生、長大。

九、课堂活动／課堂活動

In-class activity.

Theme: My New Friend

Task: 1. Find a partner in your class and introduce each other as instructed.

2. Collect your partner's background information, and present it in class.

	Questions	Answers (in English or Chinese)
1	What is your name?	
2	How old are you?	
3	Where were you born?	
4	Which year are you (at college) in?	
5	What language do you speak at home?	
6	What are your hobbies?	

十、课外活动／課外活動

After-class activity.

Interview one of your friends or roommates and fill in the following chart in Chinese or Pinyin.

我的好朋友叫 ____________________。

她是在 ____________________ 出生的。

她是大学 ____________________ 的学生。

她早上 ____。

她晚上 ____。

她喜欢 ____。

她不喜欢 ______________________________________。

LESSON 2

第二课
我的家

“凡凡，饭好了，叫你爸爸吃饭。你爸爸天天上班用电脑，回到家还守着电脑，我看他真应该跟电脑结婚。”

我妈妈个子不高，特别爱说话。

“爸，妈说饭好了，叫您吃饭。”

“来了。”我爸爸不高不矮，平时话不多。

我和爸爸、妈妈刚要吃饭，电话响了。妈妈放下筷子去接电话。

“喂，平平啊，你想知道爷爷、奶奶什么时候来美国啊，再过一个多月吧。你能回来吗？能回来，那好。我们都好。好，再见。”

妈妈放下电话，说：“是你哥哥，问爷爷、奶奶什么时候来美国。”

4. 我不覺得我是中國人。

5. 我是在美國出生、長大。

九、课堂活动/課堂活動

In-class activity.

Theme: My New Friend

Task: 1. Find a partner in your class and introduce each other as instructed.

2. Collect your partner's background information, and present it in class.

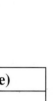

	Questions	Answers (in English or Chinese)
1	What is your name?	
2	How old are you?	
3	Where were you born?	
4	Which year are you (at college) in?	
5	What language do you speak at home?	
6	What are your hobbies?	

十、课外活动/課外活動

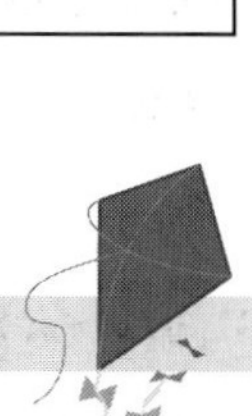

After-class activity.

Interview one of your friends or roommates and fill in the following chart in Chinese or Pinyin.

我的好朋友叫 ____________________。

她是在 ____________________ 出生的。

她是大学 ____________________ 的学生。

她早上 ____。

她晚上 ____。

她喜欢 ____。

她不喜欢 ____。

我的好朋友叫 ____________________。

她是在 ____________________ 出生的。

她是大學 __________________ 的學生。

她早上 ____。

她晚上 ____。

她喜歡 ____。

她不喜歡 ____。

十一、写作练习/寫作練習

Writing.

Write a short article (50 words) about yourself. Please include the following words.

叫，生，长大，是……的，觉得，晚上，早上，说中文

叫，生，長大，是……的，覺得，晚上，早上，說中文

十二、总结/總結

Summary.

1. Choose 5-10 of your favorite new vocabulary words from the text or reading material.

2. Quote 3-7 of your favorite sentences from the text or reading material here.

	Original sentence	**Translation of the sentence** (or make a new sentence of your own)
1		
2		
3		
4		
5		

3. From this lesson, you have learned Chinese culture, history and philosophy. They have helped you to understand,

我现在清楚了/我現在清楚了：

① ______________________________

② ______________________________

LESSON 2

第二课
我的家

“凡凡，饭好了，叫你爸爸吃饭。你爸爸天天上班用电脑，回到家还守着电脑，我看他真应该跟电脑结婚。”

我妈妈个子不高，特别爱说话。

“爸，妈说饭好了，叫您吃饭。”

“来了。”我爸爸不高不矮，平时话不多。

我和爸爸、妈妈刚要吃饭，电话响了。妈妈放下筷子去接电话。

“喂，平平啊，你想知道爷爷、奶奶什么时候来美国啊，再过一个多月吧。你能回来吗？能回来，那好。我们都好。好，再见。”

妈妈放下电话，说：“是你哥哥，问爷爷、奶奶什么时候来美国。”

LESSON 2

第二課
我的家

“凡凡，飯好了，叫你爸爸吃飯。你爸爸天天上班用電腦，回到家還守着電腦，我看他真應該跟電腦結婚。”

我媽媽個子不高，特別愛說話。

“爸，媽說飯好了，叫您吃飯。”

“來了。”我爸爸不高不矮，平時話不多。

我和爸爸、媽媽剛要吃飯，電話響了。媽媽放下筷子去接電話。

“喂，平平啊，你想知道爺爺、奶奶什麼時候來美國啊，再過一個多月吧。你能回來嗎？能回來，那好。我們都好。好，再見。”

媽媽放下電話，說：“是你哥哥，問爺爺、奶奶什麼時候來美國。”

New Words
生词表/生詞表

家		jiā	*n*	family; home
饭	飯	fàn	*n*	meal; cooked rice
爸爸		bàba	*n*	dad; pa
吃		chī	*v*	eat; have
天		tiān	*n*	day
上班		shàngbān	*vo*	go to work
用		yòng	*v*	use
电脑	電腦	diànnǎo	*n*	computer
回到		huídào	*vc*	return; go back
守		shǒu	*v*	stay with
着		zhe	*particle*	(indicating the continuation of an action or a situation)
看		kàn	*v*	think; look at; read
他		tā	*pron*	he; him
应该	應該	yīnggāi	*aux*	should; ought to
跟		gēn	*prep*	with
结婚	結婚	jiéhūn	*vo*	marry; get married
个子	個子	gèzi	*n*	height; stature
高		gāo	*adj*	tall; high
特别		tèbié	*adj/adv*	special; especially; particularly
爱	愛	ài	*v*	love; like; be apt (to do)
说话	說話	shuōhuà	*vo*	speak; talk
矮		ǎi	*adj*	short (in stature); low (in height)
平时	平時	píngshí	*adv*	ordinarily; normally
话	話	huà	*n*	talk; word; what somebody says
和		hé	*conj*	and
刚	剛	gāng	*adv*	just; just now
电话	電話	diànhuà	*n*	telephone; phone call
响	響	xiǎng	*v/adj*	sound; ring; noisy
放下		fàngxia	*vc*	lay/put down
筷子		kuàizi	*n*	chopsticks
去		qù	*v*	go to; leave for
接		jiē	*v*	receive

喂		wèi	*int*	hello
平平		Píngping	*pn*	(a given name)
啊		a	*particle*	(used after forms of address or at the end of interrogative sentences)
想		xiǎng	*v*	want/wish (to do sth); would like (to do sth); think
知道		zhīdào	*v*	know; be aware of
什么	什麽	shénme	*pron*	what
时候	時候	shíhou	*n*	time; moment
吧		ba	*particle*	(used at the end of a declarative sentence to indicate uncertainty)
能		néng	*aux*	can; be able to
回来	回來	huílai	*vc*	return; come back
吗	嗎	ma	*particle*	(interrogative particle at the end of a sentence)
那		nà	*conj/pron*	in that case; that
我们	我們	wǒmen	*pron*	we; us
都		dōu	*adv*	all; both; every
再见	再見	zàijiàn	*v*	goodbye; see you again
哥哥		gēge	*n*	elder brother
问	問	wèn	*v*	ask; inquire

的时候 just now

有时候 sometimes

弟弟 little brother

Chinese Characters
汉字一/漢字一

乛 了 子 (3)										
子	子	子	子							
丨 冂 冂 冋 回 回 (6)										
回	回	回	回							
丿 冂 月 月 用 (5)										
用	用	用	用							
丨 𠃍 口 口' 口乞 吃 (6)										
吃	吃	吃	吃							
一 丅 下 (3)										
下	下	下	下							
一 十 土 去 去 (5)										
去	去	去	去							
丿 亻 亻 什 (4)										
什	什	什	什							
丿 二 千 禾 禾 禾 和 和 (8)										
和	和	和	和							
一 十 才 木 札 机 相 相 相 相 想 想 想 (13)										
想	想	想	想							
丶 亠 亠 亩 亩 亯 高 高 高 高 (10)										
高	高	高	高							

Chinese Characters
汉字二/漢字二

家 (10)

家 家 家 家

爸 (8)

爸 爸 爸 爸

看 (9)

看 看 看 看

他 (5)

他 他 他 他

跟 (13)

跟 跟 跟 跟

能 (10)

能 能 能 能

都 (10)

都 都 都 都

到 (8)

到 到 到 到

特 (10)

特 特 特 特

别 (7)

别 别 别 别

Chinese Characters
汉字三/漢字三

飯	饭	電	电
腦	脑	結	结
問	问	時	时
話	话	麼	么
見	见	嗎	吗

Chinese Characters
汉字四／漢字四

響	响	愛	爱
剛	刚	們	们
應	应	該	该
筷	接	喂	婚
知	矮	放	道

Grammar Notes
语法简注/語法簡注

1. 了：indicating some changes have taken place

statement +了

📖 饭好了。

飯好了。

The meal is ready. (Previously Mother was cooking, but now the food is ready to be served.)

▶ 凡凡现在[xiànzài]是大学生了。

凡凡現在[xiànzài]是大學生了。

Fanfan is a college student now.

▶ 今天已经是星期五了。

今天已經是星期五了。

It is already Friday today.

2. 着：indicating some action is going on

📖 爸爸回到家还守着电脑。

爸爸回到家還守着電腦。

After Dad comes back home, he still hangs around the computer.

▶ 凡凡用着电脑。

凡凡用着電腦。

Fanfan is using the computer.

▶ 电脑开[kāi]着。

電腦開[kāi]着。

The computer is on.

3. A跟B结婚/A跟B結婚：A marries B.

📖 他真应该跟电脑结婚。

他真應該跟電腦結婚。

Indeed he should marry a computer.

▶ 他想跟我结婚。

他想跟我結婚。

He wants to marry me.

▶ 我不爱他，不想跟他结婚。

我不愛他，不想跟他結婚。

I don't love him and don't want to marry him.

4. 爱/愛：be apt (to do); love; like

① be apt (to do)

📖 我妈特别爱说话。

我媽特别愛説話。

My mom is very talkative.

② love; like

▶ 他特别爱吃中国饭。

他特别愛吃中國飯。

He loves Chinese food very much.

▶ 我不爱用筷子吃饭。

我不愛用筷子吃飯。

I don't like using chopsticks.

5. 刚要/剛要：just about to do something

📖 爸爸、妈妈刚要吃饭，电话响了。

爸爸、媽媽剛要吃飯，電話響了。

When Dad and Mom were just about to eat, the phone rang.

▶ 我刚要接电话，妈妈接了。

我剛要接電話，媽媽接了。

When I was just about to answer the phone, Mom picked it up.

▶ 我刚要起床，电话响了。

我剛要起床，電話響了。

When I was just about to get up, the phone rang.

6. V+下：下 is a complement of result here.

📖 妈妈放下电话说："你哥哥问奶奶什么时候来美国。"

媽媽放下電話説："你哥哥問奶奶什麼時候來美國。"

Mom put down the phone and said: "Your elder brother asked when Grandma would come to the US."

▶ 妈妈放下筷子去接电话。

媽媽放下筷子去接電話。

Mom put down the chopsticks and went to pick up the phone.

7. 啊：a particle used after a form of address or greeting

平平啊？

平平啊？

It is you, Pingping, right?

▶ 再见啊，凡凡。

再見啊，凡凡。

You are saying goodbye, Fanfan?

8. 什么/什麼：an interrogative pronoun

哥哥想知道爷爷、奶奶什么时候来美国。

哥哥想知道爺爺、奶奶什麼時候來美國。

Elder Brother would like to know when Grandpa and Grandma would come to the US.

▶ 爸爸什么时候回家？

爸爸什麼時候回家？

When will Dad come home?

▶ 她爱吃什么？

她愛吃什麼？

What does she like to eat?

家庭成员

在介绍自己家庭的时候，中国人一般会介绍：家里有几口人，有谁，他们做什么工作等等。宋宜凡是这么介绍她的家庭的：

我家有四口人：爸爸、妈妈、哥哥和我。我爸爸在一家电脑公司当工程师。我妈妈以前是会计，现在不工作了。我哥哥叫宋宜平，比我大五岁，在东部的一所商学院学商业管理。

我和全家人都很亲，特别是和哥哥。他是我哥哥，也是我的好朋友。

家庭成員

在介紹自己家庭的時候，中國人一般會介紹：家裏有幾口人，有誰，他們做什麼工作等等。宋宜凡是這麼介紹她的家庭的：

我家有四口人：爸爸、媽媽、哥哥和我。我爸爸在一家電腦公司當工程師。我媽媽以前是會計，現在不工作了。我哥哥叫宋宜平，比我大五歲，在東部的一所商學院學商業管理。

我和全家人都很親，特別是和哥哥。他是我哥哥，也是我的好朋友。

家庭		jiātíng	family; household
工程师	工程師	gōngchéngshī	engineer
会计	會計	kuàijì	accountant
东部	東部	dōngbù	the east; the eastern part
商学院	商學院	shāngxuéyuàn	business school
商业管理	商業管理	shāngyè guǎnlǐ	business management
亲	親	qīn	be close; intimate

判断正误／判斷正誤

Identify the following statements as true or false based on the reading passage.

1. _______ 宜凡家有三口人。
2. _______ 宜凡的爸爸是电脑工程师。
3. _______ 宜凡的妈妈是会计。
4. _______ 宜凡的哥哥在东部上大学。

1. _______ 宜凡家有三口人。
2. _______ 宜凡的爸爸是電腦工程師。
3. _______ 宜凡的媽媽是會計。
4. _______ 宜凡的哥哥在東部上大學。

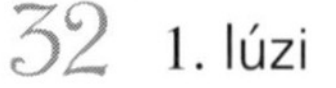

Exercises
练习/練習

一、辨音练习/辨音練習

Distinguish between the following pairs of sounds.

1. lúzi	炉子	lǘzi	驴子	2. lǜdēng	绿灯	lùdēng	路灯
3. gōngwù	公务	gōngmù	公墓	4. guìyuán	桂圆	huìyuán	会员
5. kāihuāng	开荒	kāifāng	开方	6. kōngxiǎng	空想	hōngxiǎng	轰响
7. kāihuā	开花	kāifā	开发	8. huānxīn	欢心	kuānxīn	宽心
9. hánsuān	寒酸	hánxuān	寒暄	10. Hélán	荷兰	Hé'nán	河南
1. lúzi	爐子	lǘzi	驢子	2. lǜdēng	綠燈	lùdēng	路燈
3. gōngwù	公務	gōngmù	公墓	4. guìyuán	桂圓	huìyuán	會員
5. kāihuāng	開荒	kāifāng	開方	6. kōngxiǎng	空想	hōngxiǎng	轟響
7. kāihuā	開花	kāifā	開發	8. huānxīn	歡心	kuānxīn	寬心
9. hánsuān	寒酸	hánxuān	寒暄	10. Hélán	荷蘭	Hé'nán	河南

二、标声调/標聲調

Mark the tones.

Neutral tone exercise.

1. 爸爸 baba　2. 哥哥 gege　3. 爷爷/爺爺 yeye　4. 奶奶 nainai

5. 好了 hao le　6. 是吗/是嗎 shi ma　7. 什么/什麽 shenme　8. 我的 wo de

三、根据拼音写汉字/根據拼音寫漢字

Write the Chinese characters equivalent of the following Pinyin.

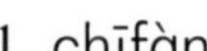

1. chīfàn　　2. diànnǎo
3. bù gāo bù ǎi　　4. píngshí
5. kuàizi　　6. Měiguó
7. jiéhūn　　8. ài shuōhuà
9. jiē diànhuà　　10. shénme shíhou
11. shàngbān　　12. zàijiàn

四、根据课文回答问题/根據課文回答問題

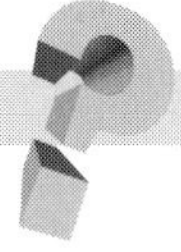

Answer the following questions by using complete sentences based on information in the text.

1. 妈妈叫谁[shéi]吃饭？
2. 凡凡的爸爸天天上班做什么？
3. 凡凡的妈妈高吗？
4. 凡凡的爸爸和妈妈都爱说话吗？
5. 为什么[wèishénme]电话响了，凡凡的妈妈去接电话？
6. 凡凡的哥哥叫什么名字？
7. 凡凡的爷爷、奶奶什么时候来美国？
8. 凡凡的哥哥能不能回家？

1. 媽媽叫誰[shéi]吃飯？
2. 凡凡的爸爸天天上班做什麽？
3. 凡凡的媽媽高嗎？
4. 凡凡的爸爸和媽媽都愛説話嗎？
5. 爲什麽[wèishénme]電話響了，凡凡的媽媽去接電話？
6. 凡凡的哥哥叫什麽名字？
7. 凡凡的爺爺、奶奶什麽時候來美國？
8. 凡凡的哥哥能不能回家？

五、填空

Fill in the blanks.

A. Fill in the blanks based on the text.

1. 我妈妈______ ______不高，特别______说话。
2. 我爸爸不______不______，平时话不______。
3. 我爸爸______ ______上班用电脑，回到家还______ 着______ ______。
4. 我和爸爸、妈妈______ ______吃饭，电话______了。
5. 我哥哥______知道爷爷、奶奶______ ______时候来美国。

1. 我媽媽______ ______不高，特别______説話。
2. 我爸爸不______不______，平時話不______。
3. 我爸爸______ ______上班用電腦，回到家還______着______ ______。
4. 我和爸爸、媽媽______ ______吃飯，電話______了。

5. 我哥哥______知道爺爺、奶奶______ ______時候來美國。

B. Fill in each of the following blanks with a. 要, b. 得, c. 能, or d. 应该/應該.

1. 这个星期天你______回家吗?

 這個星期天你______回家嗎?

 Can you come home this Sunday?

2. 你______跟奶奶说话吗?

 你______跟奶奶說話嗎?

 Do you want to talk with Grandma?

3. 我爸爸真______跟电脑结婚。

 我爸爸真______跟電腦結婚。

 My dad should really marry a computer.

4. 爷爷就______来美国了，是不是?

 爺爺就______來美國了，是不是?

 Grandpa is coming to the US, isn't he?

5. 妈妈说："从今天起，你______多吃饭了。"

 媽媽說："從今天起，你______多吃飯了。"

 Mom said, "Starting from today you must eat more."

C. Put 了 in the appropriate blanks.

1. 凡凡的爸爸天天用电脑______，上班用______，下班______回到家也用______。
2. 奶奶说______："凡凡，饭好______，叫你哥哥吃饭______。"
3. 爷爷、奶奶刚要睡觉______，电话响______，是爸爸来______的电话______。
4. 就要吃饭______，爸爸还没回家______，妈妈刚要打______电话，爸爸就回来______。

1. 凡凡的爸爸天天用電腦______，上班用______，下班______回到家也用______。
2. 奶奶說______："凡凡，飯好______，叫你哥哥吃飯______。"
3. 爺爺、奶奶剛要睡覺______，電話響______，是爸爸來______的電話______。
4. 就要吃飯______，爸爸還没回家______，媽媽剛要打______電話，爸爸就回來______。

六、重组/重組

Word order.

1. 刚要/响/下班/了/爸爸/电话

 剛要/響/下班/了/爸爸/電話

 The phone rang when Dad was just about to get off work.

2. 电脑/吃饭/用/我爸爸/也要/不

電腦/吃飯/用/我爸爸/也要/不

My dad wants to use the computer even if he has to skip the meals.

3. 筷子/凡凡/电话/去/放下/接

筷子/凡凡/電話/去/放下/接

Fanfan put down her chopsticks and went to answer the phone.

4. 时候/知道/回家/我/哥哥/什么/想

時候/知道/回家/我/哥哥/什麼/想

I'd like to know when Elder Brother will come home.

5. 跟/结婚/我朋友/打电话/真应该/很爱/电话/她

跟/結婚/我朋友/打電話/真應該/很愛/電話/她

My friend loves chatting on phone very much. She really should marry a phone.

七、翻译/翻譯

Translate the following sentences into Chinese.

1. Is your grandma tall?
2. Do you want to marry him?
3. Do you know when Mom will come home?
4. What does your dad especially love to eat?
5. I don't know when Grandma will come to the US.
6. Elder Brother is a college student now.

八、改错/改錯

Correct mistakes.

1. 爸爸应该结婚电脑。
2. 我妈个子是矮。
3. 我爸爸是不高，不矮。
4. 我和爸爸、妈妈刚要吃饭，电话响。
5. 爷爷、奶奶再过一个月多来美国。
6. 妈妈说："饭好。"

1. 爸爸應該結婚電腦。
2. 我媽個子是矮。

3. 我爸爸是不高，不矮。

4. 我和爸爸、媽媽剛要吃飯，電話響。

5. 爺爺、奶奶再過一個月多來美國。

6. 媽媽說：“飯好。”

九、课堂活动/課堂活動

In-class activity.

Theme: My Mother/Father

Task: 1. Consolidate the information about your mother/father.

2. Describe your mother/father as instructed in class.

	Checklist	Answers (in English or Chinese)
1	Age	
2	Place of birth	
3	Physical appearance: height, build,…	
4	Personality: Quiet? Outgoing?	
5	Current job, title, …	
6	Hobbies	
7	Relationship with you (optional)	

十、课外活动/課外活動

After-class activity.

Use your imagination to describe this family in Chinese as if you were a friend of the girl in this family.

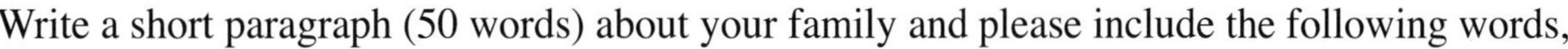

十一、写作练习/寫作練習

Writing.

Write a short paragraph (50 words) about your family and please include the following words,

有……口人，爱，爸爸，妈妈，结婚，高，矮

有……口人，愛，爸爸，媽媽，結婚，高，矮

十二、总结/總結

Summary.

1. Choose 5-10 of your favorite new vocabulary words from the text or reading material.

2. Quote 3-7 of your favorite sentences from the text or reading material here.

	Original sentence	**Translation of the sentence** (or make a new sentence of your own)
1		
2		
3		
4		
5		

3. From this lesson, you have learned Chinese culture, history, and philosophy. They have helped you to understand,

我现在清楚了/我現在清楚了：

① ______________________________

② ______________________________

第三课
我的祖父母

听妈妈说，我很小的时候，姥姥、姥爷就都去世了。但是，我爷爷、奶奶还都健在。听爸爸说，一九四九年以前，奶奶跟她的家人住在香港，爷爷住在上海。一九四九年以后他们就都搬到台北去了。现在爷爷、奶奶都退休了。他们退休以后，我们全家都希望他们能到美国来住一段时间。

我有十多年没见到爷爷、奶奶了。记得小时候，我和哥哥每次到台北去看他们，奶奶总是给我们做好吃的，爷爷常常给我们讲故事。

上个周末妈妈打电话告诉我，爷爷、奶奶已经到美国了。今天是星期五，我盼着早点儿下课，好赶快飞回家去看爷爷、奶奶！

第三課
我的祖父母

聽媽媽説，我很小的時候，姥姥、姥爺就都去世了。但是，我爺爺、奶奶還都健在。聽爸爸説，一九四九年以前，奶奶跟她的家人住在香港，爺爺住在上海。一九四九年以後他們就都搬到臺北去了。現在爺爺、奶奶都退休了。他們退休以後，我們全家都希望他們能到美國來住一段時間。

我有十多年沒見到爺爺、奶奶了。記得小時候，我和哥哥每次到臺北去看他們，奶奶總是給我們做好吃的，爺爺常常給我們講故事。

上個周末媽媽打電話告訴我，爺爺、奶奶已經到美國了。今天是星期五，我盼着早點兒下課，好趕快飛回家去看爺爺、奶奶！

New Words
生词表/生詞表

祖父母		zǔfùmǔ	*n*	paternal grandparents
听	聽	tīng	*v*	listen to; hear
小		xiǎo	*adj*	small; little; young
姥姥		lǎolao	*n*	maternal grandma
姥爷	姥爺	lǎoye	*n*	maternal grandpa
去世		qùshì	*v*	die; pass away
但是		dànshì	*conj*	but; however
健在		jiànzài	*v*	(of a person of advanced age) be still living and in good health
年		nián	*n*	year
以前		yǐqián	*n*	earlier times
她		tā	*pron*	she; her
家人		jiārén	*n*	family member
住		zhù	*v*	live; reside
香港		Xiānggǎng	*pn*	Hong Kong
上海		Shànghǎi	*pn*	Shanghai
以后	以後	yǐhòu	*n*	after; afterwards
他们	他們	tāmen	*pron*	they
搬		bān	*v*	move; remove
到		dào	*v*	arrive; reach; (a directional preposition or a resultative verb complement)
台北	臺北	Táiběi	*pn*	Taipei
现在	現在	xiànzài	*n*	now; at present
退休		tuìxiū	*v*	retire
全		quán	*n*	whole; entire
希望		xīwàng	*v/n*	hope; wish
段		duàn	*m*	period (of time); section
时间	時間	shíjiān	*n*	(concept of) time; (duration of) time
有		yǒu	*v*	have; possess; there is
十		shí	*nu*	ten
见	見	jiàn	*v*	meet; see; meet with
记得	記得	jìde	*vc*	remember

小时候	小時候	xiǎoshíhou	*n*	childhood
每		měi	*pron*	each; every
次		cì	*m*	time; occurrence
总是	總是	zǒngshì	*adv*	always
给	給	gěi	*v/prep*	give; by; with; to
做		zuò	*v*	make; do
好吃的		hǎo chī de		delicious food
常常		chángcháng	*adv*	often
讲	講	jiǎng	*v*	say; speak; tell
故事		gùshi	*n*	story; tale
上		shàng	*adj/v*	preceding; previous; go to; leave for
周末		zhōumò	*n*	weekend
打		dǎ	*v*	make (a phone call); hit
告诉	告訴	gàosu	*v*	tell (someone); inform
星期五		xīngqīwǔ	*n*	Friday
盼		pàn	*v*	long for; look forward to
早点儿	早點兒	zǎodiǎnr	*adv*	earlier
下课	下課	xiàkè	*vo*	dismiss a class; finish a class
好		hǎo	*v*	so as to; so that
赶快	趕快	gǎnkuài	*adv*	quickly; hastily
飞	飛	fēi	*v*	fly
回家		huíjiā	*vo*	come/return home

Chinese Characters
汉字一/漢字一

ノ ハ ク 父 (4)
父
ㄥ 𠂊 𠃋 毋 母 (5)
母
㇇ ㇇ ㇇ 艮 艮 艮 ㇏艮 ㇏艮 退 (9)
退
ノ 亻 仁 什 什 休 (6)
休
亅 小 小 (3)
小
ㄑ 女 女 如 她 她 (6)
她
ノ 亻 亻 仁 仨 住 住 (7)
住
ノ ㇀ 𠂉 仁 乍 年 (6)
年
丶 丷 丷 䒑 前 前 前 前 前 (9)
前
丨 ㅓ 爿 北 北 (5)
北

Chinese Characters
汉字二/漢字二

以		以	以	以							
有		有	有	有							
希		希	希	希							
望		望	望	望							
每		每	每	每							
次		次	次	次							
但		但	但	但							
告		告	告	告							
世		世	世	世							
快		快	快	快							

以 (4)

有 (6)

希 (7)

望 (11)

每 (7)

次 (6)

但 (7)

告 (7)

世 (5)

快 (7)

Chinese Characters
汉字三/漢字三

記	记	聽	听
爺	爷	後	后
訴	诉	給	给
總	总	飛	飞
講	讲	趕	赶

Chinese Characters
汉字四/漢字四

間	间	臺	台
健	港	得	海
到	做	段	常
祖	都	搬	姥
故	事	周	盼

Grammar Notes
语法简注/語法簡注

1. 听……说/聽……説：hear that...；hear somebody say that...

📖 听妈妈说，我很小的时候，姥姥、姥爷就都去世了。

聽媽媽説，我很小的時候，姥姥、姥爺就都去世了。

I heard Mom say that both my maternal grandma and grandpa passed away when I was a very little child.

▶ 听爸爸说，爷爷、奶奶这个星期来美国。

聽爸爸説，爺爺、奶奶這個星期來美國。

I heard Dad say that my grandpa and grandma would come to the US this week.

▶ 我听说你做的饭很好吃。

我聽説你做的飯很好吃。

I heard that your cooking is very good.

2. 就……了：something happens as early as…

📖 我很小的时候，姥姥、姥爷就都去世了。

我很小的時候，姥姥、姥爺就都去世了。

When I was a very little child, both my maternal grandma and grandpa (already) passed away.

▶ 我妈妈今天早上五点就起床了。

我媽媽今天早上五點就起床了。

My mom got up as early as five o'clock this morning.

▶ 我爸爸五十岁就退休了。

我爸爸五十歲就退休了。

My dad retired when he was barely fifty years old.

3. verb+了：Here 了 indicates that an action has been completed.

▶ 你爸爸退休了吗？

你爸爸退休了嗎？

Has your dad retired?

▶ 他退休了。

He has retired.

▶ 他还没退休。

他還没退休。

He has not retired yet.

4. 到+ place +来（來）/去：come to；go to

📖 我们全家都希望他们能到美国来住一段时间。

我們全家都希望他們能到美國來住一段時間。

My whole family hopes that they can come to America and stay for some time.

▶ 你奶奶什么时候到美国来?

你奶奶什麽時候到美國來?

When is your grandma coming to the US?

▶ 我明年要到中国去。

我明年要到中國去。

I want to go to China next year.

5. V+到：The verb 到 is a complement of result here. Common examples of "V + 到" include 见到/見到(to have seen)，听到/聽到(to have heard)，看到(to have seen).

📖 我有十多年没见到爷爷、奶奶了。

我有十多年没見到爺爺、奶奶了。

I haven't seen Grandpa and Grandma for over ten years.

▶ 她听到电话响了。

她聽到電話響了。

She heard the phone ring.

▶ 我没看到你朋友。

I didn't see your friend.

6. 好……：in order to；so as to；so that

📖 我盼着早点儿下课，好赶快飞回家去看爷爷奶奶。

我盼着早點兒下課，好趕快飛回家去看爺爺奶奶。

I hope the class ends earlier so that I can fly home to see Grandpa and Grandma.

▶ 我盼着爷爷、奶奶来美国，好跟他们说中文。

我盼着爺爺、奶奶來美國，好跟他們説中文。

I look forward to Grandpa and Grandma's visit to the US so that I can speak Chinese with them.

▶ 我盼着哥哥打电话来，好跟他说话。
我盼着哥哥打電話來，好跟他說話。
I look forward to Elder Brother's call so that I can talk to him.

亲属的称呼

称呼亲属的方式，南方人和北方人不太一样。比如：
爸爸的爸爸：北方人叫爷爷；南方人叫公公。
爸爸的妈妈：北方人叫奶奶；南方人叫婆婆。
妈妈的爸爸：北方人叫姥爷；南方人叫外公。
妈妈的妈妈：北方人叫姥姥；南方人叫外婆。

親屬的稱呼

稱呼親屬的方式，南方人和北方人不太一樣。比如：
爸爸的爸爸：北方人叫爺爺；南方人叫公公。
爸爸的媽媽：北方人叫奶奶；南方人叫婆婆。
媽媽的爸爸：北方人叫姥爺；南方人叫外公。
媽媽的媽媽：北方人叫姥姥；南方人叫外婆。

亲属	親屬	qīnshǔ	relative
称呼	稱呼	chēnghu	form of address; call; address
方式		fāngshì	way; style
南方		nánfāng	the south
北方		běifāng	the north

回答问题/回答問題

Answer the following questions.

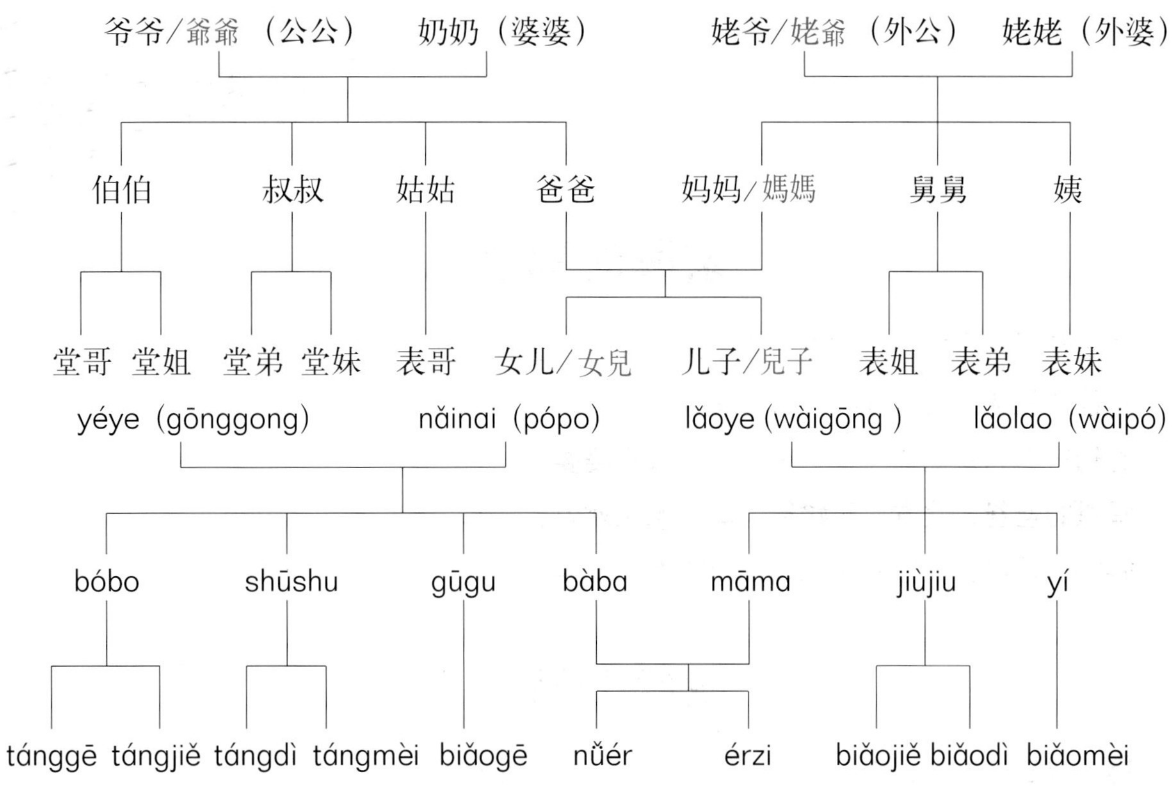

1. 你怎么称呼你爸爸的姐姐和妹妹？
2. 你怎么称呼你爸爸的弟弟？
3. 你怎么称呼你爸爸的哥哥？
4. 你怎么称呼你妈妈的哥哥、弟弟？
5. 你怎么称呼你妈妈的姐姐，妹妹？
6. 你怎么称呼你伯伯、叔叔和姑姑的孩子？
7. 你怎么称呼你舅舅和姨的孩子？

1. 你怎麼稱呼你爸爸的姐姐和妹妹？
2. 你怎麼稱呼你爸爸的弟弟？
3. 你怎麼稱呼你爸爸的哥哥？
4. 你怎麼稱呼你媽媽的哥哥、弟弟？
5. 你怎麼稱呼你媽媽的姐姐，妹妹？
6. 你怎麼稱呼你伯伯、叔叔和姑姑的孩子？
7. 你怎麼稱呼你舅舅和姨的孩子？

Exercises
练习/練習

一、辨音练习/辨音練習

Distinguish between the following pairs of sounds.

1. zhìzào	制造	zìzào	自造	2. zhàn zhù	站住	zànzhù	赞助
3. zhāi huā	摘花	zāi huā	栽花	4. zhǎyǎn	眨眼	jiǎ yǎn	假眼
5. zhěngzhì	整治	chěngzhì	惩治	6. chāzi	叉子	shāzi	沙子
7. chìzì	赤字	shìzi	柿子	8. zhàn shí	战时	zànshí	暂时
9. shào shēng	哨声	xiào shēng	笑声	10. shōu lǐ	收礼	xiūlǐ	修理
1. zhìzào	製造	zìzào	自造	2. zhànzhù	站住	zànzhù	贊助
3. zhāi huā	摘花	zāi huā	栽花	4. zhǎyǎn	眨眼	jiǎ yǎn	假眼
5. zhěngzhì	整治	chěngzhì	懲治	6. chāzi	叉子	shāzi	沙子
7. chìzì	赤字	shìzi	柿子	8. zhàn shí	戰時	zàn shí	暫時
9. shào shēng	哨聲	xiào shēng	笑聲	10. shōu lǐ	收禮	xiūlǐ	修理

二、儿声练习/兒聲練習

Pronunciation exercise using "r".

1. 早点儿 2. 样儿
3. 哪儿 4. 高个儿
5. 这儿 6. 今儿
7. 晚点儿 8. 一下儿

1. 早點兒 2. 樣兒
3. 哪兒 4. 高個兒
5. 這兒 6. 今兒
7. 晚點兒 8. 一下兒

三、根据拼音写汉字/根據拼音寫漢字

Write the Chinese characters equivalent of the following Pinyin.

1. tuìxiū 2. gàosu
3. tīngshuō 4. dǎ diànhuà

5. hǎo chī de 6. jiànzài

7. pànzhe 8. gǎnkuài

9. qùshì 10. xīwàng

四、根据课文回答问题/根據課文回答問題

Answer the following questions by using complete sentences based on information in the text.

1. 宜凡的姥姥、姥爷现在住在哪儿?
2. 一九四九年以前宜凡的爷爷、奶奶住在哪儿?
3. 一九四九年以后宜凡的爷爷、奶奶住在哪儿?
4. 宜凡的爷爷、奶奶现在还工作吗?
5. 宜凡有多少年没见到她爷爷、奶奶了?
6. 宜凡小时候，每次到台北去，爷爷、奶奶总是做什么?
7. 星期五，宜凡为什么盼着早点儿下课?
8. 你爷爷、奶奶现在怎么样?

1. 宜凡的姥姥、姥爺現在住在哪兒?
2. 一九四九年以前宜凡的爺爺、奶奶住在哪兒?
3. 一九四九年以後宜凡的爺爺、奶奶住在哪兒?
4. 宜凡的爺爺、奶奶現在還工作嗎?
5. 宜凡有多少年沒見到她爺爺、奶奶了?
6. 宜凡小時候，每次到臺北去，爺爺、奶奶總是做什麼?
7. 星期五，宜凡爲什麼盼着早點兒下課?
8. 你爺爺、奶奶現在怎麼樣?

五、填空

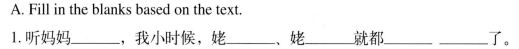

Fill in the blanks.

A. Fill in the blanks based on the text.

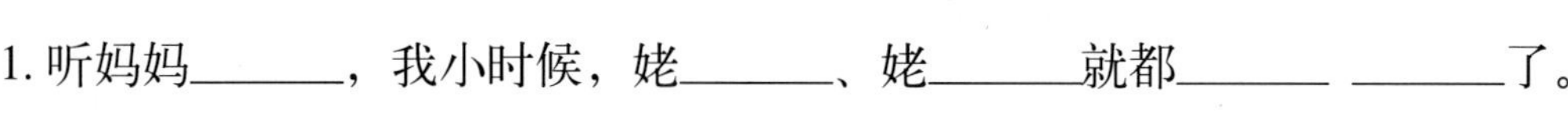

1. 听妈妈______，我小时候，姥______、姥______就都______ ______了。
2. 我爷爷、奶奶都还______在。
3. 一九四九年，奶奶住在______港，爷爷住______上______。
4. 一九四九年，他们就都搬______台北______了。
5. 爷爷、奶奶______ ______以后，我们______家都希望他们能到美国来住______ ______时间。

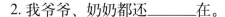

6. 小时候，我和哥哥到台北______，奶奶总是______我们做______吃______，爷爷常常______我们______故事。

1. 聽媽媽______，我小時候，姥______、姥______就都______ ______了。

2. 我爺爺、奶奶都還______在。

3. 一九四九年，奶奶住在______港，爺爺住______上______。

4. 一九四九年，他們就都搬______臺北______了。

5. 爺爺、奶奶______ ______以後，我們______家都希望他們能到美國來住______ ______時間。

6. 小時候，我和哥哥到臺北______，奶奶總是______我們做______吃______，爺爺常常______我們______故事。

B. Fill in each of the following blanks with 来/來 or 去（Note: The speaker is in the US.）

1. 凡凡的爷爷和奶奶都是一九四九年以后搬到台北______的。

2. 爷爷和奶奶这个星期就要到美国______了。

3. 小时候，每年妈妈都带我和哥哥到台北______看爷爷、奶奶。

4. 我盼着早点儿下课，好飞回家______看爷爷奶奶。

5. 上星期爷爷打电话______，问我们什么时候到台北______。

1. 凡凡的爺爺和奶奶都是一九四九年以後搬到臺北______的。

2. 爺爺和奶奶這個星期就要到美國______了。

3. 小時候，每年媽媽都帶我和哥哥到臺北______看爺爺、奶奶。

4. 我盼着早點兒下課，好飛回家______看爺爺奶奶。

5. 上星期爺爺打電話______，問我們什麽時候到臺北______。

C. Put 了 in the appropriate places in the following paragraph.

我已经很多年没去台北。记得上一次去台北是在五年前。那时候爷爷还没有退休，可是奶奶已经退休。每天爷爷一去上班，奶奶就给我做好吃的，还给我讲故事。我真希望能再回到那个时候去。每天不用上课，不用早起床，能常常给朋友打电话。有一次，我一天打十个电话。

我已經很多年没去臺北。記得上一次去臺北是在五年前。那時候爺爺還没有退休，可是奶奶已經退休。每天爺爺一去上班，奶奶就給我做好吃的，還給我講故事。我真希望能再回到那個時候去。每天不用上課，不用早起床，能常常給朋友打電話。有一次，我一天打十個電話。

六、重组/重組

Word order.

1. 中国/我姥爷/以前/姥姥/住在/和/去世

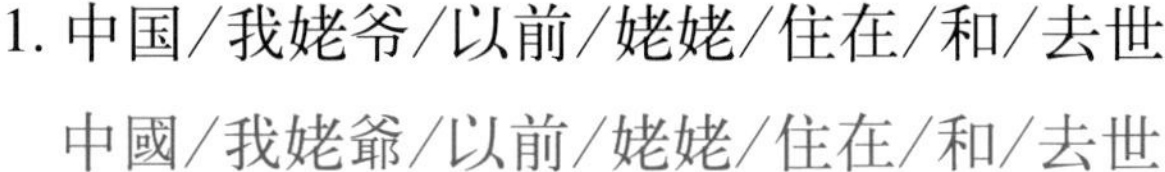

   中國/我姥爺/以前/姥姥/住在/和/去世

   My maternal grandfather and grandmother lived in China before they passed away.

2. 飞/去看/我想/爷爷/回家/赶快

   飛/去看/我想/爺爺/回家/趕快

   I want to fly home to see my grandpa and grandma.

3. 姥姥/的时候/我/就/去世了/很小

   姥姥/的時候/我/就/去世了/很小

   My maternal grandma died when I was very young.

4. 我们了/到美国/下星期/看/爷爷、奶奶/来/就要

   我們了/到美國/下星期/看/爺爺、奶奶/來/就要

   My grandpa and grandma are coming to the US to see us next week.

5. 以后/去/退休/搬到/我爸爸/想要/上海/住

   以後/去/退休/搬到/我爸爸/想要/上海/住

   After retirement my dad would like to move to Shanghai.

七、翻译/翻譯

Translate the following sentences into Chinese.

1. I heard that you love to speak Chinese, don't you?
2. How have you been? I haven't seen you for over ten years.
3. My maternal grandpa lived in Taipei before he retired.
4. I long for the class's ending so that I can go home. (use "pànzhe...")
5. My dad called me today to tell me that Grandpa had passed away the day before.

八、改错/改錯

Correct mistakes.

1. 爷爷、奶奶搬台北住一九四九年以后。
2. 我爷爷、奶奶今个星期就要来美国。
3. 我已经没记得爷爷、奶奶了。
4. 我希望老师今天下课早一点儿。
5. 奶奶做很多好吃常常。

6. 我有十年多没见爷爷、奶奶了。
1. 爺爺、奶奶搬臺北住一九四九年以後。
2. 我爺爺、奶奶今個星期就要來美國。
3. 我已經没記得爺爺、奶奶了。
4. 我希望老師今天下課早一點兒。
5. 奶奶做很多好吃常常。
6. 我有十年多没見爺爺、奶奶了。

九、课堂活动/課堂活動

In-class activity.

Theme: My Grandparents

Task: 1. Find a partner to form an instant family. Either of you plays grandma or grandpa.

2. Create a mini skit and play it in class. Pay attention to the tone differences between the two generations.

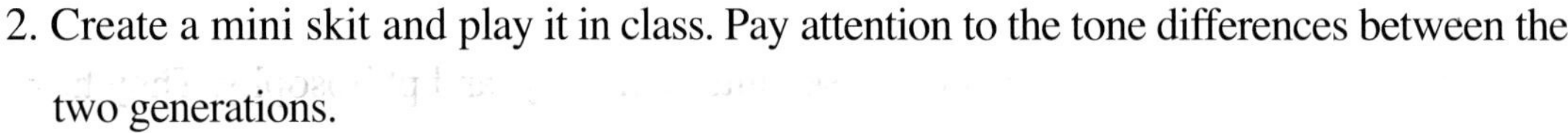

十、课外活动/課外活動

After-class activity.

Create a family tree of your family including name, age, job and home address, etc. You may ask for help from your parents and relatives.

爷爷/爺爺, ______________________________

奶奶 ______________________________

____

____

____

十一、写作练习/寫作練習

writing.

Write a short paragraph (50 words) about your Grandpa and Grandma. Please include the following words: 听说，去世，健在……/聽說，去世，健在……

十二、总结/總結

Summary.

1. Choose 5-10 of your favorite new vocabulary words from the text or reading material.

2. Quote 3-7 of your favorite sentences from the text or reading material here.

	Original sentence	**Translation of the sentence** (or make a new sentence of your own)
1		
2		
3		
4		
5		

3. From this lesson, you have learned Chinese culture, history, and philosophy. They have helped you to understand,

我现在清楚了/我現在清楚了：

① ______________________________

② ______________________________

LESSON 4

第四课
我的大学生活

星期五回到家，爷爷、奶奶一见到我，就拉着我的手问长问短。

爷爷：凡凡，你现在是大学生了，快给爷爷讲讲，你的大学生活怎么样？

凡凡：好。每天都能学习新东西，又能交新朋友，觉得很开心。

爷爷：噢?！让你最开心的是什么呢？

凡凡：自由！住得离家远，有自由。很多事情，像什么时候起床、什么时候睡觉、什么时候做作业、选什么课都自己做主，再也不用听妈妈唠叨了、让妈妈管着了。

奶奶：原来你上离家远的大学，是不想听你妈妈唠叨、让你妈妈管着啊?！

凡凡：我哥哥也一样呀，他比我跑得更远。

奶奶：他比你大嘛！

爷爷：学校里有没有不开心的事？

凡凡：有。餐厅的饭不好吃，我做梦都想吃妈妈做的菜。还有，有时候不到月底，钱就都花完了。

奶奶起床起得很早。

哥哥比我跑得更远。

不到月底钱就花完了。

离开家以后再也不要妈妈管着了。

我最开心的事

我长得像爷爷。

第四課
我的大學生活

星期五回到家，爺爺、奶奶一見到我，就拉着我的手問長問短。

爺爺：凡凡，你現在是大學生了，快給爺爺講講，你的大學生活怎麼樣？

凡凡：好。每天都能學習新東西，又能交新朋友，覺得很開心。

爺爺：噢?！讓你最開心的是什麼呢？

凡凡：自由！住得離家遠，有自由。很多事情，像什麼時候起床、什麼時候睡覺、什麼時候做作業、選什麼課都自己做主，再也不用聽媽媽嘮叨了、讓媽媽管着了。

奶奶：原來你上離家遠的大學，是不想聽你媽媽嘮叨、讓你媽媽管着啊?！

凡凡：我哥哥也一樣呀，他比我跑得更遠。

奶奶：他比你大嘛！

爺爺：學校裏有沒有不開心的事？

凡凡：有。餐廳的飯不好吃，我做夢都想吃媽媽做的菜。還有，有時候不到月底，錢就都花完了。

New Words
生词表/生詞表

生活		shēnghuó	*n/v*	life; livelihood; live
拉		lā	*v*	pull; draw; shake (hands)
手		shǒu	*n*	hand
问长问短	問長問短	wèncháng-wènduǎn	*idiom*	take the trouble to make detailed enquiries
快		kuài	*adj/adv*	quick; fast
怎么样	怎麼樣	zěnmeyàng	*pron*	how about; what about
每天		měitiān	*adv*	every day
学习	學習	xuéxí	*v*	study
新		xīn	*adj*	new
东西	東西	dōngxi	*n*	thing
又		yòu	*adv*	again; both…and
交		jiāo	*v*	associate with; be friend
开心	開心	kāixīn	*adj*	happy
噢		ō	*int*	oh (indicating realization)
让	讓	ràng	*v*	allow; let
最		zuì	*adv*	most
呢		ne	*particle*	(used at the end of interrogative sentences to indicate special, altenative or rhetorical question)
自由		zìyóu	*n/adj*	freedom; liberty; free
得		de	*particle*	(structural particle used after a verb or adjective to introduce a complement)
离	離	lí	*v/prep*	leave; part from; be at a distance from
远	遠	yuǎn	*adj*	far; distant; remote
事情		shìqing	*n*	thing; affair; matter
像		xiàng	*v*	resemble; be like; such as
睡觉	睡覺	shuìjiào	*v*	sleep
作业	作業	zuòyè	*n*	homework
选	選	xuǎn	*v*	choose; select; elect
做主		zuòzhǔ	*vo*	decide; make the decision; have the final say
也		yě	*adv*	also; too
不用		bùyòng	*adv*	need not

唠叨	嘮叨	láodao	*v*	be garrulous; nag; chatter
管		guǎn	*v*	control; discipline
原来	原來	yuánlái	*adv/adj*	as it turns out; originally; original
一样	一樣	yīyàng	*adj*	the same; equal; alike
呀		ya	*particle*	(used at the end of a sentence to express agreement, defensiveness, urge, etc.)
比		bǐ	*v/prep*	compare; contrast; than
跑		pǎo	*v*	run; run away; escape
更		gèng	*adv*	more; even more
嘛		ma	*particle*	(used to indicate that something is obvious)
学校	學校	xuéxiào	*n*	school; educational institution
里	裏	lǐ	*n*	inside; inner
事		shì	*n*	matter; affair; thing
餐厅	餐廳	cāntīng	*n*	dining hall; restaurant
做梦	做夢	zuòmèng	*vo*	dream; have a dream
菜		cài	*n*	dish; course; vegetables
有时候	有時候	yǒushíhou	*adv*	sometimes
月底		yuèdǐ	*n*	end of a month
钱	錢	qián	*n*	money
花		huā	*v/n*	spend; flower
完		wán	*v*	run out; use up (used at the end of a verb as a resultative complement); finish; complete

丶 丶 氵 氵 汗 汗 活 活 活 (9)
活 活 活 活
一 十 扌 扌 扌 扌 扩 拉 (8)
拉 拉 拉 拉
一 二 三 手 (4)
手 手 手 手
丿 𠂉 亠 手 矢 矢 矢 矢 矩 矩 短 短 (12)
短 短 短 短
丶 亠 六 六 交 交 (6)
交 交 交 交
丿 𠂉 午 乍 乍 乍 怎 怎 怎 (9)
怎 怎 怎 怎
丶 心 心 心 (4)
心 心 心 心
丨 冂 日 日 旦 早 是 是 是 是 最 最 (12)
最 最 最 最
丨 冂 曰 由 由 (5)
由 由 由 由
丶 亠 三 丰 主 (5)
主 主 主 主

Chinese Characters
汉字二/漢字二

一 厂 厂 厉 历 盾 原 原 原 原 (10)

原 原 原 原

丁 わ 也 (3)

也 也 也 也

一 匕 比 比 (4)

比 比 比 比

丶 口 口 早 早 足 足 足 趵 趵 趵 跑 (12)

跑 跑 跑 跑

一 十 艹 艹 艹 艹 艹 苎 苹 苹 菜 (11)

菜 菜 菜 菜

丿 𠂉 𠂉 牛 生 (5)

生 生 生 生

丨 口 口 口 口 口 呎 呢 (8)

呢 呢 呢 呢

フ 又 (2)

又 又 又 又

一 十 才 木 木 木 杧 杧 校 校 (10)

校 校 校 校

一 十 艹 ナ 芢 花 花 (7)

花 花 花 花

Chinese Characters
汉字三/漢字三

選	选	東	东
樣	样	業	业
夢	梦	開	开
離	离	遠	远
嘮	唠	錢	钱

Chinese Characters
汉字四/漢字四

裏	里	讓	让
廳	厅	習	习
噢	呀	候	情
新	管	叨	更
像	餐	底	嘛

Grammar Notes
语法简注/語法簡注

1. 一……就：as soon as…

① subject + 一 + action1 + 就 + action2

📖 奶奶一见到我，就拉着我的手，问长问短。

奶奶一見到我，就拉着我的手，問長問短。

As soon as Grandma saw me, she held my hand and asked all kinds of questions.

▶ 今天我一下（了）课就回家。

今天我一下（了）課就回家。

I will go home today as soon as the class is over.

▶ 昨天我一回（了）家就睡觉了。

昨天我一回（了）家就睡覺了。

I went to bed as soon as I returned home yesterday.

▶ 她一打电话就高兴。

她一打電話就高興。

She is happy the moment she starts talking on the phone.

② subject1 + 一 + action 1，(subject 2) + 就 + action 2

▶ 我一到家，我朋友就来了。

我一到家，我朋友就來了。

As soon as I got home, my friend came.

2. 让/讓：make；let；permit

① make somebody feel…

📖 让你最开心的是什么呢?

讓你最開心的是什麽呢?

What pleases you the most?

▶ 让我最开心的是我有自由。

讓我最開心的是我有自由。

What makes me happiest is that I'm very free.

▶ 学校的饭让我不开心。

學校的飯讓我不開心。

The food at school makes me unhappy.

② let or allow somebody to do something

(subject) + 让/讓 + somebody + verb + (object)

▶ 妈妈让我从今天起多说中文。
媽媽讓我從今天起多說中文。
Mom asks me to speak more Chinese from today on.

▶ 选什么课，爸爸让我自己做主。
選什麼課，爸爸讓我自己做主。
Dad lets me decide which courses I will enroll in.

3. 得：It is a marker for the complement of degree or the descriptive or predicative complement.

subject + verb + 得 + complement（adjective/adjective phrase）

📖 他比我跑得更远。
他比我跑得更遠。
He is even farther away from home than me.

▶ 奶奶起得很早。
Grandma gets up very early.

▶ 他跑得很快。
He runs very fast.

subject + verb + object + verb + 得 + complement（adjective/adjective phrase）

▶ 奶奶起床起得很早。
Grandma gets up very early.

▶ 他跑步跑得很快。
He runs very fast.

4. A 比 B……：A is more "adjective" than B.

A + 比 + B + adjective

📖 他比你大嘛！
(Because) He is older than you!

▶ 哥哥比我高。
Elder Brother is taller than me.

A + 比 + B + verb

▶ 妈妈比爸爸爱说话。
媽媽比爸爸愛說話。
Mom is more talkative than Dad.

▶ 哥哥比我喜欢打电话。
哥哥比我喜歡打電話。
Elder Brother likes to make phone calls more than I do.

A + verb + 得 + 比 + B + (adverb) + adjective + (complement)

▶ 他跑得比我远得多。
他跑得比我遠得多。
He is even farther away from home than me.

▶ 哥哥吃得比我快得多。
My elder brother eats much faster than me.

A + verb + objective + verb + 得 + 比 + B + adjective + (complement)

▶ 哥哥说中文说得比我好得多。
哥哥說中文說得比我好得多。
My elder brother speaks Chinese much better than I do.
Note: This sentence can also be phrased as follows:

▶ 哥哥说中文比我说得好得多。
哥哥說中文比我說得好得多。

▶ 哥哥比我说中文说得好得多。
哥哥比我說中文說得好得多。

5. 有没有：the affirmative-negative (verb-not-verb) question pattern

📖 学校里有没有不开心的事？
學校裏有沒有不開心的事？
Is there anything at school that makes you unhappy?

▶ 你今天有没有课？
你今天有沒有課？
Do you have any class today?

▶ 你交没交新朋友?

Did you make any new friends?

Subject + verb + 不 + verb + (object) ?

▶ 你是不是大学生?

你是不是大學生?

Are you a college student?

▶ 你爱不爱吃餐厅的饭?

你愛不愛吃餐廳的飯?

Do you love to eat the food at the dinning-hall?

Subject + adjective + 不 + adjective?

▶ 你开心不开心?

你開心不開心?

Are you happy?

▶ 你爸爸高不高?

Is your dad tall?

6. 原来：It is an adverb indicating that the speaker, who originally may have had some false assumptions, now discovers the true situation.

📖 原来你上离家远的大学，是不想听你妈妈唠叨呀!

原來你上離家遠的大學，是不想聽你媽媽嘮叨呀!

So it is because you don't want to put up with your mom's nagging that you attended a college so far from home!

▶ 原来你喜欢自己做主呀!

原來你喜歡自己做主呀!

So you like making decisions by yourself!

▶ 原来你的钱都花完了呀!

原來你的錢都花完了呀!

So you spent all your money!

7. V+完：finish an action

完 is a verb complement of result here.

(subject) + verb + 完 + (object)

钱花完了。

錢花完了。

The money is spent up.

▶ 你做完作业了吗？

你做完作業了嗎？

Have you finished your homework?

▶ A: 你吃完饭了没有？

你吃完飯了沒有？

Have you finished eating?

B: 我吃完(饭)了。

我吃完(飯)了。

I finished eating.

C: 我还没吃完(饭)呢。

我還沒吃完(飯)呢。

I haven't finished eating yet.

Reading Passage 阅读/閱讀

中文角

我们学校里有很多学生社团。我参加了一个叫“中文角”的社团。“中文角”又叫“汉语俱乐部”。每个星期五晚上，我和一些对中国感兴趣的同学就聚在一起。有时候我们聊中国的风土人情；有时候我们请去过中国的同学介绍他们在中国的见闻，或者看他们在中国照的照片；还有时候我们唱中文卡拉OK或者学做中国菜。

中文角

我們學校裏有很多學生社團。我參加了一個叫“中文角”的社團。“中文角”又叫“漢語俱樂部”。每個星期五晚上，我和一些對中國感興趣的同學就聚在一起。有時候我們聊中國的風土人情；有時候我們請去過中國的同學介紹他們在中國的見聞，或者看他們在中國照的照片；還有時候我們唱中文卡拉OK或者學做中國菜。

中文角		Zhōngwénjiǎo	Chinese Corner
社团	社團	shètuán	club; organization
参加	參加	cānjiā	join
汉语	漢語	Hànyǔ	Chinese language
俱乐部	俱樂部	jùlèbù	club
感兴趣	感興趣	gǎn xìngqù	be interested (in)
风土人情	風土人情	fēngtǔ-rénqíng	local conditions and customs
见闻	見聞	jiànwén	what one sees and hears

Chinese Corner

Friday, October 15, 6:30 p.m.
at Rome Café, Price Center
汉语俱乐部
10月15日，星期五，下午六点半
在Price Center's Rome 咖啡厅
大家都来说汉语！
不管你是什么人，我们都欢迎！
来认识学汉语的朋友，
有问题吗？
请给我打电话或发电子邮件
博瑞
858-232-2252

Chinese Corner

Friday, October 15, 6:30 p.m.
at Rome Café, Price Center
漢語俱樂部
10月15日，星期五，下午六點半
在Price Center's Rome 咖啡廳
大家都來說漢語！
不管你是什麼人，我們都歡迎！
來認識學漢語的朋友，
有問題嗎？
請給我打電話或發電子郵件
博瑞
858-232-2252

判断正误／判斷正誤

Identify the following statements as true or false based on the reading passage.

1. _______ 宜凡的大学里学生社团很多。
2. _______ 宜凡去过北京。
3. _______ “中文角”也叫“汉语俱乐部”。
4. _______ 学生在“中文角”做中国菜。
5. _______ 学生在“中文角”聊与中国有关的事。

1. _______ 宜凡的大學裏學生社團很多。
2. _______ 宜凡去過北京。
3. _______ “中文角”也叫“漢語俱樂部”。
4. _______ 學生在“中文角”做中國菜。
5. _______ 學生在“中文角”聊與中國有關的事。

Exercises
练习/練習

一、辨音练习/辨音練習

Distinguish between the following pairs of sounds.

1. shuǐniú 水牛 shuǐliú 水流 2. shānchéng 山城 sān céng 三层
3. zǎozi 枣子 jiǎozi 饺子 4. zīshì 姿势 zhīshi 知识
5. zuòyè 作业 zuòniè 作孽 6. chéngkè 乘客 zhèngkè 政客
7. chénjiù 陈旧 chéngjiù 成就 8. shànxīn 善心 sànxīn 散心
9. shīrén 诗人 sīrén 私人 10. shìdài 世代 sì dài 四代

1. shuǐniú 水牛 shuǐliú 水流 2. shānchéng 山城 sān céng 三層
3. zǎozi 棗子 jiǎozi 餃子 4. zīshì 姿勢 zhīshi 知識
5. zuòyè 作業 zuòniè 作孽 6. chéngkè 乘客 zhèngkè 政客
7. chénjiù 陳舊 chéngjiù 成就 8. shànxīn 善心 sànxīn 散心
9. shīrén 詩人 sīrén 私人 10. shìdài 世代 sì dài 四代

二、标声调/標聲調

Mark the tone.

Mark the tone for the first syllable.

"Yī" prior to the lst, 2nd and 3rd tones.

	prior to the 1st tone	prior to the 2nd tone	prior to the 3rd tone
1	yizhāng	yinián	yidiǎnr
2	yiqiān	yihuí	yibǎ
3	yitiān	yipíng	yihuǐr
4	yishēng	yizhí	yiběn

三、根据拼音写汉字/根據拼音寫漢字

Write the Chinese characters equivalent of the following Pinyin.

1. shēnghuó
2. zìjǐ
3. xuéxí
4. guǎn zhe
5. kāixīn
6. zěnmeyàng
7. zìyóu
8. wèncháng-wènduǎn
9. láodao
10. zuòmèng
11. zuòzhǔ
12. yuèdǐ

四、根据课文回答问题/根據課文回答問題

Answer the following questions by using complete sentences based on information in the text.

1. 爷爷、奶奶见到宜凡做什么了?
2. 宜凡觉得她的大学生活怎么样?
3. 为什么宜凡觉得上大学后很开心?
4. 什么事情让宜凡最开心?
5. 宜凡的自由是什么?
6. 宜凡为什么想上离家远的大学?
7. 宜凡有什么不开心的事?
8. 你的大学生活怎么样? 你开心不开心?

1. 爺爺、奶奶見到宜凡做什麼了?
2. 宜凡覺得她的大學生活怎麼樣?
3. 爲什麼宜凡覺得上大學後很開心?
4. 什麼事情讓宜凡最開心?
5. 宜凡的自由是什麼?
6. 宜凡爲什麼想上離家遠的大學?
7. 宜凡有什麼不開心的事?
8. 你的大學生活怎麼樣? 你開心不開心?

五、填空

Fill in the blanks.

A. Fill in the blanks based on the text.

1. 爷爷、奶奶一见______我，就拉______我的手，问______问______。
2. 我觉得住______离家远，有______ ______。很多事情，______什么时候______床、什么时______睡觉、什么时候______作业、______什么课都自己______ ______。
3. 每天______能学习______东西，又能______新朋友，觉得很______ ______。
4. 学校里也有不开心的______，______厅的饭不好吃；还有，有时候不到月______，钱就都______ ______了。

1. 爺爺、奶奶一見______我，就拉______我的手，問______問______。
2. 我覺得住______離家遠，有______ ______。很多事情，______什麼時候______床、什麼時______睡覺、什麼時候______作業、______什麼課都自己______ ______。

3. 每天______能學習______東西，又能______新朋友，覺得很______ ______。

4. 學校裏也有不開心的______，______廳的飯不好吃；還有，有時候不到月______，錢就都______ ______了。

B. Insert the words on the left to the sentences on the right.

1. 就　哥哥一看见我，走过来问长问短。

2. 都　我做梦想去中国。

3. 让　她上离家远的大学是不想妈妈管着。

4. 离　原来你上家远的大学，是不想听你妈妈唠叨啊。

5. 比　哥哥我大，可是我哥哥跑得快。

1. 就　哥哥一看見我，走過來問長問短。

2. 都　我做夢想去中國。

3. 讓　她上離家遠的大學是不想媽媽管着。

4. 離　原來你上家遠的大學，是不想聽你媽媽嘮叨啊。

5. 比　哥哥我大，可是我哥哥跑得快。

C. Fill in the blanks with 看/看完，讲（講）/讲（講）完，吃/吃完，花/花完 and use each only once.

1. 昨天爷爷的故事还没______，电话就响了。今天我一定请爷爷再______。

2. 奶奶做的菜真好______，我们一下子就______了。

3. 小王很能______钱，每个月还没到月底，她的钱就______了。

4. 我不知道你也喜欢______书。这本书我一______，就给你。

1. 昨天爺爺的故事還没______，電話就響了。今天我一定請爺爺再______。

2. 奶奶做的菜真好______，我們一下子就______了。

3. 小王很能______錢，每個月還没到月底，她的錢就______了。

4. 我不知道你也喜歡______書。這本書我一______，就給你。

六、重组/重組

Word order.

1. 家里/学校里/住在/自由/我觉得/比/住在

   家裏/學校裏/住在/自由/我覺得/比/住在

   I think that it is more free living at school than living at home.

2. 就/上了大学/她/很开心/一/觉得

   就/上了大學/她/很開心/一/覺得

   As soon as she started her university life, she felt happy.

3. 给奶奶/大学生活/快/你的/讲讲/怎么样

给奶奶/大學生活/快/你的/講講/怎麽樣

Hurry up and tell Grandma how your university life is.

4. 你搬到/原来/唠叨啊/香港去/听妈妈/是不想

你搬到/原來/嘮叨啊/香港去/聽媽媽/是不想

So it turns out that the reason you moved to Hong Kong is that you don't want to put up with our mom's nagging.

5. 自己/什么时候/做主/睡觉/什么时候/都/做作业/凡凡

自己/什麽時候/做主/睡覺/什麽時候/都/做作業/凡凡

Fanfan makes the decision herself on when to go to bed and when to do the homework.

七、翻译/翻譯

Translate the following sentences into Chinese.

1. As soon as I get home today, I will go to bed.
2. Did you make any new friends when you were at the university? (use the affirmative-negative question pattern)
3. He is older than me. However, I run faster than he, and I take more course at the college than he (use "bǐ")
4. When Little Sister came home last time, she said that what made her happy at the college was that the food at the cafeteria was delicious, and however, what made her unhappy was she had already spent all her money.
5. When I asked my friend how she liked her life at the university, my friend said that she really liked it, and that she didn't have to listen to her dad's chatter any more. I said, "So it is because you don't want to put up with your dad's chatter that you attended a university far away from home!"

八、改错/改錯

Correct mistakes.

1. 你现在是大学生，你的大学生活怎么样？
2. 你爷爷奶奶是什么时候来美国？
3. 哥哥说他不想妈妈唠叨。
4. 我做梦想吃妈妈做的菜。
5. 我觉得他的生活比你的很好。
6. 我觉得住在学校比住在家里自由很多。

7. 我奶奶做菜比我爷爷好很多。

8. 我哥哥说中文比我好很多。

1. 你現在是大學生，你的大學生活怎麼樣？

2. 你爺爺奶奶是什麼時候來美國？

3. 哥哥說他不想媽媽嘮叨。

4. 我做夢想吃媽媽做的菜。

5. 我覺得他的生活比你的很好。

6. 我覺得住在學校比住在家裏自由很多。

7. 我奶奶做菜比我爺爺好很多。

8. 我哥哥說中文比我好很多。

九、课堂活动／課堂活動

In-class activity.

Group work: exchange your college life experiences within your group.

	Routine Event	Special Event/Weekend Event
6:00a.m.—8:00a.m.		
8:00a.m.—12:00a.m.		
1:00p.m.—3:00p.m.		
4:00p.m.—6:00p.m.		
6:00p.m.—10:00p.m.		
10:00p.m.—		

十、课外活动／課外活動

After-class activity.

1. Design a full size poster for an upcoming "Chinese Corner" meeting. Fill in the worksheet first.

Chinese Corner
Time:
Location:
Topic:
Contact:
Convincing words:

2. Design an advertisement for your club.

十一、写作练习/寫作練習

Writing.

Theme: One Day of My College Life

Write a short essay about your college life (60—70 words). Please include the following words,

自己做主，自由，交新朋友，做作业，花钱，开心

自己做主，自由，交新朋友，做作業，花錢，開心

十二、总结/總結

Summary.

1. Choose 5-10 of your favorite new vocabulary words from the text or reading material.

2. Quote 3-7 of your favorite sentences from the text or reading material here.

	Original sentence	**Translation of the sentence** (or make a new sentence of your own)
1		
2		
3		
4		
5		

3. From this lesson, you have learned Chinese culture, history, and philosophy. They have helped you to understand,

我现在清楚了/我現在清楚了：

① ______________________________

② ______________________________

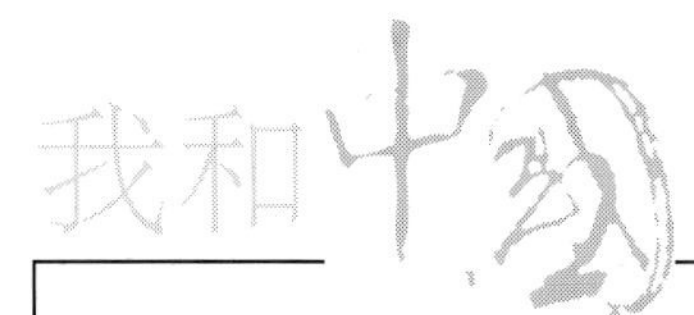

LESSON 5

第五课

接风

为了给爷爷、奶奶接风，妈妈在我家附近最好的中餐馆订了座位。为了吃饭的时候能用中文给大家点菜，首先，我请爸爸把爷爷、奶奶喜欢吃的菜，用电子邮件发给我。然后，我把那些菜名用电脑打出来，并请我的中文老师给我纠正了发音。最后，我把那些菜名念了一遍又一遍，一直到把它们都背下来。

吃饭那天，我用中文点了八个菜。听我点完菜，奶奶笑得眼睛眯成了一条缝儿；爷爷高兴得不停地点头；爸爸、妈妈没说话，只是看着我笑；哥哥竖起大拇指，说："小妹，你中文说得真好！"看着家人这高兴的样子，我觉得那天的饭真好吃！

第五課
接風

爲了給爺爺、奶奶接風，媽媽在我家附近最好的中餐館訂了座位。爲了吃飯的時候能用中文給大家點菜，首先，我請爸爸把爺爺、奶奶喜歡吃的菜，用電子郵件發給我。然後，我把那些菜名用電腦打出來，并請我的中文老師給我糾正了發音。最後，我把那些菜名念了一遍又一遍，一直到把它們都背下來。

吃飯那天，我用中文點了八個菜。聽我點完菜，奶奶笑得眼睛眯成了一條縫兒；爺爺高興得不停地點頭；爸爸、媽媽沒說話，只是看着我笑；哥哥豎起大拇指，説：“小妹，你中文説得真好！”看着家人這高興的樣子，我覺得那天的飯真好吃！

New Words
生词表/生詞表

接风	接風	jiēfēng	*vo*	give a dinner of welcome (to a visitor from afar)
为了	爲了	wèile	*conj*	for; for the sake of; in order to
附近		fùjìn	*n/adj*	vicinity; nearby; neighboring
中餐馆	中餐館	zhōngcānguǎn	*n*	Chinese restaurant
订	訂	dìng	*v*	reserve; order; book
座位		zuòwèi	*n*	seat
大家		dàjiā	*pron*	all of us; everybody
点菜	點菜	diǎn cài		order dishes
首先		shǒuxiān	*adv/conj*	first; first of all
请	請	qǐng	*v*	request; ask (a favor); please
把		bǎ	*prep*	(used to advance the object of a verb to the position before it)
喜欢	喜歡	xǐhuan	*v*	like; be fond of
电子邮件	電子郵件	diànzǐ yóujiàn		email
发	發	fā	*v*	deliver; send out
然后	然後	ránhòu	*conj*	then; afterwards; after that
菜名		cài míng		name of a dish
打(印)		dǎ(yìn)	*v*	print
出来		chūlai	*vc*	come out; (used as a complement after a verb to indicate an outward movement or result)
并		bìng	*conj*	and; furthermore
老师	老師	lǎoshī	*n*	teacher
纠正	糾正	jiūzhèng	*v*	correct; rectify
发音	發音	fāyīn	*n/vo*	pronunciation; pronounce
最后	最後	zuìhòu	*adv*	finally; eventually
念		niàn	*v*	read aloud; study; attend school
遍		biàn	*m*	(for actions) once through; one time
一直到		yīzhí dào		until; up to
它们	它們	tāmen	*pron*	they; them
背		bèi	*v*	recite from memory; learn by heart
下来	下來	xiàlai	*vc*	come down; (used after a verb to indicate the completion or result of an action)
点	點	diǎn	*v*	select; choose

笑		xiào	*v*	smile; laught
眼睛		yǎnjing	*n*	eye(s)
眯		mī	*v*	narrow one's eyes
成		chéng	*v*	become; turn into
条	條	tiáo	*m*	(used for something long, narrow or thin)
缝	縫	fèng	*n*	a narrow opening; crack; fissure
高兴	高興	gāoxìng	*adj*	glad; happy; cheerful
停		tíng	*v*	stop; halt; pause
地		de	*particle*	(an adverbial particle)
点头	點頭	diǎntóu	*vo*	nod one's head
只是		zhǐshì	*adv*	only; just; merely
竖	豎	shù	*v*	set upright; erect
大拇指		dàmǔzhǐ	*n*	thumb
小妹		xiǎomèi	*n*	little sister; younger sister
这	這	zhè	*pron*	this
样子	樣子	yàngzi	*n*	appearance; manner; shape

Chinese Characters
汉字一/漢字一

丨 阝 阝 阝 阝 附 附 (7)
附 附 附 附
′ 厂 斤 斤 䜣 䜣 近 (7)
近 近 近 近
丶 亠 广 广 広 庅 庅 座 座 座 (10)
座 座 座 座
ノ 亻 亻 仁 仁 位 位 (7)
位 位 位 位
丶 丷 丷 䒑 䒑 首 首 首 首 (9)
首 首 首 首
ノ 𠂉 ⺧ 生 生 先 (6)
先 先 先 先
丶 丷 丷 兰 并 并 (6)
并 并 并 并
一 十 士 吉 吉 吉 吉 吉 壴 喜 喜 喜 (12)
喜 喜 喜 喜
一 扌 扌 扌 扣 扣 把 (7)
把 把 把 把
ノ ク 夕 夕 名 名 (6)
名 名 名 名

Chinese Characters
汉字二/漢字二

一 丅 下 正 正 (5)

正

丶 亠 亠 立 立 产 音 音 音 (9)

音

丿 人 八 今 今 念 念 念 (8)

念

一 厂 万 成 成 成 (6)

成

一 十 𠃊 古 古 有 直 直 (8)

直

丨 丬 丬 丬 北 北 背 背 背 (9)

背

一 十 扌 扌 打 (5)

打

丿 ⺈ ⺮ 竹 竹 竹 竺 竺 笑 笑 (10)

笑

丨 口 口 只 只 (5)

只

乚 凵 中 出 出 (5)

出

Chinese Characters
汉字三/漢字三

爲	为	風	风
訂	订	糾	纠
請	请	歡	欢
發	发	縫	缝
師	师	郵	邮

Chinese Characters
汉字四/漢字四

興	兴	頭	头
對	对	館	馆
條	条	豎	竖
這	这	地	停
眼	睛	遍	指

Grammar Notes
语法简注/語法簡注

1. 为了……/爲了……：in order to…; for the sake of…

📖 为了给爷爷、奶奶接风，妈妈在我家附近最好的中餐馆订了座位。
爲了給爺爺、奶奶接風，媽媽在我家附近最好的中餐館訂了座位。
In order to give a dinner of welcome for Grandpa and Grandma (who are coming from afar), Mom reserved seats in the best Chinese restaurant near our home.

▶ 为了让妈妈开心，我每天给她打个电话。
爲了讓媽媽開心，我每天給她打個電話。
In order to make Mom happy, I call her every day.

▶ 为了学中文，哥哥去了北京。
爲了學中文，哥哥去了北京。
In order to study Chinese, Elder Brother went to Beijing.

Note: The sentences above can also be phrased as follows:

▶ 妈妈在我家附近最好的中餐馆订了座位，是为了给爷爷、奶奶接风。
媽媽在我家附近最好的中餐館訂了座位，是爲了給爺爺、奶奶接風。

▶ 我每天给妈妈打电话，是为了让她开心。
我每天給媽媽打電話，是爲了讓她開心。

▶ 哥哥去了北京，是为了学中文。
哥哥去了北京，是爲了學中文。

2. 首先：first；然后/然後：then；最后/最後：at last; finally; in the end

📖 首先，我请爸爸把爷爷、奶奶喜欢吃的菜，用电子邮件发给我。
首先，我請爸爸把爺爺、奶奶喜歡吃的菜，用電子郵件發給我。
Firstly, I asked Dad to send (a list of) Grandpa and Grandma's favorite dishes to me by email.

▶ 然后，我把那些菜名用电脑打出来。
然後，我把那些菜名用電腦打出來。
Then, I typed those dishes' names on a computer.

▶ 最后，我把那些菜名念了一遍又一遍。
最後，我把那些菜名念了一遍又一遍。
Finally, I read out those dishes' names loud many times.

3. 把：It is used to advanced the object of a verb to the position before it to show the influence on something or to show how something is handled.

subject + (adverb/negative) + 把 + object + verb phrase

📖 我请爸爸把爷爷、奶奶喜欢吃的菜，用电子邮件发给我。

我請爸爸把爺爺、奶奶喜歡吃的菜，用電子郵件發給我。

I asked Dad to send (a list of) Grandpa and Grandma's favorite dishes to me by email.

▶ 他把那些菜名用电脑打出来了。

他把那些菜名用電腦打出來了。

He typed those dishes' names on a computer.

▶ 他还没把那些菜名用电脑打出来。

他還沒把那些菜名用電腦打出來。

He hasn't typed those dishes' names on a computer yet.

▶ 我把那些菜名念了一遍又一遍。

我把那些菜名念了一遍又一遍。

I read out those dishes' names loud over and over again.

▶ 我把奶奶做的菜都吃了。

I ate all the dishes Grandma made.

4. 给/給：for；to

📖 我想用中文给大家点菜。

我想用中文給大家點菜。

I would like to order dishes for everybody in Chinese.

▶ 我的中文老师给我纠正发音。

我的中文老師給我糾正發音。

My Chinese teacher corrected my pronunciation for me.

▶ 妈妈每天给我们做饭。

媽媽每天給我們做飯。

Mom cooks for us every day.

5. verb + 得 + complement：indicating the result or degree

📖 奶奶笑得眼睛眯成一条缝儿。

奶奶笑得眼睛眯成一條縫兒。

Grandma narrowed her eyes in a smile.

▶ 爷爷高兴得不停地点头。

爺爺高興得不停地點頭。

Grandpa was so glad that he kept nodding his head.

6. verb ＋ 下来：indicating completion or result of an action

背下來：completely memorize something by repeating or reciting it many times

▶ 请把那些菜名背下来。

請把那些菜名背下來。

Please memorize the names of those dishes.

▶ 请把这些字写下来。

請把這些字寫下來。

Please write down these characters.

中国人的口味

中国地大人多，人们的口味也很不一样。一般来说，南方人喜欢吃甜的，做菜少不了放糖；北方人爱吃咸的，做菜放盐放得多。四川人、湖南人、湖北人喜欢吃辣的，菜里常有辣椒；山西人爱吃酸的，做菜离不开醋。所以，中国有“南甜、北咸、东辣、西酸”的说法。

下边是宋宜凡为她家人点的菜，你知道宋家是什么地方的口味吗？

宫保鸡丁、鱼香肉丝、梅菜扣肉、京都排骨、干烧黄鱼、红烧狮子头、麻婆豆腐、干煸四季豆、炒年糕、虾仁儿炒米饭，还有海鲜汤。

中國人的口味

中國地大人多，人們的口味也很不一樣。一般來說，南方人喜歡吃甜的，做菜少不了放糖；北方人愛吃鹹的，做菜放鹽放得多。四川人、湖南人、湖北人喜歡吃辣的，菜裏常有辣椒；山西人愛吃酸的，做菜離不開醋。所以，中國有“南甜、北鹹、東辣、西酸”的說法。

下邊是宋宜凡爲她家人點的菜，你知道宋家是什麽地方的口味嗎？

宮保鷄丁、魚香肉絲、梅菜扣肉、京都排骨、乾燒黃魚、紅燒獅子頭、麻婆豆腐、乾煸四季豆、炒年糕、蝦仁兒炒米飯，還有海鮮湯。

口味		kǒuwèi	one's taste; taste of food
甜		tián	sweet
糖		táng	sugar; candy
咸	鹹	xián	salty
盐	鹽	yán	salt
辣椒		làjiāo	hot pepper; chili; red pepper
酸		suān	sour; tart
醋		cù	vinegar
鸡丁	鷄丁	jīdīng	chicken cube
肉丝	肉絲	ròusī	shredded meat
黄鱼	黃魚	huángyú	yellow croaker (a kind of fish)
炒		chǎo	stir-fry
海鲜汤	海鮮湯	hǎixiāntāng	seafood soup

判断正误／判斷正誤

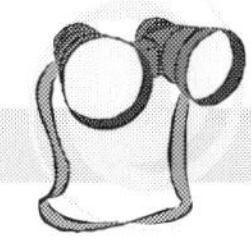

Identify the following statements as true or false based on the reading passage.

1. _______ 南方人喜欢吃酸的，做菜少不了放糖。
2. _______ 北方人爱吃辣的，做菜放盐放得多。
3. _______ 四川人、湖南人、湖北人喜欢吃甜的，菜里常有辣椒。
4. _______ 山西人爱吃咸的，做菜离不开醋。

1. _______ 南方人喜歡吃酸的，做菜少不了放糖。
2. _______ 北方人愛吃辣的，做菜放鹽放得多。
3. _______ 四川人、湖南人、湖北人喜歡吃甜的，菜裏常有辣椒。
4. _______ 山西人愛吃鹹的，做菜離不開醋。

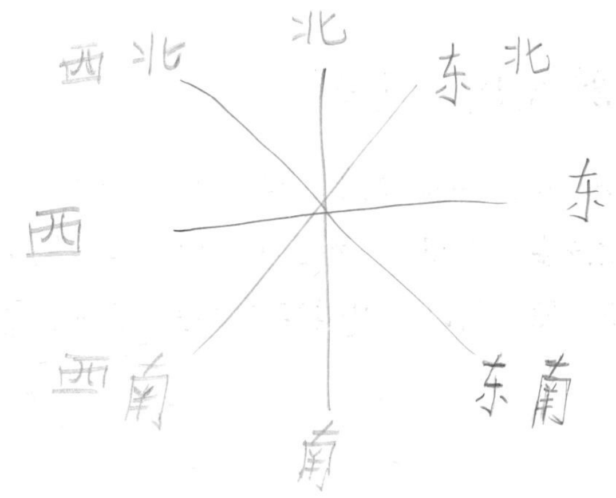

Exercises
练习／練習

一、辨音练习／辨音練習

Distinguish between the following pairs of sounds.

1. cánsī 蚕丝 chánshī 禅师 2. cā chē 擦车 chāchē 叉车
3. cōngtóu 葱头 kōngtóu 空投 4. sùshè 宿舍 sùshè 素色
5. qíncài 芹菜 qīngcài 青菜 6. yǎnjing 眼睛 yǎnjìng 眼镜
7. yījiù 依旧 yīxiù 衣袖 8. yíngjiù 营救 réngjiù 仍旧
9. wǔnǚ 舞女 mǔnǚ 母女 10. wénruò 文弱 wénluò 纹络

1. cánsī 蠶絲 chánshī 禪師 2. cā chē 擦車 chāchē 叉車
3. cōngtóu 葱頭 kōngtóu 空投 4. sùshè 宿舍 sùshè 素色
5. qíncài 芹菜 qīngcài 青菜 6. yǎnjing 眼睛 yǎnjìng 眼鏡
7. yījiù 依舊 yīxiù 衣袖 8. yíngjiù 營救 réngjiù 仍舊
9. wǔnǚ 舞女 mǔnǚ 母女 10. wénruò 文弱 wénluò 紋絡

二、声调练习／聲調練習

Tonal changes.

Mark the tones.

A. "Bù" prior to the 1st , 2nd and 3rd tones.

bu shūo bu jiē bu gāo bu shēng bu duō
bu lái bu xué bu fán bu liú bu huí
bu shǒu bu hǎo bu zǎo bu ǎi bu shǎo

B. "Bù" prior to the 4th tone.

bu shì bu yào bu jiàn bu wèn
bu qù bu huì bu shèng bu ài

三、根据拼音写汉字／根據拼音寫漢字

Write the Chinese characters equivalent of the following Pinyin.

1. jiēfēng 2. shǒuxiān 3. zuòwèi 4. jiūzhèng 5. lǎoshī
6. diǎncài 7. diǎntóu 8. diànzǐ yóujiàn 9. fāyīn 10. gāoxìng

四、根据课文回答问题/根據課文回答問題

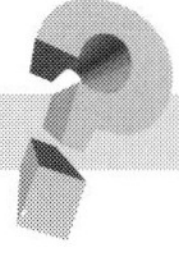

Answer the following questions by using complete sentences base on information in the text.

1. 为什么宜凡的妈妈在她家附近最好的中餐馆订了座位?
2. 为了给爷爷、奶奶接风，宜凡首先做了什么？然后做了什么？最后做了什么?
3. 宜凡是怎么知道爷爷、奶奶爱吃什么菜的?
4. 宜凡那天都点了几个菜?
5. 宜凡点完菜，宜凡的爸爸妈妈说什么了?
6. 宜凡的爷爷奶奶说什么了?
7. 宜凡的哥哥说什么了?
8. 为什么宜凡觉得那天的饭很好吃?
9. 你家吃饭的时候谁点菜？你们喜欢点什么菜?

1. 爲什麼宜凡的媽媽在她家附近最好的中餐館訂了座位?
2. 爲了給爺爺、奶奶接風，宜凡首先做了什麼？然後做了什麼？最後做了什麼?
3. 宜凡是怎麼知道爺爺、奶奶愛吃什麼菜的?
4. 宜凡那天都點了幾個菜?
5. 宜凡點完菜，宜凡的爸爸媽媽説什麼了?
6. 宜凡的爺爺奶奶説什麼了?
7. 宜凡的哥哥説什麼了?
8. 爲什麼宜凡覺得那天的飯很好吃?
9. 你家吃飯的時候誰點菜？你們喜歡點什麼菜?

五、填空

Fill in the blanks.

A. Fill in the blanks based on the text.

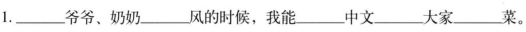

1. ______爷爷、奶奶______风的时候，我能______中文______大家______菜。
2. 首先，我请爸爸______爷爷、奶奶喜欢吃______菜，______电子邮件发______我。
3. 然后，我______那些菜名______电脑______出来，并请我的中文老师______我______ ______了发音。
4. 最后，我______那些菜______念了一______又一______，一直到把______们都______下来。
5. 吃饭的那天，我______中文______了八个菜。

6. 听我点______菜，奶奶笑______眼睛眯______了一______缝儿。

7. 哥哥竖______大拇指，说我中文说______真好。

1. ______爺爺、奶奶______風的時候，我能______中文______大家______菜。

2. 首先，我請爸爸______爺爺、奶奶喜歡吃______菜，______電子郵件發______我。

3. 然後，我______那些菜名______電腦______出來，并請我的中文老師______我______ ______了發音。

4. 最後，我______那些菜______念了一______又一______，一直到把______們都______下來。

5. 吃飯的那天，我______中文______了八個菜。

6. 聽我點______菜，奶奶笑______眼睛眯______了一______縫兒。

7. 哥哥豎______大拇指，説我中文説______真好。

B. Choose the appropriate de（的，得 or 地）for each blank.

1. 奶奶笑______眼睛眯成了一条缝儿。

2. 爷爷没说话，只是不停______点头。

3. 小妹高兴______说："哥哥说______真好！"

4. 奶奶做______饭最好吃，爷爷讲______故事最好听。

5. 他的同学住______比他远______多。

6. 我觉______那天______饭真好吃！

7. 我是在美国出生、美国长大______。

8. 妈妈高兴______不停______笑。

1. 奶奶笑______眼睛眯成了一條縫兒。

2. 爺爺没説話，只是不停______點頭。

3. 小妹高興______説："哥哥説______真好！"

4. 奶奶做______飯最好吃，爺爺講______故事最好聽。

5. 他的同學住______比他遠______多。

6. 我覺______那天______飯真好吃！

7. 我是在美國出生、美國長大______。

8. 媽媽高興______不停______笑。

六、改写/改寫

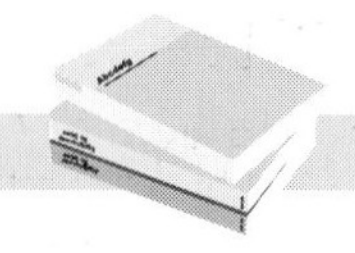

Rewrite the following sentences.

A. Rewrite the following sentences with “把”.

1. 我用电脑打出菜名来。
2. 那些菜名我念了很多遍。
3. 奶奶喜欢吃的菜爷爷都告诉我了。
4. 我请爸爸发给我奶奶喜欢吃的菜。
5. 妈妈说，她已经订好座位了。

1. 我用電腦打出菜名來。
2. 那些菜名我念了很多遍。
3. 奶奶喜歡吃的菜爺爺都告訴我了。
4. 我請爸爸發給我奶奶喜歡吃的菜。
5. 媽媽説，她已經訂好座位了。

B. Put the following three sentences in a chronological order by using the appropriate conjunctions.

1. 把菜名都背下来。
2. 把菜名用电脑打出来。
3. 请爸爸把爷爷奶奶爱吃的菜告诉我。

1. 把菜名都背下來。
2. 把菜名用電腦打出來。
3. 請爸爸把爺爺奶奶愛吃的菜告訴我。

七、重组/重組

Word order.

1. 告诉我/他喜欢/我请/把/爷爷/吃的菜

   告訴我/他喜歡/我請/把/爺爺/吃的菜

   I ask Grandpa to tell me the dishes he likes.

2. 菜名/点菜/为了/我把/背下来了/用中文/都

   菜名/點菜/爲了/我把/背下來了/用中文/都

   In order to order dishes in Chinese, I memorized all the names of the dishes.

3. 不停地/高兴得/点完/妈妈/菜/听我/点头

   不停地/高興得/點完/媽媽/菜/聽我/點頭

   After hearing me order the dishes, Mom was so glad that she kept nodding her head.

4. 老师叫我/我的发音/为了/背下来/纠正/把菜名/先
老師叫我/我的發音/爲了/背下來/糾正/把菜名/先
In order to correct my pronunciation, the teacher asked me memorize the dishes' names first.
5. 听我/奶奶/眼睛/说完/一条缝儿/中文/眯成了/笑得
聽我/奶奶/眼睛/説完/一條縫兒/中文/眯成了/笑得
Hearing me speak Chinese, Grandma narrowed her eyes in a smile.

八、翻译/翻譯

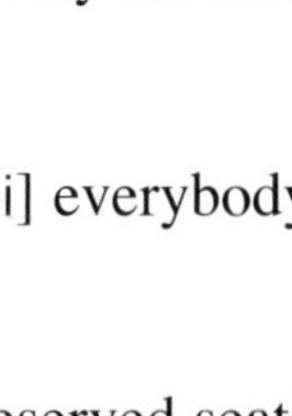

Translate the following sentences into Chinese.

1. I don't speak Chinese well. In order to speak Chinese well, I want to speak more Chinese starting from tomorrow.
2. My elder brother sent an email to me today. He asked me to send him the names of my favorite dishes by email.
3. At the Chinese restaurant, my Chinese teacher requested that I order food for [gěi] everybody in Chinese.
4. In order to [wèile] give a dinner of welcome [jiēfēng] for Dad's friend, my dad reserved seats in the best Chinese restaurant.
5. Grandma cooks for [gěi] us every day. In order to make her happy, I always finish the dishes she makes. (use "bǎ") When she sees me finish all the food she makes, she would always be so happy that she keeps smiling.
6. I read out those dishes' names loud many times until I memorized all of them. (use "bǎ")

九、改错/改錯

Correct mistakes.

1. 我要点菜用中文，为了让爷爷、奶奶高兴。
2. 妈妈订了座位在附近的中餐馆。
3. 我打出来中文菜名用电脑。
4. 点菜完，爷爷说我点菜得好。
5. 是为了学好中文，明年我去中国。
6. 我念那些菜名一遍又一遍。
7. 我都背那些菜名下来了。
8. 爷爷、奶奶吃完了我点的菜。

1. 我要點菜用中文，爲了讓爺爺、奶奶高興。

2. 媽媽訂了座位在附近的中餐館。

3. 我打出來中文菜名用電腦。

4. 點菜完，爺爺説我點菜得好。

5. 是爲了學好中文，明年我去中國。

6. 我念那些菜名一遍又一遍。

7. 我都背那些菜名下來了。

8. 爺爺、奶奶吃完了我點的菜。

十、课堂活动／課堂活動

In-class activity.

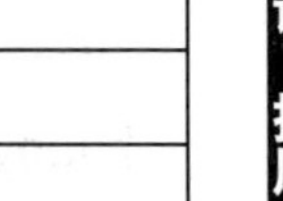

Theme: My Favorite Chinese Dishes

Task: 1. Conduct a survey on "What is your favorite Chinese food?" in class.

2. Report the survey results and compare the top five dishes among teams in class.

Worksheet:

	Team 1	Team 2	Team 3
1			
2			
3			
4			
5			

十一、课外活动／課外活動

After-class activity.

Task: Design a menu of your family's.

十二、总结/總結

Summary.

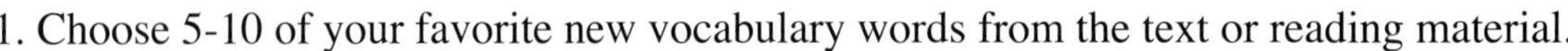

1. Choose 5-10 of your favorite new vocabulary words from the text or reading material.

2. Quote 3-7 of your favorite sentences from the text or reading material here.

	Original sentence	**Translation of the sentence** (or make a new sentence of your own)
1		
2		
3		
4		
5		

3. From this lesson, you have learned Chinese culture, history, and philosophy. They have helped you to understand,

   我现在清楚了/我現在清楚了：

   ① ______________________________

   ② ______________________________

字词复习（一）/字詞複習（一）

请你找一找，从第一课到第五课，你学过哪些带下列偏旁部首的字。

請你找一找，從第一課到第五課，你學過哪些帶下列偏旁部首的字。

Find characters with the following radicals from Lesson 1 to Lesson 5.

1. 人 亻

2. 彳

3. 女

4. 口 囗

5. 日

6. 言 讠

7. 扌

8. 木

9. 王

10. 糸 纟

11. 門 门

12. 艹

13. 目

14. 月

15. 心

16. 金 钅

17. 攵

18. 灬

19. 辶

20. 水 氵

第二单元 第二單元

历史 文化 歷史 文化

Unit Two Chinese History and Culture

LESSON 6

第六课
面积大 人口多

从饭馆回到家，我和爷爷坐在客厅里聊天儿。

凡凡：爷爷，上星期五，我们“中文角”的人为中国大还是美国大的事争论起来。有人说，中国的面积比美国的大；也有人说，美国的面积比中国的大。爷爷，您说，到底是中国的面积大还是美国的面积大？

爷爷：其实，中国的面积跟美国的差不多。我记得，中国的面积大约是九百六十万平方公里，美国的面积差不多有九百三十多万平方公里。按这个计算，中国是亚洲最大的，世界第三大的国家。可是，也有人说美国的面积是九百六十三万平方公里。

凡凡：那人口呢？我听说中国是世界上人口最多的国家，是吗？

爷爷：是啊，现在至少有十三亿吧。

凡凡：爷爷，您是说中国和美国的面积差不多一样大，可是中国的人口却大约是美国的四五倍。这就是说，像我们家这么大的房子，要是在中国，这里边会住十八九个人，是吗？

LESSON 6

第六課

面積大 人口多

從飯館回到家，我和爺爺坐在客廳裏聊天兒。

凡凡：爺爺，上星期五，我們“中文角”的人爲中國大還是美國大的事爭論起來。有人說，中國的面積比美國的大；也有人說，美國的面積比中國的大。爺爺，您說，到底是中國的面積大還是美國的面積大？

爺爺：其實，中國的面積跟美國的差不多。我記得，中國的面積大約是九百六十萬平方公里，美國的面積差不多有九百三十多萬平方公里。按這個計算，中國是亞洲最大的，世界第三大的國家。可是，也有人說美國的面積是九百六十三萬平方公里。

凡凡：那人口呢？我聽說中國是世界上人口最多的國家，是嗎？

爺爺：是啊，現在至少有十三億吧。

凡凡：爺爺，您是說中國和美國的面積差不多一樣大，可是中國的人口却大約是美國的四五倍。這就是說，像我們家這麼大的房子，要是在中國，這裏邊會住十八九個人，是嗎？

New Words
生词表/生詞表

面积	面積	miànjī	*n*	surface area
人口		rénkǒu	*n*	human population
饭馆	飯館	fànguǎn	*n*	small restaurant
坐		zuò	*v*	sit; take a seat
客厅	客廳	kètīng	*n*	living room
聊天儿	聊天兒	liáotiānr	*vo*	chat
中文角		Zhōngwénjiǎo	*n*	Chinese Corner
争论	爭論	zhēnglùn	*v*	dispute; argue; debate
起来	起來	qǐlai	*v*	(used after a verb or an adjective to indicate the beginning and continuation of an action)
到底		dàodǐ	*adv*	at last; on earth (used in question for emphasis)
还是	還是	háishi	*conj*	or
其实	其實	qíshí	*adv*	actually; in fact; as a matter of fact
差不多		chàbuduō	*adj*	similar
大约	大約	dàyuē	*adv*	approximately; about
九百		jiǔbǎi	*nu*	nine hundred
六十		liùshí	*nu*	sixty
万	萬	wàn	*nu*	ten thousand
平方公里		píngfāng gōnglǐ		square kilometer
三十		sānshí	*nu*	thirty
按		àn	*prep*	according to; in accordance with
计算	計算	jìsuàn	*v*	count; calculate
亚洲	亞洲	Yàzhōu	*pn*	Asia
世界		shìjiè	*n*	world
国家	國家	guójiā	*n*	country; nation
可是		kěshì	*conj*	but; however
十三		shísān	*nu*	thirteen
听说	聽說	tīngshuō	*v*	hear about
至少		zhìshǎo	*adv*	at (the) least
亿	億	yì	*nu*	a hundred million
却		què	*adv*	but; yet
倍		bèi	*m*	time; fold
这就是说	這就是說	zhè jiù shì shuō	*idiom*	this is to say…
这么	這麼	zhème	*adv*	so; such; like this
房子		fángzi	*n*	house; building
要是		yàoshi	*conj*	if; suppose; in case
里边	裏邊	lǐbian	*n*	interior; inside
会	會	huì	*aux*	be likely to; can; be able to
十八九		shíbā-jiǔ	*nu*	eighteen or nineteen

二百五 250 also stupid　　成千上万 10s of thousands　　千万不要 don't do it

Chinese Characters
汉字一/漢字一

xiōng dì
兄弟　　很大方 generous

从…至 from to there　　公平 fair　　A X, subject B 却 Y

AX, 却Y
他是中国人,
却不会说
中文.

丿 ㇇ 𠆢 从 从 坐 坐 (7)

坐 坐 坐 坐

丶 丶 宀 宀 peak 安 客 客 客 (9)

客 客 客 客

一 丆 丆 丙 而 而 而 面 面 (9)

面 面 面 面

丿 ⺈ ⺈ 角 角 角 角 (7)

角 角 角 角

丿 八 公 公 (4)

公 公 公 公

丿 ⺈ 㔾 刍 刍 争 (6)

争 争 争 争

丶 ㇇ 之 (3)

之 之 之 之

一 十 廾 廾 甘 甘 其 其 (8)

其 其 其 其

丶 丷 丷 兰 兰 羊 差 差 差 (9)

差 差 差 差

一 丆 丆 百 百 百 (6)

百 百 百 百

Chinese Characters
汉字二/漢字二

一 ㄗ 五 至 至 至 (6)

至 至 至 至

丨 ㄐ 小 少 (4)

少 少 少 少

丿 亻 亻 仁 亻 位 位 倍 倍 倍 (10)

倍 倍 倍 倍

一 ㄧ 立 平 平 (5)

平 平 平 平

丶 ㄧ ㄔ 户 户 戶 房 房 (8)

房 房 房 房

丨 ㄇ 口 (3)

口 口 口 口

丶 二 亍 方 (4)

方 方 方 方

丨 ㄇ 日 田 田 罒 罕 界 界 (9)

界 界 界 界

丿 ㄏ ㄅ ㄅ 竹 竹 笁 笃 笃 第 第 (11)

第 第 第 第

一 ㄧ ㄇ 可 可 (5)

可 可 可 可

Chinese Characters
汉字三/漢字三

論	论	億	亿
會	会	邊	边
實	实	約	约
萬	万	計	计
積	积	亞	亚

Grammar Notes
语法简注/語法簡注

1. A还是B／A還是B：either A or B

This is an alternative question and may form part of another sentence which is not an alternative question.

📖 我们“中文角”的人为中国大还是美国大的问题争论起来。
我們“中文角”的人爲中國大還是美國大的問題争論起來。
We, the people from the Chinese Corner, began to argue over the issue of whether China or the US is bigger.

▶ 中国的人口多还是美国的人口多？
中國的人口多還是美國的人口多？
Which is larger, China's population or America's?

▶ 你喜欢美国菜还是喜欢中国菜？
你喜歡美國菜還是喜歡中國菜？
Do you like American food or Chinese food?

2. 为……争论起来／爲……争論起來：dispute about something; argue over

📖 我们“中文角”的人为中国大还是美国大的事争论起来。
我們“中文角”的人爲中國大還是美國大的事争論起來。
We, the people from the Chinese Corner, began to argue over the issue of whether China or the US is bigger.

▶ 我和爸爸为我上哪个大学的事争论起来。
我和爸爸爲我上哪個大學的事争論起來。
Dad and I argue over the issue of which university I should attend.

3. 到底……：It is used in questions for emphasis.

📖 到底是中国的面积大还是美国的面积大？
到底是中國的面積大還是美國的面積大？
In the final analysis, is the surface area of China larger than that of the US or vice versa?

▶ 你到底来不来？
你到底來不來？
Are you coming or not?

▶ 他到底是美国人还是中国人？

他到底是美國人還是中國人？

Is he American or Chinese?

4. A跟／和B……：a pattern of comparison

① A is about the same as B; A is the same as B

A跟／和B差不多（一样）

A跟／和B差不多（一樣）

▶ 你的问题跟我的一样。

你的問題跟我的一樣。

Your question is the same as mine.

▶ 那个电脑跟这个差不多（一样）。

那個電腦跟這個差不多（一樣）。

That computer is about the same as this one.

② A is about the same "adjective" as B; A is the same "adjective" as B

A跟B差不多／一样 ＋adjective

A跟B差不多／一樣 ＋adjective

📖 其实，中国的面积跟美国的差不多（一样）大。

其實，中國的面積跟美國的差不多（一樣）大。

In fact, the surface area of China is about as big as that of the US.

▶ 我哥哥跟你（差不多）一样高。

我哥哥跟你（差不多）一樣高。

My elder brother is about as tall as you are.

▶ 美国的面积跟中国的一样大吗？

美國的面積跟中國的一樣大嗎？

Is the surface area of the US as large as that of China?

5. 按……计算，……／按……計算，……：calculated according to…

📖 按这个计算，中国是亚洲最大的，世界第三大的国家。

按這個計算，中國是亞洲最大的，世界第三大的國家。

Calculated according to this, China is the largest country in Asia, (and) the third largest in the world.

▶ 按美国人的计算，美国的面积比中国大。

按美國人的計算，美國的面積比中國大。

Calculated according to Americans, the surface area of the US is bigger than that of China.

6. …… 呢：an abbreviated question with 呢

📖 那人口呢？ Then, what about population?

▶ 你妈妈爱打电话，你爸爸呢？

你媽媽愛打電話，你爸爸呢？

Your mom loves chatting on phone. What about your dad?

▶ 我妈妈爱唠叨，你妈妈呢？

我媽媽愛嘮叨，你媽媽呢？

My mom is garrulous. How about your mom?

7. 要是……，就……：if…, then…

📖 像我们家这么大的房子，要是在中国，这里边会住十八九个人。

像我們家這麼大的房子，要是在中國，這裏邊會住十八九個人。

As for a house as big as ours, if it were in China, it would accommodate eighteen or nineteen people.

▶ 要是我有时间，我就为你订座位。

要是我有時間，我就爲你訂座位。

If I have time, I will reserve a seat for you.

▶ 要是我住得离家远，我就不用听妈妈唠叨了。

要是我住得離家遠，我就不用聽媽媽嘮叨了。

If I lived far away from home, I wouldn't have to listen to my mother's natters.

8. ……，是吗/……，是嗎：…, right? …, is it?

statement，是吗（是不是）？/statement，是嗎（是不是）？

📖 这里边会住十八九个人，是吗？

這裏邊會住十八九個人，是嗎？

The house would have to accommodate eighteen or nineteen people, right?

▶ 你喜欢北京，是吗？

你喜歡北京，是嗎？

You like Beijing, right?

▶ 他比我矮，是不是？

He's shorter than me, right?

Reading Passage
阅读/閱讀

珠穆朗玛峰

珠穆朗玛，藏语是“第三神女”的意思。传说，很早很早以前，天上有五神女姐妹。她们羡慕西藏人的生活，就从天上下到人间。在这五神女姐妹中，第三神女“珠穆朗玛”最漂亮，也最善良。

后来，第三神女把自己变成一座高山，每天看护着西藏人民。西藏人民为了纪念这位又漂亮又善良的第三神女，就把她变成的高山叫做“第三神女峰”——这就是现在海拔8844.43米的世界最高峰——珠穆朗玛峰。

珠穆朗瑪峰

珠穆朗瑪，藏語是“第三神女”的意思。傳説，很早很早以前，天上有五神女姐妹。她們羨慕西藏人的生活，就從天上下到人間。在這五神女姐妹中，第三神女“珠穆朗瑪”最漂亮，也最善良。

後來，第三神女把自己變成一座高山，每天看護着西藏人民。西藏人民爲了紀念這位又漂亮又善良的第三神女，就把她變成的高山叫做“第三神女峰”——這就是現在海拔8844.43米的世界最高峰——珠穆朗瑪峰。

珠穆朗玛峰	珠穆朗瑪峰	Zhūmùlǎngmǎfēng	Mount Qomolangma
藏语	藏語	Zàngyǔ	Tibetan (language)
神女		shénnǚ	goddess
意思		yìsi	meaning
传说	傳説	chuánshuō	it is said; legend
天上		tiānshàng	sky; heaven
羡慕		xiànmù	envy
西藏		Xīzàng	Tibet
漂亮		piàoliang	pretty; beautiful
善良		shànliáng	good and honest; kind-hearted
纪念	紀念	jìniàn	commemorate/remember
海拔		hǎibá	elevation
米		mǐ	meter

判断正误/判斷正誤

Identify the following statements as true or false based on the reading passage.

1. _______ 这是一个真实的故事。
2. _______ 珠穆朗玛，藏语是“第三神女”的意思。
3. _______ “第三神女”是五姐妹神女中最漂亮，最善良的。
4. _______ “第三神女”就是现在海拔8844.43米的世界最高峰。

1. _______ 這是一個真實的故事。
2. _______ 珠穆朗瑪，藏語是“第三神女”的意思。
3. _______ “第三神女”是五姐妹神女中最漂亮，最善良的。
4. _______ “第三神女”就是現在海拔8844.43米的世界最高峰。

Exercises
练习/練習

一、发音练习/發音練習

Pronunciation exercise.

绕口令/繞口令 Tongue Twister

Sì shì sì, shí shì shí,
Shísì shì shísì, sìshí shì sìshí.
Sìshí jiǎn shísì, zài chéng sìshísì, shì yìqiān yìbǎi sìshísì,
Xiànzài qǐng nǐ shì yi shì.

四是四，十是十，
十四是十四，四十是四十。
四十减十四，再乘四十四，是一千一百四十四，
现在请你试一试。

四是四，十是十，
十四是十四，四十是四十。
四十減十四，再乘四十四，是一千一百四十四，
現在請你試一試。

二、词语练习/詞語練習

Vocabulary exercise.

	Chinese Character	Pinyin	Make a Sentence of Your Own
1		miànjī	
2		liáotiānr	
3		dàodǐ	
4		chàbuduō	
5		dàyuē	
6		tīngshuō	
7		zuì	
8		zhìshǎo	

三、根据课文回答问题/根據課文回答問題

Answer the following questions by using complete sentences based on information in the text.

1. “中文角”的人为什么事争论起来?
2. 中国的面积有多大?
3. 美国的面积有多大?
4. 哪个国家是亚洲最大的国家?
5. 中国是世界上第几大的国家?
6. 中国现在大约有多少人口?

1. “中文角”的人爲什麽事争論起來?
2. 中國的面積有多大?
3. 美國的面積有多大?
4. 哪個國家是亞洲最大的國家?
5. 中國是世界上第幾大的國家?
6. 中國現在大約有多少人口?

四、填空

Fill in the blanks.

A. Fill in the blanks based on the text.

1. 我们“中文角”的人，______中国大______ ______美国大的事争论______ ______。
2. ______人说，中国的面积______美国______大；也有人说，美国的面积比中国______大。
3. 中国是______洲______大的，世界______三大的国家，现在______ ______有十三亿人口。
4. 中国和美国的面积______ ______ ______一样大，可是中国的人口却______ ______是美国的五______。

1. 我們“中文角”的人，______中國大______ ______美國大的事争論______ ______。
2. ______人説，中國的面積______美國______大；也有人説，美國的面積比中國______大。

3. 中國是______洲______大的，世界______三大的國家，現在______ ______有十三億人口。
4. 中國和美國的面積______ ______ ______一樣大，可是中國的人口却______ ______是美國的五______。

B. Choose the appropriate word for each blank.

1. 我______（要是；就是）在中国出生的就好了。
2. ______（还是；其实），中国跟美国差不多大。
3. ______（你说；据说）中国有十三亿人口。
4. 你知道中国______（到底；其实）有多少人吗？
5. 小王跟小马为什么时候去中国的事______（争论；听）起来。

1. 我______（要是；就是）在中國出生的就好了。
2. ______（還是；其實），中國跟美國差不多大。
3. ______（你說；據説）中國有十三億人口。
4. 你知道中國______（到底；其實）有多少人嗎？
5. 小王跟小馬爲什麼時候去中國的事______（争論；聽）起來。

五、重组/重組

Word order.

1. 五倍/中国的/美国的/我的中文老师/人口/大约是/说
   五倍/中國的/美國的/我的中文老師/人口/大約是/説
   My Chinese teacher said that the population of China is approximately five times as great as that of US.
2. 是/面积大/还是/中国的/美国的/你知道/大
   是/面積大/還是/中國的/美國的/你知道/大
   Do you know whether China is bigger than the US or vice versa?
3. 十三亿/有人说/有/现在/没那么多/中国的人口/也有人说/中国的人口
   十三億/有人説/有/現在/没那麽多/中國的人口/也有人説/中國的人口
   Some people said that there are 1.3 billion people in China now, while some said there are fewer than that.
4. 争论/为/爸爸和我/问题/我上/哪一所大学的/起来
   争論/爲/爸爸和我/問題/我上/哪一所大學的/起來
   Dad and I argued over the issue of which university I should attend.

5. 像/听说/四五个人/要是/这里边会住/这么大的房间/在中国的大学/我住的

像/聽說/四五個人/要是/這裏邊會住/這麼大的房間/在中國的大學/我住的

I heard that (as for) a room as big as mine, if it were at a university in China, it would accommodate four or five people.

六、翻译/翻譯

Translate the following sentences into Chinese.

1. Does your mom love Chinese food or American food?
2. Elder Brother said that his Chinese teacher is better than my Chinese teacher, but I feel that my Chinese teacher is as good as his Chinese teacher.
3. Last month you said you could come home this Friday. Three days ago you called me and said you could come home either this weekend or next weekend. When can you come home after all?
4. Dad said he and Mom would come to visit me next Saturday, and would like to dine with me at the restaurant near my university. I said, "If I have time, I will reserve seats for all of us."
5. The Americans said that the surface area of the US is bigger than that of China. However, according to the calculation of the Chinese, the surface area of the US is smaller than that of China. In the final analysis, is the surface area of China bigger or the surface area of US bigger?

七、改错/改錯

Correct mistakes.

1. 中国的面积比美国的差不多。	1. 中國的面積比美國的差不多。
2. 中国的面积不跟美国的一样大。	2. 中國的面積不跟美國的一樣大。
3. 中国的面积比美国的有一点儿大。	3. 中國的面積比美國的有一點兒大。
4. 中国是最大的国家在亚洲。	4. 中國是最大的國家在亞洲。
5. 美国的人口跟中国小一点儿。	5. 美國的人口跟中國小一點兒。
6. 你现在去学校或者[huòzhě]去饭馆?	6. 你現在去學校或者[huòzhě]去飯館?

八、课堂活动/課堂活動

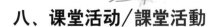

In-class activity.

Theme: Contest on "How much do you know about China?"

Worksheet:

	Checklist
1	Name five large cities in China and point them out on the map.
2	Name the two longest rivers in China and indicate where they are on the map.
3	Find the location of Mount Qomolangma（珠穆朗玛峰）on the map.

九、课外活动/課外活動

After-class activity.

A. Before starting Lesson 6, go online to find answers to the following questions.

1. 中国的面积有多大？人口有多少？
2. 美国的面积有多大？人口有多少？
3. 世界上面积最大的国家是哪个？第二大的国家是哪个？第三大的国家是哪个？
4. 人口最多的国家是哪个？第二多的国家是哪个？第三多的国家是哪个？
5. 世界上面积最小的国家是哪个？人口最少的国家是哪个？

1. 中國的面積有多大？人口有多少？
2. 美國的面積有多大？人口有多少？
3. 世界上面積最大的國家是哪個？第二大的國家是哪個？第三大的國家是哪個？
4. 人口最多的國家是哪個？第二多的國家是哪個？第三多的國家是哪個？
5. 世界上面積最小的國家是哪個？人口最少的國家是哪個？

B. Compare China with the US.

	中国/中國	美国/美國
面积/面積(Area)		
人口（Population）		
首都（Capital City）		
语言/語言（Language）		
食物（Food）		

十、写作练习/寫作練習

Writing.

Design a birthday card for either your parent, sibling, friend, or other relatives.

For example:

亲爱的美美：

祝你生日快乐！从今天起你就是大人了！以后什么事你都可以自己作主了，再也不用听你妈妈唠叨，让你妈妈管着了！！！！为你高兴！

友：丑丑

Suggested words：亲爱的　祝　生日　快乐　希望　健康　长寿

親愛的美美：

祝你生日快樂！從今天起你就是大人了！以後什麼事你都可以自己作主了，再也不用聽你媽媽嘮叨，讓你媽媽管着了！！！！爲你高興！

友：醜醜

Suggested words：親愛的　祝　生日　快樂　希望　健康　長壽

十一、总结/總結

Summary.

1. Choose 5-10 of your favorite new vocabulary words from the text or reading material.
2. Quote 3-7 of your favorite sentences from the text or reading material here.

	Original sentence	Translation of the sentence (or make a new sentence of your own)
1		
2		
3		
4		
5		

3. From this lesson, you have learned Chinese culture, history, and philosophy. They have helped you to understand,

① 我现在清楚了/我現在清楚了：__________

② 我现在知道了/我現在知道了：__________

LESSON 7

第七课
历史长

吃过早饭，妈妈带奶奶到中国城去了。我陪爷爷到公园去散步。爷爷喜欢一边散步，一边讲故事。

“爷爷，美国已经有两百多年的历史了，中国呢？”

爷爷喝了一口水，说：“中国的历史可长喽！五六千年以前，中国人的祖先就已经开始生活在黄河、长江两岸了。那时候中国有一百多个小国，这些小国之间不断地打仗。到了战国时期就剩下七个比较大的国家了。公元前二百二十一年，秦始皇统一了中国，建立了秦朝。

秦朝以后，中国又经历了汉、三国、隋、唐、宋、元、明、清等朝代。一九一一年，清朝结束；一九一二年，中华民国建立，孙中山先生任总统。”爷爷停了一下，接着说：“一九四九年，中华人民共和国成立……”

“爷爷，我们已经走了一个小时了。”

“噢，是吗？！”爷爷总是这样，一讲到中国历史就忘了时间！

第七課
歷史長

吃過早飯，媽媽帶奶奶到中國城去了。我陪爺爺到公園去散步。爺爺喜歡一邊散步，一邊講故事。

“爺爺，美國已經有兩百多年的歷史了，中國呢？”

爺爺喝了一口水，說：“中國的歷史可長嘍！五六千年以前，中國人的祖先就已經開始生活在黃河、長江兩岸了。那時候中國有一百多個小國，這些小國之間不斷地打仗。到了戰國時期就剩下七個比較大的國家了。公元前二百二十一年，秦始皇統一了中國，建立了秦朝。

秦朝以後，中國又經歷了漢、三國、隋、唐、宋、元、明、清等朝代。一九一一年，清朝結束；一九一二年，中華民國建立，孫中山先生任總統。”爺爺停了一下，接着說：“一九四九年，中華人民共和國成立……”

“爺爺，我們已經走了一個小時了。”

“噢，是嗎？！”爺爺總是這樣，一講到中國歷史就忘了時間！

New Words
生词表/生詞表

历史	歷史	lìshǐ	*n*	history
早饭	早飯	zǎofàn	*n*	breakfast
带	帶	dài	*v*	take; bring
中国城	中國城	Zhōngguóchéng	*n*	Chinatown
陪		péi	*v*	keep (someone) company; accompany
公园	公園	gōngyuán	*n*	park
散步		sànbù	*vo*	take a walk; go for a walk/stroll
一边	一邊	yībiān	*conj*	while; as
喝		hē	*v*	drink
口		kǒu	*m*	(for mouthfuls, persons, etc.)
水		shuǐ	*n*	water
可		kě	*adv*	indeed; very (used in a declarative sentence for emphasis)
喽	嘍	lou	*particle*	(used to indicate a certainty)
千		qiān	*n*	thousand
祖先		zǔxiān	*n*	ancestor
开始	開始	kāishǐ	*v*	begin; start
黄河		Huánghé	*pn*	Yellow River
长江	長江	Chángjiāng	*pn*	Yangtze River
两岸	兩岸	liǎng'àn	*n*	both banks (of the river)
一百		yībǎi	*nu*	one hundred
这些	這些	zhèxiē	*pron*	these
之间	之間	zhījiān	*n*	among; between
不断	不斷	bùduàn	*adv*	constantly; continuously
打仗		dǎzhàng	*vo*	fight a battle; wage war
战国时期	戰國時期	Zhànguó Shíqī	*pn*	the Warring States Period (475 BC—221 BC)
剩下		shèngxia	*vc*	be left (over); remain
比较	比較	bǐjiào	*adv/v*	relatively; compare
公元		gōngyuán	*n*	AD (Christian era)
秦始皇		Qín Shǐhuáng	*pn*	the first emperor of Qin Dynasty
统一	統一	tǒngyī	*v*	unify; unite

建立		jiànlì	*v*	build; establish; found
秦朝		Qíncháo	*pn*	Qin Dynasty (221 BC—206 BC)
经历	經歷	jīnglì	*v/n*	go through; undergo; experience
汉	漢	Hàn	*pn*	Han Dynasty (206 BC—220 AD)
三国	三國	Sānguó	*pn*	Three Kingdoms (220—280): Wei (220—265), Shu (221—263), and Wu (222—280)
隋		Suí	*pn*	Sui Dynasty (581—618)
唐		Táng	*pn*	Tang Dynasty (618—907)
宋		Sòng	*pn*	Song Dynasty (960—1279)
元		Yuán	*pn*	Yuan Dynasty (1206—1368)
明		Míng	*pn*	Ming Dynasty (1368—1644)
清		Qīng	*pn*	Qing Dynasty (1616—1911)
等		děng	*particle*	and so on; and so forth; etc.
朝代		cháodài	*n*	dynasty
结束	結束	jiéshù	*v*	end; finish; conclude
中华民国	中華民國	Zhōnghuá Mínguó	*pn*	Republic of China (1912—1949)
孙中山	孫中山	Sūn Zhōngshān	*pn*	Sun Yat-sen, the founder of the Republic of China
先生		xiānsheng	*n*	Mr.; sir; one's husband
一下		yīxià	*m*	one time; once; in a short while
中华人民共和国	中華人民共和國	Zhōnghuá Rénmín Gònghéguó	*pn*	People's Republic of China
成立		chénglì	*v*	found; establish
走		zǒu	*v*	walk; go; leave
小时	小時	xiǎoshí	*n*	hour
任		rèn	*v*	assume; take up
总统	總統	zǒngtǒng	*n*	president
这样	這樣	zhèyàng	*pron*	so; such; like this; this way
忘		wàng	*v*	forget

Chinese Characters
汉字一/漢字一

丶 口 口 史 史 (5)

史 史 史 史

一 厂 万 成 成 成 (6)

成 成 成 成

丨 ⺊ 屮 屮 屮 屮 步 (7)

步 步 步 步

丨 山 山 (3)

山 山 山 山

一 十 廾 廾 廾 廾 苗 苗 苗 黄 黄 (11)

黄 黄 黄 黄

丶 亠 亠 亠 立 (5)

立 立 立 立

亅 ⺢ 水 水 (4)

水 水 水 水

丨 山 山 山 岸 岸 岸 岸 (8)

岸 岸 岸 岸

丿 二 千 (3)

千 千 千 千

丿 亻 亻 什 仗 (5)

仗 仗 仗 仗

Chinese Characters
汉字二/漢字二

ㄑ ㄠ 女 女' 女' 女' 始 始 (8)										
始	始	始	始							
丶 丶 氵 氵 氵 沪 沪 河 (8)										
河	河	河	河							
丶 丶 氵 氵 汀 江 (6)										
江	江	江	江							
一 十 廾 廾 共 共 (6)										
共	共	共	共							
ノ 亻 白 白 白 皁 皁 皁 皇 (9)										
皇	皇	皇	皇							
一 十 亡 古 古 古 直 卓 卓 朝 朝 朝 (12)										
朝	朝	朝	朝							
丶 丶 宀 宀 宇 宋 宋 (7)										
宋	宋	宋	宋							
ノ 亻 亻 代 代 (5)										
代	代	代	代							
丶 亠 亡 亡 忘 忘 忘 (7)										
忘	忘	忘	忘							
一 二 亍 元 (4)										
元	元	元	元							

Chinese Characters
汉字三/漢字三

歷	历	帶	带
戰	战	斷	断
統	统	孫	孙
漢	汉	華	华
較	较	嘍	喽

Chinese Characters
汉字四/漢字四

圓	园	两	兩
東	明	陪	城
期	剩	政	散
任	清	等	秦
唐	喝	走	民

Grammar Notes
语法简注/語法簡注

1. 过/過：It is used after another verb indicating "passing by".

   Affirmative sentence：verb+过/過+（object）

   Negative sentence：没有+verb+过/過+（object）

   Interrogative sentence：Verb+没+verb+过/過+(object)?

   Verb+过/過+(object)+没有?

📖 吃过早饭，妈妈带奶奶到中国城去了。

吃過早飯，媽媽帶奶奶到中國城去了。

Aften breakfast, Mom brought Grandma to Chinatown.

▶ A: 你们去没去过上海?

你們去沒去過上海?

Have you ever been to Shanghai?

B: 我去过上海。

我去過上海。

I have been to Shanghai.

C: 我没去过上海。

我沒去過上海。

I have never been to Shanghai.

2. 一边+V1，一边+V2/一邊+V1，一邊+V2：The subject does V2, while doing V1.

📖 爷爷喜欢一边散步，一边讲故事。

爺爺喜歡一邊散步，一邊講故事。

Grandpa likes telling stories while taking a walk.

▶ 她一边用电脑，一边打电话。

她一邊用電腦，一邊打電話。

She makes phone calls while using the computer.

▶ 他一边吃饭，一边听音乐。

他一邊吃飯，一邊聽音樂。

He listens to music while eating.

3. 可……：It means "indeed" and is used in a declarative sentence for emphasis.

📖 中国的历史可长喽！

中國的歷史可長嘍！

China's history is indeed very long. (China's history is longer than you expected.)

▶ 中国人可多了。

中國人可多了。

There are a lot of Chinese people! (More than you can imagine.)

▶ 这个电影可好看了。

這個電影可好看了。

This movie is great! (Better than you expected.)

4. ……之间/……之間：among; between

| plural nouns ＋ 之间/之間 |

| noun 1 + 和/跟 + noun 2 ＋ 之间/之間 |

📖 这些小国之间不断打仗。

這些小國之間不斷打仗。

These small states fought continuously against each other.

▶ 他们之间不亲。

他們之間不親。

They are not close to each other.

▶ 那个母亲和她女儿之间很亲。

那個母親和她女兒之間很親。

That mother is very close to her daughter.

5. ……上：in

When 上 comes after an abstract noun, it can indicate the area or the aspect of the noun.

📖 秦始皇统一了中国，建立了中国历史上第一个王朝——秦朝。

秦始皇統一了中國，建立了中國歷史上第一個王朝——秦朝。

Qin Shihuang unified China and established the first dynasty in Chinese history—the Qin Dynasty.

▶ 世界上有多少国家？

世界上有多少國家？

How many countries are there in the world?

▶ 中文报纸上有中国菜谱。

中文報紙上有中國菜譜。

There are Chinese menus in Chinese-language newspapers.

Reading Passage
阅读/閱讀

女皇帝——武则天

从秦始皇统一中国到最后一个封建王朝——清朝——结束，中国历史上有过二百多位皇帝，但是女皇帝却只有一个，这就是唐朝的武则天。

武则天，名叫武曌 [zhào]，山西文水人，在位十五年。武则天死后，人们在她的墓前为她树了一块大石碑。但是因为武则天活着的时候说过："我的碑上不要刻字。我做的事是好是坏，由后人评价。"所以，我们今天看到的武则天的碑上一个字也没有。这块一个字也没刻的石碑就是有名的"无字碑"。

女皇帝——武則天

從秦始皇統一中國到最後一個封建王朝——清朝——結束，中國歷史上有過二百多位皇帝，但是女皇帝却只有一個，這就是唐朝的武則天。

武則天，名叫武曌 [zhào]，山西文水人，在位十五年。武則天死後，人們在她的墓前爲她樹了一塊大石碑。但是因爲武則天活着的時候説過："我的碑上不要刻字。我做的事是好是壞，由後人評價。"所以，我們今天看到的武則天的碑上一個字也没有。這塊一個字也没刻的石碑就是有名的"無字碑"。

女皇帝		nǚ huángdì	empress
墓		mù	grave; tomb
树	樹	shù	erect (a stone tablet); tree
石碑		shíbēi	stone tablet; stele
因为	因爲	yīnwèi	because; on account of
活		huó	live
刻		kè	carve; engrave
评价	評價	píngjià	evaluate; appraise

判断正误/判斷正誤

Identify the following statements as true or false based on the reading passage.

1. _______ 中国历史上，皇帝都是男的。

2. _______ 武则天是山西人。

3. ______ 武则天的碑上的字不多。

4. ______ 人们为武则天树“无字碑”，是因为人们不知道她做的事是好还是坏。

1. ______ 中國歷史上，皇帝都是男的。

2. ______ 武則天是山西人。

3. ______ 武則天的碑上的字不多。

4. ______ 人們爲武則天樹“無字碑”，是因爲人們不知道她做的事是好還是壞。

Exercises 练习/練習

一、发音练习/發音練習

Pronunciation exercise.

绕口令/繞口令 Tongue Twister

Băndèng kuān, biăndan cháng, biăndan băng zài băndèng shang.

Băndèng bú ràng biăndan băng zài băndèng shang,

biăndan piān yào băng zài băndèng shang.

板凳宽，扁担长，扁担绑在板凳上。

板凳不让扁担绑在板凳上，

扁担偏要绑在板凳上。

板凳寬，扁擔長，扁擔綁在板凳上。

板凳不讓扁擔綁在板凳上，

扁擔偏要綁在板凳上。

二、词语练习/詞語練習

Vocabulary exercise.

	Chinese Character	Pinyin	Make a Sentence of Your Own
1		jiéshù	
2		péi	
3		bĭjiào	
4		búduàn de	
5		zŏngshì	
6		yĭjing	
7	开始	kāishĭ	上大学
8		shèngxia	

三、根据课文回答问题/根據課文回答問題

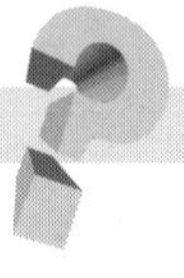

Answer the following questions by using complete sentences based on information in the text.

1. 中国有多少年的历史了？
2. 中国人的祖先五千年前就开始在什么地方生活了？
3. 是谁统一了中国，建立了秦朝？
4. 秦朝以后，中国又经历了哪些朝代？
5. 清朝是什么时候结束的？

1. 中國有多少年的歷史了？
2. 中國人的祖先五千年前就開始在什麼地方生活了？
3. 是誰統一了中國，建立了秦朝？
4. 秦朝以後，中國又經歷了哪些朝代？
5. 清朝是什麼時候結束的？

四、填空

Fill in the blanks.

A. Fill in the blanks based on the text.

1. 五六千年______ ______，中国人的______先就已经______ ______生活在黄河、长江两______了。
2. 那时候中国有一百多个小______，这些小国______ ______不断地______仗，到了______ ______时期就剩______七个______ ______大的国家了。
3. 公元______二百二十一年，秦始皇______ ______了中国，______立了______朝 。
4. 一九一一年，______朝结束；一九一二年，______立了中华民国，孙______ ______先生任总统。
5. 一九四九年，中华人民共和国______ ______。

1. 五六千年______ ______，中國人的______先就已經______ ______生活在黃河、長江兩______了。
2. 那時候中國有一百多個小______，這些小國______ ______不斷地______仗，到了______ ______時期就剩______七個______ ______大的國家了。
3. 公元______二百二十一年，秦始皇______ ______了中國，______立了______朝 。
4. 一九一一年，______朝結束；一九一二年，______立了中華民國，孫______ ______先生任總統。
5. 一九四九年，中華人民共和國______ ______。

B. Fill in each of the following blanks with “以前” or “以后/以後”.

1. 听说大约四十年______， 爷爷、奶奶就搬到中国台湾去了。

2. 唐朝______，中国又经历了宋、元、明等朝代。

3. 公元前二百二十一年______，中国不是一个统一的国家。

1. 聽説大約四十年______， 爺爺、奶奶就搬到中國臺灣去了。

2. 唐朝______，中國又經歷了宋、元、明等朝代。

3. 公元前二百二十一年______，中國不是一個統一的國家。

五、重组/重組

Word order.

1. 去/早饭/我陪/吃/散步/爷爷/到公园/过

   去/早飯/我陪/吃/散步/爺爺/到公園/過

   After breakfast, I accompanied Grandpa to take a walk in a park.

2. 结束/记得/的/一九一一年/她/清朝/是/才

   結束/記得/的/一九一一年/她/清朝/是/纔

   She remembers that the Qing Dynasty didn't end until 1911.

3. 喜欢/时候/一边/妈妈/吃晚饭的/说话/吃饭/一边/总是

   喜歡/時候/一邊/媽媽/吃晚飯的/説話/吃飯/一邊/總是

   At dinner Mom always likes talking while eating.

4. 剩下的/不断地/国家/战国时期/七个/打仗/之间

   剩下的/不斷地/國家/戰國時期/七個/打仗/之間

   In the Warring States Period, the remaining seven countries continuously fought with each other.

5. 中国人的祖先/听说/就/五六千年/生活/已经/以前/在黄河长江两岸/开始/了

   中國人的祖先/聽説/就/五六千年/生活/已經/以前/在黃河長江兩岸/開始/了

   It is said that five or six thousand years ago the ancestors of Chinese people began to live along both shores of the Yellow River and the Yangtze River.

六、翻译/翻譯

Translate the following sentences into Chinese.

1. When I am in my own room, I like to make phone calls while using the computer.
2. At my university's cafeteria as soon as I start eating, I miss my mom's cooking.
3. My teacher asked me, "Do you know how many countries there are in the world? Which country has the longest history?"
4. I asked my American friend, "Have you ever been to Chinatown?" He said he hadn't been to Chinatown. I said, "As soon as we finish breakfast, I will take you to Chinatown."
5. My friend asked me, "Would you like to come to my home to have dinner with us tonight? My mom is making Chinese food tonight. The Chinese food my mom makes is indeed delicious!"

七、改写/改寫

Rewrite the following sentences with the patterns in the parentheses.

1. 我喜欢走路的时候听音乐。（一边……一边……）
2. 爷爷讲起中国历史忘了时间。（一……就……）
3. 一九一一年，中国最后一个王朝结束。（才）
4. 在中国历史上，大大小小的朝代有三十几个。（过）
5. 战国时期，那些小国之间打仗不停。（一……就……）

1. 我喜歡走路的時候聽音樂。（一邊……一邊……）
2. 爺爺講起中國歷史忘了時間。（一……就……）
3. 一九一一年，中國最後一個王朝結束。（纔）
4. 在中國歷史上，大大小小的朝代有三十幾個。（過）
5. 戰國時期，那些小國之間打仗不停。（一……就……）

八、改错/改錯

Correct mistakes.

1. 我有去过中国台湾。
2. 我有吃过那个饭馆。
3. 我有听过孙中山的名字。
4. 我没有过黄河、长江。
5. 我有学过中国历史。

6. 老师，你有没有看见我朋友？
7. 爷爷讲一个故事给我了。
8. 我们从八点到十点，走两个小时了。
9. 我一看电视就忘时间了。
10. 吃早饭我陪爷爷去了公园散步。
1. 我有去過中國臺灣。
2. 我有吃過那個飯館。
3. 我有聽過孫中山的名字。
4. 我没有過黄河、長江。
5. 我有學過中國歷史。
6. 老師，你有没有看見我朋友？
7. 爺爺講一個故事給我了。
8. 我們從八點到十點，走兩個小時了。
9. 我一看電視就忘時間了。
10. 吃早飯我陪爺爺去了公園散步。

九、课堂活动/課堂活動

In-class activity.

Before starting Lesson 7, go online to find the following information.

1. 战国时期是从_____年到_____年。那时候的名人有：____________________
2. 战国时期的七国是(1)_____ (2)_____ (3)_____ (4)_____ (5)_____ (6)_____ (7)_____
3. 三国是指哪三个国家____ ____ ____。那时候的名人有：____________________
4. 唐朝是从_____年到_____年。那时候的名人有：____________________
5. 孙中山是_____年生，_____年去世的，人们叫他_____。
6. 黄河在哪儿(在中国的北边还是南边)？多长？为什么人们把它叫做黄河？
7. 长江在哪儿(在中国的北边还是南边)？多长？
1. 戰國時期是從_____年到_____年。那時候的名人有：____________________
2. 戰國時期的七國是(1)_____ (2)_____ (3)_____ (4)_____ (5)_____ (6)_____ (7)_____
3. 三國是指哪三個國家____ ____ ____。那時候的名人有：____________________
4. 唐朝是從_____年到_____年。那時候的名人有：____________________
5. 孫中山是_____年生，_____年去世的，人們叫他_____。

6. 黄河在哪兒(在中國的北邊還是南邊)? 多長? 爲什麼人們把它叫做黄河?

7. 長江在哪兒(在中國的北邊還是南邊)? 多長?

十、课外活动/課外活動

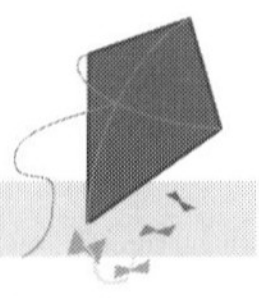

After-class activity.

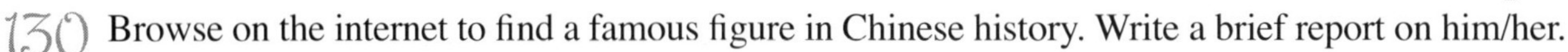

Browse on the internet to find a famous figure in Chinese history. Write a brief report on him/her.

For example:

秦始皇、武则天、诸葛亮、屈原、孔子、老子、孙中山……

秦始皇、武則天、諸葛亮、屈原、孔子、老子、孫中山……

十一、写作练习/寫作練習

Writing.

Design a Mother's Day or Father's Day card.

For example:

Suggested words: 爱　感谢　辛苦了　世上只有妈妈好

愛　感謝　辛苦了　世上只有媽媽好

十二、总结/總結

Summary.

1. Choose 5-10 of your favorite new vocabulary words from the text or reading material.

2. Quote 3-7 of your favorite sentences from the text or reading material here.

	Original sentence	**Translation of the sentence** (or make a new sentence of your own)
1		
2		
3		
4		
5		

3. From this lesson, you have learned Chinese culture, history, and philosophy. They have helped you to understand,

① 我现在清楚了/我現在清楚了：________________________

② 我现在知道了/我現在知道了：________________________

LESSON 8

第八课
汉字

星期六跟几个高中的同学吃完午饭回到家，我看见爷爷正在写毛笔字。爷爷看见我回来了，停下手里的毛笔对我说："凡凡，过来看看认识不认识爷爷写的这些字。"我指着其中的三个字说："我的名字——宋宜凡，别的字我就不认识了。"爷爷笑着说："不错，能认识自己的名字也很不错呀。"

"爷爷，我觉得记汉字真难。每次上中文课学了新字，我总是写啊写、记啊记，可是第二天一起床就又忘了。"

"其实，记汉字的办法很多。请教一下你的中文老师，他们一定有好办法。"

"那认识多少字就能看得懂中文报纸了？"

"汉字一共有大约六七万个，但是最常用的不过两三千个。据说，如果能认识这两千个常用字，就能认识报纸上百分之九十七的字。就是认识了前五百个，也能认识报纸上百分之七十五点八的字。当然，学会了前五百个字，以后再学别的字也就容易多了。"

"那多长时间才能学会这两千个常用字呢？"

"这……你还是得去请教你的中文老师。"

LESSON 8

第八課

漢字

星期六跟幾個高中的同學吃完午飯回到家，我看見爺爺正在寫毛筆字。爺爺看見我回來了，停下手裏的毛筆對我說：“凡凡，過來看看認識不認識爺爺寫的這些字。”我指着其中的三個字說：“我的名字——宋宜凡，別的字我就不認識了。”爺爺笑着說：“不錯，能認識自己的名字也很不錯呀。”

“爺爺，我覺得記漢字真難。每次上中文課學了新字，我總是寫啊寫、記啊記，可是第二天一起床就又忘了。”

“其實，記漢字的辦法很多。請教一下你的中文老師，他們一定有好辦法。”

“那認識多少字就能看得懂中文報紙了？”

“漢字一共有大約六七萬個，但是最常用的不過兩三千個。據說，如果能認識這兩千個常用字，就能認識報紙上百分之九十七的字。就是認識了前五百個，也能認識報紙上百分之七十五點八的字。當然,學會了前五百個字，以後再學別的字也就容易多了。”

“那多長時間纔能學會這兩千個常用字呢？”

“這……你還是得去請教你的中文老師。”

New Words
生词表/生詞表

汉字	漢字	hànzì	*n*	Chinese character
几	幾	jǐ	*nu*	several
高中		gāozhōng	*n*	high school
同学	同學	tóngxué	*n*	schoolmate
午饭	午飯	wǔfàn	*n*	lunch
看见	看見	kànjiàn	*vc*	catch sight of; see
正在		zhèngzài	*adv*	in the process of; in the course of
写	寫	xiě	*v*	write; compose; depict
毛笔	毛筆	máobǐ	*n*	Chinese writing brush
毛笔字	毛筆字	máobǐzì	*n*	characters written with a writing brush
停下		tíngxia	*vc*	stop; pause
对	對	duì	*prep*	to; towards
过来	過來	guòlai	*v*	come here
认识	認識	rènshi	*v*	know; recognize; be acquainted with
指		zhǐ	*v*	point at; point to
其中		qízhōng	*n*	within; among them
名字		míngzi	*n*	name or given name
别		bié	*pron*	other; another
不错	不錯	bùcuò	*adj*	correct; right; not bad; pretty good
记	記	jì	*v*	commit to memory; remember
难	難	nán	*adj*	difficult; hard; troublesome
请教	請教	qǐngjiào	*v*	consult; seek advice (from someone)
一定		yīdìng	*adv*	surely; certainly; necessarily
多少		duōshao	*pron*	how many; how much
报纸	報紙	bàozhǐ	*n*	newspaper
一共		yīgòng	*adv*	altogether; in all
常用		cháng yòng		often used; in common use
不过	不過	bùguò	*adv*	only; merely; no more than
据说	據說	jùshuō	*v*	it is said; allegedly
如果		rúguǒ	*conj*	if; in case; in the event of
百分之		bǎifēn zhī		percentage
点	點	diǎn	*n*	decimal point
容易		róngyì	*adj*	easy; likely; liable

Chinese Characters
汉字一/漢字一

丶 丷 宀 宀 字 字 (6)

字 字 字 字

丿 𠂉 𠂉 午 (4)

午 午 午 午

丿 二 三 毛 (4)

毛 毛 毛 毛

丨 冂 冂 冂 同 同 (6)

同 同 同 同

𡿨 女 女 如 如 如 (6)

如 如 如 如

丶 丷 宀 宀 宀 宀 定 定 (8)

定 定 定 定

丨 口 日 日 旦 甲 果 果 (8)

果 果 果 果

丿 八 分 分 (4)

分 分 分 分

丶 丷 宀 宀 宀 穸 突 突 容 容 (10)

容 容 容 容

丨 冂 日 日 旦 易 易 易 (8)

易 易 易 易

Chinese Characters
汉字二/漢字二

寫	写	筆	笔
認	认	識	识
難	难	當	当
錯	错	報	报
紙	纸	據	据

Grammar Notes
语法简注/語法簡注

1. verb + resultative complement：verb + 见/見，verb + 下，verb + 完，verb + 到

📖 那多长时间才能学会两千个最常用字呢？

那多長時間纔能學會兩千個最常用字呢？

Then how long does it take for one to master the usage of the 2,000 most commonly used characters?

▶ 跟同学吃完午饭回到家，我看见爷爷正在写毛笔字。

跟同學吃完午飯回到家，我看見爺爺正在寫毛筆字。

When I returned home after lunch with my schoolmates, I saw Grandpa writing characters with a brush.

▶ 爷爷看见我回来了，停下手里的毛笔。

爺爺看見我回來了，停下手裏的毛筆。

When Grandpa saw me come back, he put down the brush in his hand.

▶ 他学中文学了一年了，但是他还没学会写自己的名字。

他學中文學了一年了，但是他還沒學會寫自己的名字。

He has learnt Chinese for one year, but he still doesn't know how to write his own name.

▶ 这本历史书我已经看了两遍了，可是还没看到"秦始皇"这三个字。

這本歷史書我已經看了兩遍了，可是還沒看到"秦始皇"這三個字。

I have read this history book twice, but I haven't seen the three characters "Qin Shihuang" yet.

▶ 我一写完字，就去公园散步。

我一寫完字，就去公園散步。

As soon as I finished writing characters, I went to the park to take a walk.

▶ 请你们把笔放下。

請你們把筆放下。

Please put down your pens.

2. 正在……：be doing something；in the process of doing something

📖 我看见爷爷正在写毛笔字。

我看見爺爺正在寫毛筆字。

I saw Grandpa writing characters with a brush.

▶ 他们正在上电脑课。
他們正在上電腦課。
They are attending a computer class.

▶ 今天早上我到家的时候，我看见爸爸正在用电脑。
今天早上我到家的時候，我看見爸爸正在用電腦。
When I returned home this morning, I saw my dad using the computer.

3. verb + 啊 + verb：The phrase 写啊写/寫啊寫，记啊记/記啊記 means 写了又写/寫了又寫，记了又记/記了又記. The multi-functional modal particle 啊 emphasizes the repetition of the action, and in this case implies impatience and frustration.

▶ 我总是写啊写、记啊记，可是一起床就又忘了。
我總是寫啊寫、記啊記，可是一起床就又忘了。
I've always kept writing and memorizing (the new characters). However, as soon as I get up, I forget them all.

▶ 我每天背啊背，可是还是背不下来。
我每天背啊背，可是還是背不下來。
I have been reciting every day, but I still can't memorize them.

▶ 妈妈说啊说，老是说不完。
媽媽說啊說，老是說不完。
Mom has been talking endlessly.

4. 一下："Verb + 一下" indicates that the action is short and casual.

▶ 你应该请教一下你的中文老师。
你應該請教一下你的中文老師。
You should consult your Chinese language teacher.

▶ 我想认识一下你的中文老师。
我想認識一下你的中文老師。
I'd like to get to know your Chinese teacher.

▶ 我能看一下你的书吗?
我能看一下你的書嗎?
May I take a look at your book?

5. 不过……/不過……： merely; no more than

📖 但是最常用的不过两三千个字。
但是最常用的不過兩三千個字。

However, the most commonly used Chinese characters amount to no more than two or three thousand.

▶ 那个老师不过二十岁。

那個老師不過二十歲。

That teacher is merely 20 years old.

▶ 他在中国台湾住了不过一年。

他在中國臺灣住了不過一年。

He lived in Taiwan of China for no more than one year.

6. 据(sb)说/據(sb)說：it is said that…；they say…；allegedly

📖 据说，如果能认识最常用的两千字，就可以认识报纸上百分之九十七的字。

據說，如果能認識最常用的兩千字，就可以認識報紙上百分之九十七的字。

It is said that if you can recognize the 2,000 most commonly used characters, you would be able to recognize 97% of the characters in newspapers.

▶ 据说，这个学校很好。

據說，這個學校很好。

It is said that this is a good school.

▶ 据我朋友说，你会说中文。

據我朋友說，你會說中文。

My friend says that you can speak Chinese.

7. 百分之：…percent

百分之+ number

▶ 百分之五十八：58%；fifty eight percent

▶ 百分之百：100%；one hundred percent

8. 如果……，就……：if…，then…

This pattern of the conditional sentence is similar to the pattern “要是……就……” in Lesson 6.

① When there is only one subject in the sentence, the sentence pattern is as follow,

(S1) 如果……，S1就……	If ... S1，then S1 ...
如果(S1) ……，S1就……	

▶ (我) 如果能认识常用的两千个字，我就可以看报纸了。

(我) 如果能認識常用的兩千個字，我就可以看報紙了。

如果（我）能认识常用的两千个字，我就可以看报纸了。

如果（我）能認識常用的兩千個字，我就可以看報紙了。

If I can recognize the most often used 2,000 characters, I will be able to read newspapers.

② When there are two subjects in the sentence, the sentence pattern is as follow,

如果S1……，S2就…… ———— If S1…, then S2 …

▶ 如果你去北京，我就跟你去。

If you go to Beijing, I'll go with you.

▶ 如果我能看中文报纸，我妈妈就高兴了。

如果我能看中文報紙，我媽媽就高興了。

If I can read Chinese newspapers, my mom would be delighted.

9. 就是……，也……：even if…, still…

就是 + supposition, (subject) + 也 + verb

📖 就是认识了前五百个，也能认识报纸上百分之七十五点八的字。

就是認識了前五百個，也能認識報紙上百分之七十五點八的字。

Even if you recognize just the first 500 characters, you'd still be able to recognize 75.8% of the characters in newspapers.

▶ 就是你给我钱，我也不去看电影。

就是你給我錢，我也不去看電影。

Even if you give me money, I won't go to see a movie.

▶ 就是我不学中文，我也要去北京。

就是我不學中文，我也要去北京。

Even if I don't study Chinese, I still want to go to Beijing.

Reading Passage
阅读/閱讀

仓颉造字

传说黄帝(大约公元前二千六百年) 时，黄帝手下有个人叫仓颉，非常聪明。

有一天下大雪，仓颉和几个朋友出去打猎。他看见雪地上有很多动物的脚印，受到启发，于是造出了汉字。

谁都知道，一种文字的产生，是要经过很长很长时间的，绝不是一个人一下子就能造出来的。不过，“仓颉造字”的传说有一点还是“传”对了，那就是，最早的汉字都是由图画演变来的。这从三千多年前最早的文字——甲骨文——就可以看出来。如：

山 ；人 ；口 ；门

汉字后来又经过了金文（商代和西周时）、小篆（秦始皇统一中国后）、隶书（秦始皇统一中国后 ——汉代）、一直到现在的楷书（汉代晚期到现在）。

倉頡造字

傳說黄帝（大約公元前二千六百年）時，黄帝手下有個人叫倉頡，非常聰明。

有一天下大雪，倉頡和幾個朋友出去打獵。他看見雪地上有很多動物的脚印，受到啓發，于是造出了漢字。

誰都知道，一種文字的産生，是要經過很長很長時間的，絶不是一個人一下子就能造出來的。不過，“倉頡造字”的傳說有一點還是“傳”對了，那就是，最早的漢字都是由圖畫演變來的。這從三千多年前最早的文字——甲骨文——就可以看出來。如：

山 ；人 ；口 ；門

漢字後來又經過了金文（商代和西周時）、小篆（秦始皇統一中國後）、隸書（秦始皇統一中國後——漢代）、一直到現在的楷書（漢代晚期到現在）。

造字		zào zì	create (Chinese) characters
雪		xuě	snow
打猎	打獵	dǎliè	go hunting
动物	動物	dòngwù	animal
脚印		jiǎoyìn	footprint
受到		shòudào	be subjected to

启发	啓發	qǐfā	inspire
产生	產生	chǎnshēng	come into being; emerge
图画	圖畫	túhuà	drawing; picture; painting
演变	演變	yǎnbiàn	develop; evolve
甲骨文		jiǎgǔwén	inscriptions on bones or tortoise shells

判断正误/判斷正誤

Identify the following statements as true or false based on the reading passage.

1. _______ 皇帝就是黄帝。
2. _______ 中国的汉字是仓颉造的。
3. _______ 汉字是由图画演变来的。
4. _______ 甲骨文是中国最早的汉字。
5. _______ 我们今天看见的汉字都是楷书体的。

1. _______ 皇帝就是黃帝。
2. _______ 中國的漢字是倉頡造的。
3. _______ 漢字是由圖畫演變來的。
4. _______ 甲骨文是中國最早的漢字。
5. _______ 我們今天看見的漢字都是楷書體的。

一、发音练习/發音練習

Pronunciation exercise.

A Tang poem of Li Bai (701-762)

Jìng Yè Sī

Chuáng qián míngyuè guāng,
Yí shì dì shang shuāng.
Jǔ tóu wàng míngyuè,
Dī tóu sī gùxiāng.

静夜思

床前明月光，

疑是地上霜。

举头望明月，

低头思故乡。

静夜思

床前明月光，

疑是地上霜。

舉頭望明月，

低頭思故鄉。

二、词语练习／詞語練習

Vocabulary exercise.

	Chinese character	Pinyin	Make a Sentence of Your Own
1		kànjiàn	
2		zhèngzài	
3		rènshi	
4		qǐngjiào	
5		juéde	
6		búcuò	
7		tóngxué	
8		xuéhuì	

三、根据课文回答问题／根據課文回答問題

Answer the following questions by using complete sentences based on information in the text.

1. 汉字一共有多少个？
2. 最常用汉字有多少个？
3. 认识两千个最常用字能认识报纸上百分之多少的字？
4. 认识前五百个最常用字能认识报纸上百分之多少的字？
5. 你现在认识多少个汉字了？
6. 你是怎么记汉字的？

1. 漢字一共有多少個？
2. 最常用漢字有多少個？
3. 認識兩千個最常用字能認識報紙上百分之多少的字？
4. 認識前五百個最常用字能認識報紙上百分之多少的字？
5. 你現在認識多少個漢字了？
6. 你是怎麼記漢字的？

四、填空

Fill in the blanks.

A. Fill in the blanks based on the text.

1. 爷爷看______我回来了，停______手里的毛笔______我说："凡凡，来看看这些字。"
2. 我指着______ ______的三个字说："我的名字——宋宜凡。"
3. 我______ ______记汉字______难。每次上中文课学了______字，我总是______啊写，______啊记，可是第二天一起床______又忘了。
4. 汉字一共有______ ______六七万个，但是最______ ______的不______两三千个。

1. 爺爺看______我回來了，停______手裏的毛筆______我說："凡凡，來看看這些字。"
2. 我指着______ ______的三個字說："我的名字——宋宜凡。"
3. 我______ ______記漢字______難。每次上中文課學了______字，我總是______啊寫，______啊記，可是第二天一起床______又忘了。
4. 漢字一共有______ ______六七萬個，但是最______ ______的不______兩三千個。

B. Insert the words from the left in appropriate place in the sentence.

1. 但是　我记汉字记得很快，忘得也很快，真没办法。
2. 就　　听说如果能认识两千个常用汉字，可以看报纸了。
3. 一下　你写毛笔字已经写了很长时间了，停吧。
4. 也　　只要每天能记住二十个汉字，就是不吃饭、不睡觉，我很开心。
5. 据说　常写毛笔字的人，汉字都写得很漂亮。

1. 但是　我記漢字記得很快，忘得也很快，真沒辦法。
2. 就　　聽說如果能認識兩千個常用漢字，可以看報紙了。
3. 一下　你寫毛筆字已經寫了很長時間了，停吧。
4. 也　　只要每天能記住二十個漢字，就是不吃飯、不睡覺，我很開心。
5. 據說　常寫毛筆字的人，漢字都寫得很漂亮。

C. Multiple choices.

1. 你知道多长时间才能（a. 学，b. 学会，c. 学不会）两千个常用字吗？
2. 我一回家，就（a. 看，b. 看见，c. 看得见）爷爷在写毛笔字。
3. 爷爷怎么总是有（a. 讲，b. 讲完，c. 讲不完）的故事？
4. 毛笔字好难写，我已经跟爷爷学了半年了，可是还是（a. 写得好，b. 写好，c. 写不好）。

1. 你知道多長時間纔能（a. 學，b. 學會，c. 學不會）兩千個常用字嗎?
2. 我一回家，就（a. 看，b. 看見，c. 看得見）爺爺在寫毛筆字。
3. 爺爺怎麽總是有（a. 講，b. 講完，c. 講不完）的故事?
4. 毛筆字好難寫，我已經跟爺爺學了半年了，可是還是（a. 寫得好，b. 寫好，c. 寫不好）。

五、重组/重組

Word order.

1. 了/跟朋友/午饭/回学校/就/哥哥/吃完/一
   了/跟朋友/午飯/回學校/就/哥哥/吃完/一
   As soon as Elder Brother finished lunch with his friends, he went to school.
2. 最常用的/看报纸了/可以/认识/就/两千字/了/听说/你
   最常用的/看報紙了/可以/認識/就/兩千字/了/聽說/你
   It is said that if you know the most commonly used 2,000 characters, you'll then be able to read newspapers.
3. 不是/据/记住/的/办法/只有/汉字/这些/说/我朋友
   不是/據/記住/的/辦法/只有/漢字/這些/說/我朋友
   According to my friend, the methods to memorize Chinese characters are by no means limited to only these.
4. 去/一/应该/你/有/老师/问题/请教/就/你的
   去/一/應該/你/有/老師/問題/請教/就/你的
   If you have questions, you should go consult your teacher.
5. 也/不让我/就是/去香港/我/我妈妈/要去/我女朋友/香港/在/因为
   也/不讓我/就是/去香港/我/我媽媽/要去/我女朋友/香港/在/因爲
   Even if my mom wouldn't let me go to Hong Kong , I'll still want to go because my girlfriend is in Hong Kong.

六、翻译/翻譯

Translate the following sentences into Chinese.

1. I asked my grandpa, "How long does it take for you to finish writing 200 characters with a brush?"

2. Because I have a Chinese class tomorrow, I must finish my homework even if I can't go to bed tonight.
3. It is said that that university is very good. Therefore, even if I don't have money, I'll still want to find out a way to attend that university.
4. Teacher Song is merely twenty-five years old. However, I heard that he knows a few new methods for memorizing Chinese characters. If I have time, I'll go consult him.
5. My friend feels that learning Chinese characters is truly difficult. She said, "Each time I learn a new character, I would keep writing and memorizing it. However, I would forget it when I get up the next day."

七、改错/改錯

Correct mistakes.

1. 我回家的时候看了爷爷在写毛笔字。
2. 爷爷笑了说，"不错，你认识汉字真不少。"
3. 这些汉字真难，我记得不住。
4. 报纸的汉字我都没认识。
5. 我想请教中文老师一下儿。
6. 新学的字，我要是一写就记了，就我高兴了。
7. 我如果能看中文报纸，就高兴了。

1. 我回家的時候看了爺爺在寫毛筆字。
2. 爺爺笑了說，"不錯，你認識漢字真不少。"
3. 這些漢字真難，我記得不住。
4. 報紙的漢字我都沒認識。
5. 我想請教中文老師一下兒。
6. 新學的字，我要是一寫就記了，就我高興了。
7. 我如果能看中文報紙，就高興了。

八、课堂活动/課堂活動

In-class activity.

1. Circle the characters you recognize in the table below of the first 100 characters taken from the List of the 3500 Most Commonly Used Hanzi.

	1	2	3	4	5	6	7	8	9	10
1	的	一	是	了	不	我	这	人	有	在
2	个	你	他	就	来	大	儿	上	们	要
3	国	中	和	说	那	么	也	到	地	子
4	为	会	以	出	对	得	年	生	好	着
5	时	家	可	去	发	能	过	作	还	工
6	自	行	下	都	经	多	没	学	方	理
7	里	现	业	看	后	成	起	小	事	用
8	什	天	开	她	呢	民	定	同	实	法
9	进	主	于	老	分	心	长	日	面	点
10	样	产	把	本	当	十	部	问	三	吧

	1	2	3	4	5	6	7	8	9	10
1	的	一	是	了	不	我	這	人	有	在
2	個	你	他	就	來	大	兒	上	們	要
3	國	中	和	說	那	麼	也	到	地	子
4	爲	會	以	出	對	得	年	生	好	着
5	時	家	可	去	發	能	過	作	還	工
6	自	行	下	都	經	多	没	學	方	理
7	裏	現	業	看	後	成	起	小	事	用
8	什	天	開	她	呢	民	定	同	實	法
9	進	主	於	老	分	心	長	日	面	點
10	樣	產	把	本	當	十	部	問	三	吧

2. Group work: introduce and exchange your methods to memorize Chinese characters.

九、课外活动/課外活動

After-class activity.

Do you know the Famous Four Inventions made by Chinese people throughout history? Search for the answers online and fill in the table below.

	Invention	Who invented it?	When was it invented?
1			
2			
3			
4			

十、写作练习/寫作練習

Writing.

Design a Chinese New Year's or a Christmas card.

For example:

冬冬哥哥：

祝你新春愉快！在新的一年里万事如意！

妹：夏夏

Suggested words: 新年　圣诞节　春节　愉快　万事如意

冬冬哥哥：

祝你新春愉快！在新的一年裏萬事如意！

妹：夏夏

Suggested words: 新年　聖誕節　春節　愉快　萬事如意

十一、总结/總結

Summary.

1. Choose 5-10 of your favorite new vocabulary words from the text or reading material.

2. Quote 3-7 of your favorite sentences from the text or reading material here.

	Original sentence	**Translation of the sentence** (or make a new sentence of your own)
1		
2		
3		
4		
5		

3. From this lesson, you have learned Chinese culture, history, and philosophy. They have helped you to understand,

① 我现在清楚了/我現在清楚了：________________________________

② 我现在知道了/我現在知道了：________________________________

LESSON 9

第九课
百家姓

星期天中午，我和哥哥回学校以前，我们全家人到中国城去饮茶。

我从小就喜欢饮茶。我喜欢一边喝茶，一边吃点心，一边聊天儿。我也喜欢看服务员推着小车忙来忙去的。

“我姓司马，是这里的经理。请问各位对今天的饭菜满意吗？”

“满意！满意！”全家人异口同声地回答。

“多谢各位，请慢用。”那位经理说完，向另一张桌子走去。

“他的姓怎么有两个字呀？”我小声地问。

“司马是复姓。那位经理姓的是复姓。”妈妈回答。

“爷爷，中国人有多少个姓啊？”哥哥问。

“常见的有四百多个。”

“听说‘李’是最大的姓，全世界差不多有一亿的中国人姓‘李’。”奶奶说。

“我们家的‘宋’，在《百家姓》里排第一百一十八位。”一向不爱说话的爸爸，今天却开口了。

“爸，您是怎么知道的？”我问。

“网上查的，网上什么都查得到。”

LESSON 9

第九課
百家姓

星期天中午，我和哥哥回學校以前，我們全家人到中國城去飲茶。

我從小就喜歡飲茶。我喜歡一邊喝茶，一邊吃點心，一邊聊天兒。我也喜歡看服務員推着小車忙來忙去的。

“我姓司馬，是這裏的經理。請問各位對今天的飯菜滿意嗎？”

“滿意！滿意！”全家人异口同聲地回答。

“多謝各位，請慢用。”那位經理説完，向另一張桌子走去。

“他的姓怎麼有兩個字呀？”我小聲地問。

“司馬是複姓。那位經理姓的是複姓。”媽媽回答。

“爺爺，中國人有多少個姓啊？”哥哥問。

“常見的有四百多個。”

“聽説‘李’是最大的姓，全世界差不多有一億的中國人姓‘李’。”奶奶説。

“我們家的‘宋’，在《百家姓》裏排第一百一十八位。”一向不愛説話的爸爸，今天却開口了。

“爸，您是怎麼知道的？”我問。

“網上查的，網上什麼都查得到。”

五星級 jí

排名第

向前

排在……名

but/lower

S + 却 que

New Words
生词表/生詞表

百家姓		Bǎijiāxìng	*pn*	*Book of China's Family Names* (literally, "a hundred surnames")
中午		zhōngwǔ	*n*	noon
从小	從小	cóng xiǎo		since childhood
饮茶	飲茶	yǐnchá	*vo*	eat dim sum (literally, "drink tea")
茶		chá	*n*	tea
点心	點心	diǎnxin	*n*	dim sum; pastry; dessert
服务员	服務員	fúwùyuán	*n*	attendant; waiter/waitress
推		tuī	*v*	push
小车	小車	xiǎochē	*n*	small cart
忙来忙去	忙來忙去	mánglái-mángqù	*idiom*	be busy doing this and that
姓		xìng	*n/v*	surname; be surnamed
司马	司馬	Sīmǎ	*pn*	(a compound surname)
经理	經理	jīnglǐ	*n*	manager
请问	請問	qǐngwèn	*v*	excuse me; it may be asked
各		gè	*n*	each; every; all
位		wèi	*m*	(used to refer to people)
饭菜	飯菜	fàncài	*n*	meal; food
满意	滿意	mǎnyì	*adj*	be satisfied; be pleased
异口同声	異口同聲	yìkǒu-tóngshēng	*idiom*	with one voice; in unison
回答		huídá	*n/v*	reply; answer; response
多谢	多謝	duō xiè		thanks a lot
慢		màn	*adj*	slow
向		xiàng	*prep*	to; towards
另		lìng	*pron*	another; other
张	張	zhāng	*m*	(measure word for tables, paper)
桌子		zhuōzi	*n*	table; desk
怎么	怎麼	zěnme	*pron*	how; what; why

小声	小聲	xiǎoshēng	*n*	low voice
复姓	複姓	fùxìng	*n*	compound surname
常见	常見	cháng jiàn		be commonly seen
李		Lǐ	*pn*	(a surname)
排		pái	*v*	put in order
一向		yīxiàng	*adv*	always
开口	開口	kāikǒu	*vo*	open one's mouth; start to talk
网上	網上	wǎngshàng	*n*	online; on the internet
查		chá	*v*	check; examine; look up

在

早上

我姓木子李.

上午 8-12

中午

下午

向 _ _ 开口要钱.

忙忘了

公司 company

马上 immediately

shuang 木 林

pāi pì

拍马屁 flatter

怎么 走 route

怎么 去 method

单 dan 女生

Chinese Characters
汉字一/漢字一

ㄑ 女 女 女' 女𠂉 女𠂉 姓 姓 (8)

姓 姓 姓 姓

ㄱ コ 巳 巳 异 异 (6)

异 异 异 异

一 十 艹 艹 艾 苁 荼 茶 茶 (9)

茶 茶 茶 茶

丿 刀 月 月 月 肌 服 服 (8)

服 服 服 服

丿 ク 夂 夂 各 各 (6)

各 各 各 各

丶 丶 忄 忄 忙 忙 (6)

忙 忙 忙 忙

丨 ⺊ ⺊ 占 占 占 卓 卓 桌 桌 (10)

桌 桌 桌 桌

丿 𠂉 𥫗 𥫗 ⺮ ⺮ 笁 笒 笒 笒 答 答 (12)

答 答 答 答

丶 丶 忄 忄 㤕 㤕 㤕 㤕 愠 愠 愠 愠 慢 慢 (14)

慢 慢 慢 慢

丨 冂 冂 冋 回 回 (6)

回 回 回 回

Chinese Characters
汉字二/漢字二

ノ 丿 冂 向 向 向 (6)
向 向 向 向
丶 口 口 号 另 (5)
另 另 另 另
一 十 才 木 本 李 李 (7)
李 李 李 李
一 十 才 木 木 杏 杏 杳 查 (9)
查 查 查 查
一 丨 扌 扌 扌 扌 扌 扌 排 排 排 (11)
排 排 排 排
丶 亠 亠 立 立 产 音 音 音 音 意 意 意 (13)
意 意 意 意
丁 コ 司 司 司 (5)
司 司 司 司

Chinese Characters
汉字三/漢字三

飲	饮	務	务
員	员	馬	马
謝	谢	張	张
滿	满	網	网
複	复	推	理

Grammar Notes
语法简注/語法簡注

1. V来V去/V來V去：do an action repeatedly；over and over

我也喜欢看服务员推着小车忙来忙去的样子。

我也喜歡看服務員推着小車忙來忙去的樣子。

I also enjoy watching the waiters busy themselves with pushing small carts.

▶ 他想来想去，可是还是想不出一个好办法。

他想來想去，可是還是想不出一個好辦法。

He thought and thought, but was still unable to figure out a good solution.

▶ 我看来看去，还是不认识这些字。

我看來看去，還是不認識這些字。

I read them over and over again, but I still can't recognize these characters.

2. 对……满意/對……滿意：be pleased/satisfied with…

请问各位对今天的饭菜满意吗？

請問各位對今天的飯菜滿意嗎？

May I ask, are you satisfied with the dishes today?

▶ 我对自己写的毛笔字很满意。

我對自己寫的毛筆字很滿意。

I am very satisfied with the characters that I have written with a brush.

▶ 他对自己的中文很不满意。

他對自己的中文很不滿意。

He is very dissatisfied with his Chinese.

3. 向……：to；toward

那位经理说完，向另一张桌子走去。

那位經理說完，向另一張桌子走去。

Having finished speaking, that manager walked towards another table.

▶ 小妹一看到我就向我跑过来。

小妹一看到我就向我跑過來。

As soon as she saw me, Little Sister ran toward me.

▶ 他向我走过来。

他向我走過來。

He walked towards me.

4. 怎么/怎麼：why；how come

📖 他的姓怎么有两个字啊？

他的姓怎麼有兩個字啊？

How come there are two Chinese characters in his surname?

▶ 他怎么不停地喝茶？

他怎麼不停地喝茶？

How come he drinks tea continuously?

5. 地：地 is a structural particle to form an adverbial modifier.

adverb + 地+verb

📖 我小声地问。

我小聲地問。

I asked in a low voice.

▶ 全家人异口同声地回答。

全家人异口同聲地回答。

My entire family replied in unison.

▶ 爷爷大声地说：“我很满意。”

爺爺大聲地說：“我很滿意。”

Grandpa said loudly, “I’m very pleased.”

▶ 他不停地喝茶。

He drinks tea continuously.

6. 一向：always

📖 一向不爱说话的爸爸，今天却开口了。

一向不愛說話的爸爸，今天卻開口了。

My dad, who is liable to keep silent, nevertheless spoke out today.

▶ 我妈妈一向爱说话。

我媽媽一向愛說話。

My mom is always talkative.

▶ 周末，我一向起床起得晚。

I always get up late on weekends.

7. 什么/谁/怎么/哪儿……都/也

什麽/誰/怎麽/哪兒……都/也

The question words 谁/誰，什么/什麽，那儿/哪兒，怎么/怎麽 mean "anyone/everyone", "anything/everything", "anywhere/everywhere" and "no matter how" respectively.

网上什么都查得到。

網上什麽都查得到。

One can find everything by surfing online.

▶ 在中国城什么点心都吃得到。

在中國城什麽點心都吃得到。

One can get to eat every kind of dim sum in Chinatown.

▶ 谁都喜欢饮茶。

誰都喜歡飲茶。

Everyone likes to eat dim sum.

▶ 来美国以后，爷爷哪儿都想去看看。

來美國以後，爺爺哪兒都想去看看。

My paternal grandpa wants to visit every place after he came to the US.

▶ 这个问题真难。我想来想去，可是怎么都想不出一个好办法。

這個問題真難。我想來想去，可是怎麽都想不出一個好辦法。

This problem is truly difficult. I thought about it over and over again, but couldn't figure out a good solution.

8. V + 得 + 到：The patten "V + 得 + 到" indicates the possibility of an action to take place or to be realized.

网上什么都查得到。

網上什麽都查得到。

On line one can find everything.

▶ 在美国什么茶都喝得到。

在美國什麽茶都喝得到。

One can get to drink all kinds of tea in the US.

The negative form is "V + 不 + 到".

▶ 我在网上查不到那个汉字。

我在網上查不到那個漢字。

I can't find that Chinese character online.

Reading Passage
阅读/閱讀

中国人的姓是怎么来的

汉字的“姓”字，左边是个“女”字，右边是个“生”字，合在一起是女人生孩子的意思。

在母系社会，孩子只知道自己的母亲是谁，不知道自己的父亲。孩子的姓是随母亲的。所以最初的姓都带“女”字，如：“姜”。

到了父系社会，孩子不但知道自己的母亲是谁，而且也知道自己的父亲是谁。孩子跟父亲的关系变得清楚了，人们的姓也不只带“女”字了。

古时候，有人以自己的职业取姓，如：做陶器的人就姓“陶”；也有人以自己住的地方取姓，如：住在菜园附近的人就会姓“园”。

中國人的姓是怎麼來的

漢字的“姓”字，左邊是個“女”字，右邊是個“生”字，合在一起是女人生孩子的意思。

在母係社會，孩子只知道自己的母親是誰，不知道自己的父親。孩子的姓是隨母親的。所以最初的姓都帶“女”字，如：“姜”。

到了父係社會，孩子不但知道自己的母親是誰，而且也知道自己的父親是誰。孩子跟父親的關係變得清楚了，人們的姓也不只帶“女”字了。

古時候，有人以自己的職業取姓，如：做陶器的人就姓“陶”；也有人以自己住的地方取姓，如：住在菜園附近的人就會姓“園”。

左边	左邊	zuǒbian	left side; left-hand side
右边	右邊	yòubian	right side; right-hand side
母系社会	母係社會	mǔxì shèhuì	matriarchal society
父亲	父親	fùqīn	father
随	隨	suí	follow
最初		zuìchū	the earliest; at the beginning
关系	關係	guānxi	relation; relationship

取（名）		qǔ(míng)	name; give somebody a name
随意	隨意	suíyì	do as one pleases
职业	職業	zhíyè	occupation; profession
陶器		táoqì	pottery; earthenware
菜园	菜園	càiyuán	vegetable garden
附近		fùjìn	nearby; neighboring; vicinity

判断正误/判斷正誤

Identify the following statements as true or false based on the reading passage.

1. ______ 汉字的“姓”字，是女人生孩子的意思。
2. ______ 在母系社会，孩子只知道自己的母亲是谁，不知道父亲是谁。
3. ______ 到了父系社会，孩子不知道自己的母亲是谁，只知道自己的父亲是谁。

1. ______ 漢字的“姓”字，是女人生孩子的意思。
2. ______ 在母係社會，孩子只知道自己的母親是誰，不知道父親是誰。
3. ______ 到了父係社會，孩子不知道自己的母親是誰，只知道自己的父親是誰。

Exercises 练习/練習

一、发音练习/發音練習

Pronunciation exercise.

A Tang poem by Wang Zhihuan (688-742)

Dēng Guànquè Lóu	登鹳雀楼	登鸛雀樓
Báirì yī shān jìn,	白日依山尽，	白日依山盡，
Huánghé rù hǎi liú.	黄河入海流。	黄河入海流。
Yù qióng qiān lǐ mù,	欲穷千里目，	欲窮千里目，
Gèng shàng yì céng lóu.	更上一层楼。	更上一層樓。

二、词语练习/詞語練習

Vocabulary exercise.

	Chinese Character	Pinyin	Make a Sentence of Your Own
1		quán	
2		cóngxiǎo	
3		xǐhuan	
4		mánglái-mángqù	
5		mǎnyì	
6		yíxiàng	
7		yǐnchá	
8		xìng	

三、根据课文回答问题/根據課文回答問題

Answer the following questions by using complete sentences based on information in the text.

1. 什么时候宜凡和全家人去饮茶?
2. 宜凡为什么喜欢跟家人去饮茶?
3. 宜凡的家人对饭馆的饭菜满意不满意?
4. 饭馆的经理姓什么? 他姓的是什么姓?
5. 中国人常见的姓有多少个?
6. 中国最大的姓是什么? 世界上有多少中国人姓这个姓?
7. “宋”在《百家姓》里排第多少位? 怎么知道的?
8. 你家的姓在《百家姓》里排第多少位?

1. 什麼時候宜凡和全家人去飲茶?
2. 宜凡爲什麼喜歡跟家人去飲茶?
3. 宜凡的家人對飯館的飯菜滿意不滿意?
4. 飯館的經理姓什麼? 他姓的是什麼姓?
5. 中國人常見的姓有多少個?
6. 中國最大的姓是什麼? 世界上有多少中國人姓這個姓?
7. “宋”在《百家姓》裏排第多少位? 怎麼知道的?
8. 你家的姓在《百家姓》裏排第多少位?

四、填空

Fill in the blanks.

A. Fill in the blanks based on the text.

1. 星期天中______，我们______家人到中国______去______茶。
2. 我______ ______就喜欢饮茶。我喜欢一边______茶，一边______点心，一边______天儿。我也喜欢______服务员推______小车忙______忙______的。
3. 听______，"李"是最______的姓，全世界______ ______ ______有一亿的中国人姓李。
4. 网上______的，______上______ ______都查______到。

1. 星期天中______，我們______家人到中國______去______茶。
2. 我______ ______就喜歡飲茶。我喜歡一邊______茶，一邊______點心，一邊______天兒。我也喜歡______服務員推______小車忙______忙______的。
3. 聽______，"李"是最______的姓，全世界______ ______ ______有一億的中國人姓李。
4. 網上______的，______上______ ______都查______到。

B. Multiple choice.

1. 我爸爸平时不爱说话，______（a. 什么，b. 怎么，c. 这么）今天说个没完？
2. 他______（a. 什么，b. 怎么，c. 这么，）都没说就走了。
3. 小王慢慢地站起来______（a. 向，b. 跟，c. 对）门口走去。
4. 请问，你______（a. 向，b. 跟，c. 对）这位服务员的服务满意吗？
5. 小张 ______（a. 一向，b. 一定，c. 一起）起得很早，可是今天十点才起床。
6. 我喜欢上网，因为网上 ______（a.怎么，b.什么，c.谁）都查得到。

1. 我爸爸平時不愛說話，______（a. 什麽，b. 怎麽，c. 這麽）今天說個没完？
2. 他 ______（a. 什麽，b. 怎麽，c. 這麽）都没說就走了。
3. 小王慢慢地站起來 ______（a. 向，b. 跟，c. 對）門口走去。
4. 請問，你______（a. 向，b. 跟，c. 對）這位服務員的服務滿意嗎？
5. 小張 ______（a. 一向，b. 一定，c. 一起）起得很早，可是今天十點纔起床。
6. 我喜歡上網，因爲網上 ______（a. 怎麽，b. 什麽，c. 誰）都查得到。

C. Use the structure "V来V去/V來V去" to fill in the blanks.

1. 小王__________________，还是看不懂那本书。
2. 这个字我__________________，就是写不漂亮。
3. 我们__________________，觉得还是"老东方饭馆"的饮茶最好。

4. 经理____________________就是不同意我的看法。

5. 我最喜欢看服务员推着小车____________________的。

1. 小王____________________，還是看不懂那本書。

2. 這個字我____________________，就是寫不漂亮。

3. 我們____________________，覺得還是“老東方飯館”的飲茶最好。

4. 經理____________________就是不同意我的看法。

5. 我最喜歡看服務員推着小車____________________的。

五、重组/重組

Word order.

1. 跟朋友/电脑/一边/一向/一边/用/哥哥/聊天/喜欢

   跟朋友/電腦/一邊/一向/一邊/用/哥哥/聊天/喜歡

   Elder Brother has all along been fond of chatting with his friends while using the computer.

2. 可是/对/不满意/那个服务员/饭菜/对/我/今天的/很满意

   可是/對/不滿意/那個服務員/飯菜/對/我/今天的/很滿意

   I am satisfied with the dishes today, but dissatisfied with that waiter.

3. 差不多/中国人/据说/九千万的/姓张/全世界/有

   差不多/中國人/據説/九千萬的/姓張/全世界/有

   It is said that there are approximately ninty million Chinese people in the whole world who are surnamed Zhang.

4. 爸爸、妈妈/去饮茶/我/就/到中国城/从小/喜欢/跟

   爸爸、媽媽/去飲茶/我/就/到中國城/從小/喜歡/跟

   I've enjoyed going to Chinatown with my parents to eat dim sum since I was a little child.

5. 都/听说/得到/茶/在香港/什么/喝

   都/聽説/得到/茶/在香港/什麼/喝

   I heard that one can get to drink just every kind of tea in Hong Kong.

六、翻译/翻譯

Translate the following sentences into Chinese.

1. I have enjoyed going to the park to take a walk with my grandma ever since my childhood.
2. He was busy (doing this and that) today, but he actually didn't do anything at all.
3. My dad has all along been fond of drinking tea while reading newspapers.

4. Even if I can't speak Chinese well, I still want to go to China next year. After I go to China, I will go visit all sorts of places.
5. These two Chinese surnames are not common. I checked online over and over again, but still couldn't find these two surnames online.
6. I went to a restaurant in Chinatown with my parents to eat dim sum last Sunday. According to my parents, you can get to eat every kind of dim sum in Chinatown. However, that restaurant didn't have my favorite dim sum. I couldn't get to eat my favorite dim sum and wasn't satisfied with the food there.

七、改错/改錯

Correct mistakes.

1. 我回家以前，打一个电话给了爸爸、妈妈。	1. 我回家以前，打一個電話給了爸爸、媽媽。
2. 每个周末我们全家人饮茶去中国城。	2. 每個周末我們全家人飲茶去中國城。
3. 我的姓是李。"李"是中国最大姓。	3. 我的姓是李。"李"是中國最大姓。
4. 你把"百家姓"在电脑上查了吗？	4. 你把"百家姓"在電腦上查了嗎？
5. 小王一边吃点心和一边说话跟经理。	5. 小王一邊吃點心和一邊說話跟經理。
6. 我怎么在网上查得不到我们家的姓？	6. 我怎麽在網上查得不到我們家的姓？
7. 我今天没看得到司马经理。	7. 我今天沒看得到司馬經理。
8. 我在大学不吃到"饮茶"。	8. 我在大學不吃到"飲茶"。

八、课堂活动/課堂活動

In-class activity.

Before starting Lesson 9, go online to find the following information.

http://www.greatchinese.com/surname/surname.htm

http://host2.twes.tyc.edu.tw/~ta150012/r4.htm

1. 《百家姓》是什么？
2. 《百家姓》里有多少个姓？
3. 《百家姓》是谁写的？什么时候写的？
4. 你家的姓在《百家姓》里排第多少位？

1. 《百家姓》是什麽？
2. 《百家姓》裏有多少個姓？
3. 《百家姓》是誰寫的？什麽時候寫的？

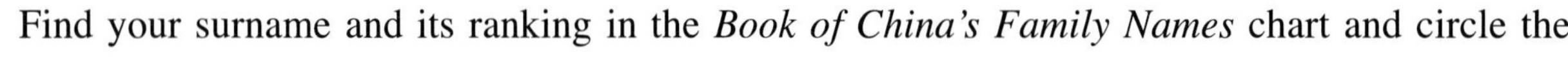

4. 你家的姓在《百家姓》裏排第多少位?

九、课外活动/課外活動

After-class activity.

Find your surname and its ranking in the *Book of China's Family Names* chart and circle the surnames of all of your classmates.

赵钱孙李	周吴郑王	冯陈诸卫	蒋沈韩杨
朱秦尤许	何吕施张	孔曹严华	金魏陶姜
趙錢孫李	周吳鄭王	馮陳諸衛	蔣沈韓楊
朱秦尤許	何呂施張	孔曹嚴華	金魏陶姜

十、写作练习/寫作練習

Writing.

Task: Write an apology email letter to someone. The letter should contain at least 50 characters and include the following information.

1. Who are you apologize to?
2. What are you apologizing for?
3. How would you like to do to make up for what you did?

For example:

贺老师:

您好!

昨天晚上我上网[wǎng]上到今天早上两点多，早上起床后又昏[hūn]头昏脑地找不到车钥匙[yàoshi]，只好去赶校车。没想到路[lù]上又堵[dǔ]车，结果我迟到了。实在[shízài]不好意思[yìsi]，我赶到教室[jiàoshì]的时候，您已经快下课[kè]了。

老师，如果明天您有时间的话，我能到您的办公室[bàngōngshì]去请您给我补补[bǔ]课吗?

敬祝

教安

您的学生：少迟

十月四号

Suggested words: 对不起　实在　不好意思　如果……的话　能不能

賀老師：

您好！

昨天晚上我上網[wǎng]上到今天早上兩點多，早上起床後又昏[hūn]頭昏腦地找不到車鑰匙[yàoshi]，只好去趕校車。没想到路[lù]上又堵[dǔ]車，結果我遲到了。實在[shízài]不好意思[yìsi]，我趕到教室[jiàoshì]的時候，您已經快下課[kè]了。

老師，如果明天您有時間的話，我能到您的辦公室[bàngōngshì]去請您給我補補[bǔ]課嗎？

敬祝

教安

您的學生：少遲

十月四號

Suggested words: 對不起　實在　不好意思　如果……的話　能不能

十一、总结/總結

Summary.

1. Choose 5-10 of your favorite new vocabulary words from the text or reading material.

2. Quote 3-7 of your favorite sentences from the text or reading material here.

	Original sentence	Translation of the sentence (or make a new sentence of your own)
1		
2		
3		
4		
5		

3. From this lesson, you have learned Chinese culture, history, and philosophy. They have helped you to understand,

① 我现在清楚了/我現在清楚了：____________________

② 我现在知道了/我現在知道了：____________________

LESSON 10

第十课
多民族

时间过得真快，转眼感恩节、圣诞节、新年都过完了。爷爷、奶奶回了台北，哥哥实习去了北京，我也回到学校，开始了新的学期。

有一天，我收到哥哥从中国寄来的一个邮包，打开一看，哇！里边装了几十张彩色图片，而且每张图片上的人穿的、戴的都非常独特。我赶快看夹在图片里的简介。看完简介，我明白了，原来中国是一个多民族的国家。图片上的人，是中国不同民族的代表！简介上还说：中国一共有五十六个民族。汉族人最多，占中国人口的百分之九十二以上。其他的五十五个民族都被叫做少数民族，不到中国人口的百分之八。在五十五个少数民族中，壮族、回族、维吾尔族、蒙古族和藏族的人数比较多。人数最少的一个少数民族只有两千人左右。这些少数民族不但有自己独特的风俗习惯，而且许多民族还有自己的语言和文字。

我得写信谢谢哥哥，他寄给我的图片真让我大开眼界！

LESSON 10

第十課
多民族

時間過得真快，轉眼感恩節、聖誕節、新年都過完了。爺爺、奶奶回了臺北，哥哥實習去了北京，我也回到學校，開始了新的學期。

有一天，我收到哥哥從中國寄來的一個郵包，打開一看，哇！裏邊裝了幾十張彩色圖片，而且每張圖片上的人穿的、戴的都非常獨特。我趕快看夾在圖片裏的簡介。看完簡介，我明白了，原來中國是一個多民族的國家。圖片上的人，是中國不同民族的代表！簡介上還說：中國一共有五十六個民族。漢族人最多，占中國人口的百分之九十二以上。其他的五十五個民族都被叫做少數民族，不到中國人口的百分之八。在五十五個少數民族中，壯族、回族、維吾爾族、蒙古族和藏族的人數比較多。人數最少的一個少數民族只有兩千人左右。這些少數民族不但有自己獨特的風俗習慣，而且許多民族還有自己的語言和文字。

我得寫信謝謝哥哥，他寄給我的圖片真讓我大開眼界！

New Words
生词表/生詞表

简体	繁體	Pinyin	Part of speech	English
民族		mínzú	*n*	ethnic group
转眼	轉眼	zhuǎnyǎn	*adv*	in the twinkling of an eye; in an instant
感恩节	感恩節	Gǎn'ēnjié	*pn*	Thanksgiving Day
圣诞节	聖誕節	Shèngdànjié	*pn*	Christmas
新年		xīnnián	*pn*	New Year
实习	實習	shíxí	*v*	practise; do fieldwork
北京		Běijīng	*pn*	Beijing
学期	學期	xuéqī	*n*	school term; semester
收		shōu	*v*	receive; accept
寄		jì	*v*	send; mail; post
邮包	郵包	yóubāo	*n*	postal parcel
打开	打開	dǎkāi	*vc*	open; uncover
哇		wa	*int*	ah; oh (used to express surprise)
装	裝	zhuāng	*v*	load; hold; pack
几十	幾十	jǐ shí		tens; dozens
彩色		cǎisè	*n*	multicolor; color
图片	圖片	túpiàn	*n*	picture; photograph
而且		érqiě	*conj*	and; but also
穿		chuān	*v*	wear; put on (clothes, shoes, etc.)
戴		dài	*v*	wear; put on (hats, gloves, glasses, etc.)
非常		fēicháng	*adv*	very; extremely
独特	獨特	dútè	*adj*	unique; distinctive
夹	夾	jiā	*v*	place in between
简介	簡介	jiǎnjiè	*n*	brief introduction; synopsis
明白		míngbai	*v/adj*	know; understand; realize; clear
不同		bùtóng	*adj*	different; distinct
代表		dàibiǎo	*n/v*	representative; represent
汉族	漢族	Hànzú	*n*	Han ethnic group
占		zhàn	*v*	constitute; make up; account for
全国	全國	quán guó		whole nation/country

以上		yǐshàng	*n*	more than; over; above
其他		qítā	*pron*	others; else
被		bèi	*prep*	by (used in the passive voice to introduce the doer of the action)
叫做		jiàozuò	*v*	be known as; be called
少数民族	少數民族	shǎoshù mínzú	*n*	minority ethnic group
中		zhōng	*n*	inside
壮族	壯族	Zhuàngzú	*pn*	Zhuang (Chuang) ethnic group
回族		Huízú	*pn*	Hui ethnic group
维吾尔族	維吾爾族	Wéiwú'ěrzú	*pn*	Uygur ethnic group
蒙古族		Ménggǔzú	*pn*	Mongolian ethnic group
藏族		Zàngzú	*pn*	Tibetan ethnic group; the Tibetans
人数	人數	rénshù	*n*	number of people
少		shǎo	*adj*	few; little; less
只		zhǐ	*adv*	only; just; merely
左右		zuǒyòu	*n*	about; or so; the left and right sides
不但		bùdàn	*conj*	not only... (but also...)
风俗	風俗	fēngsú	*n*	custom
习惯	習慣	xíguàn	*n*	habit
许多	許多	xǔduō	*adj*	many; a lot of; much
语言	語言	yǔyán	*n*	language
文字		wénzì	*n*	character; writing; written language
大开眼界	大開眼界	dàkāi-yǎnjiè	*idiom*	open a new horizon (to sb)

Chinese Characters
汉字一/漢字一

、亠亡市亯亨京京 (8)
京 京 京 京
、亠方方方方方方旌族族 (11)
族 族 族 族
丨 ㄐ 屮 屮 收 收 (6)
收 收 收 收
一 厂 厂 厂 后 后 咸 咸 咸 咸 感 感 感 (13)
感 感 感 感
丨 口 口 口 叶 吐 哇 哇 哇 (9)
哇 哇 哇 哇
丶 丷 宀 宀 宊 宊 宔 宔 寄 寄 寄 (11)
寄 寄 寄 寄
ノ 勹 句 句 包 (5)
包 包 包 包
ノ ノ ノ ノ 丝 乎 采 采 彩 彩 彩 (11)
彩 彩 彩 彩
ノ ク 乌 名 名 色 (6)
色 色 色 色
丿 丿 片 片 (4)
片 片 片 片

Chinese Characters

汉字二/漢字二

丿 人 介 介 (4)

介 介 介 介

丨 ⺊ 占 占 占 (5)

占 占 占 占

一 十 十 古 古 (5)

古 古 古 古

丿 ク 夕 夕 外 (5)

外 外 外 外

一 ナ 左 左 左 (5)

左 左 左 左

丿 亻 亻 仆 伀 伀 俗 俗 俗 (9)

俗 俗 俗 俗

一 丆 丆 丙 而 而 (6)

而 而 而 而

丨 冂 月 月 且 (5)

且 且 且 且

丶 丶 宀 穴 穴 空 空 穿 穿 (9)

穿 穿 穿 穿

丨 丨 ヨ ヨ 非 非 非 非 (8)

非 非 非 非

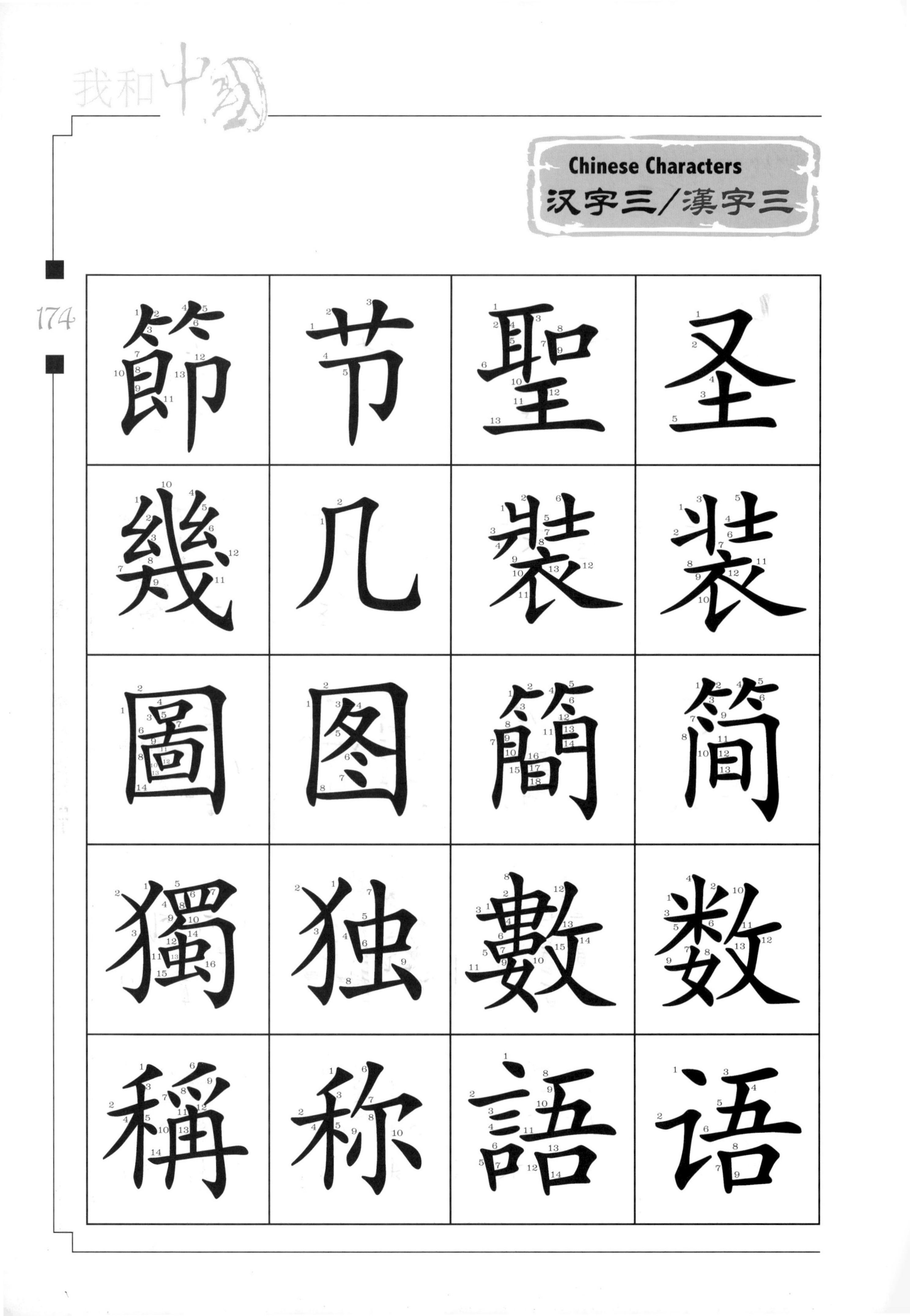

Chinese Characters

汉字三/漢字三

節	节	聖	圣
幾	几	裝	装
圖	图	簡	简
獨	独	數	数
稱	称	語	语

Chinese Characters
汉字四/漢字四

轉	转	夾	夹
許	许	慣	惯
誕	诞	壯	壮
爾	尔	維	维
風	风	代	表

Grammar Notes
语法简注/語法簡注

1. 转眼(一转眼)/轉眼(一轉眼)：in the twinkling of an eye；in an instant

📖 转眼感恩节、圣诞节、新年都过完了。
轉眼感恩節、聖誕節、新年都過完了。
In an instant, Thanksgiving, Christmas, and the New Year Holidays are all over.

▶ 转眼我已经十八岁了。
轉眼我已經十八歲了。
In an instant, I'm already eighteen years old.

▶ 转眼他们把点心都吃完了。
轉眼他們把點心都吃完了。
In an instant, they finished all the dim sum.

2. N1+占+N2+的+百分之+NU：N1 constitute… percent of N2

📖 在五十六个民族中，汉族人最多，占全国人口的百分之九十二以上。
在五十六個民族中，漢族人最多，占全國人口的百分之九十二以上。
Among the fifty-six ethnic groups, the Han ethnic group is the most numerous, and constitutes over ninty-two percent of the total population.

▶ 我们班女生占全班人数的百分之六十。
我們班女生占全班人數的百分之六十。
Female students constitute sixty percent of our entire class.

▶ 我们学校选学中文的学生占全校学生的百分之三。
我們學校選學中文的學生占全校學生的百分之三。
The students who enroll in Chinese constitute three percent of the total students in our school.

3. 被：It is used in the passive voice to introduce the doer of the actior or the action if the doer is not mentioned.

📖 其他的五十五个民族都被叫做少数民族。
其他的五十五個民族都被叫做少數民族。
All the other fifty-five ethnic groups are called minority ethnic groups.

▶ 她的早饭被她朋友吃了。
她的早飯被她朋友吃了。

Her breakfast is eaten by her friends.

▶ 爷爷的茶被爸爸喝了。

爺爺的茶被爸爸喝了。

Grandpa's tea was drunk by dad.

4. 不但……，而且……：not only…，but also…

📖 这些少数民族不但有自己独特的风俗习惯，而且许多民族还有自己的语言和文字。

這些少數民族不但有自己獨特的風俗習慣，而且許多民族還有自己的語言和文字。

Not only do these minority ethnic groups have their own unique customs, but some of them even have their own languages and local scripts.

▶ 他不但会说藏语，而且会说蒙古语。

他不但會説藏語，而且會説蒙古語。

He can speak not only Tibetan but also Mongolian.

▶ 我哥哥不但会说中文，而且会说日文。

我哥哥不但會説中文，而且會説日文。

My elder brother can speak not only Chinese but also Japanese.

5. 左右：about；or so；around

📖 人数最少的一个民族只有两千人左右。

人數最少的一個民族只有兩千人左右。

The ethnic group with the smallest population has only about 2000 people.

▶ 晚上九点左右我给你打电话。

晚上九點左右我給你打電話。

I'll give you a call at about 9pm.

▶ 他看看左右没人，就走了。

He saw there was no one around and then left.

Reading Passage
阅读/閱讀

土家族的独特婚俗——哭嫁

湖南省有一个少数民族——土家族。土家族有一个很独特的婚俗——哭嫁。土家族姑娘出嫁那天要大哭，参加婚礼的人也要跟着新娘一起哭，婚礼是在一片哭声中进行的。

土家族姑娘不但在结婚那天哭，而且在结婚以前就开始哭了，这一哭要哭上四十八天。她们哭什么呢？哭父母，说她们舍不得离开父母；哭姐妹，说她们舍不得离开亲人；哭媒人，说媒人坏，让她们与家人分开；她们还哭自己是女孩子，说女孩子命苦。

据有些学者研究，土家族哭嫁的习俗反映了土家族姑娘对婚姻不自由的不满。

如今土家族青年男女可以自由恋爱了，那土家族的姑娘出嫁时还哭什么呢？

土家族的獨特婚俗——哭嫁

湖南省有一個少數民族——土家族。土家族有一個很獨特的婚俗——哭嫁。土家族姑娘出嫁那天要大哭，參加婚禮的人也要跟着新娘一起哭，婚禮是在一片哭聲中進行的。

土家族姑娘不但在結婚那天哭，而且在結婚以前就開始哭了，這一哭要哭上四十八天。她們哭什麼呢？哭父母，説她們捨不得離開父母；哭姐妹，説她們捨不得離開親人；哭媒人，説媒人壞，讓她們與家人分開；她們還哭自己是女孩子，説女孩子命苦。

據有些學者研究，土家族哭嫁的習俗反映了土家族姑娘對婚姻不自由的不滿。

如今土家族青年男女可以自由戀愛了，那土家族的姑娘出嫁時還哭什麼呢？

婚俗		hūnsú	marriage custom
哭嫁		kūjià	(a girl) weeping because she is to be married
姑娘		gūniang	girl
婚礼	婚禮	hūnlǐ	wedding ceremony
新娘		xīnniáng	bride
舍不得	捨不得	shě bu de	unwilling to part with
离开	離開	líkāi	leave; depart from
媒人		méiren	matchmaker
命苦		mìngkǔ	having a hard lot; doomed to a life of misfortune
学者	學者	xuézhě	scholar
习俗	習俗	xísú	custom

反映		fǎnyìng	reflect
婚姻		hūnyīn	marriage
不满	不滿	bùmǎn	dissatisfied
自由恋爱	自由戀愛	zìyóu liàn'ài	have freedom to choose one's spouse

判断正误/判斷正誤

Identify the following statements as true or false based on the reading passage.

1. _______ 土家族的姑娘在婚礼上得大哭。
2. _______ 参加婚礼的人都得哭。
3. _______ 土家族姑娘只在婚礼那天才哭。
4. _______ 土家族姑娘的婚姻不自由。
5. _______ 土家族姑娘现在还不能自由恋爱。

1. _______ 土家族的姑娘在婚禮上得大哭。
2. _______ 參加婚禮的人都得哭。
3. _______ 土家族姑娘只在婚禮那天纔哭。
4. _______ 土家族姑娘的婚姻不自由。
5. _______ 土家族姑娘現在還不能自由戀愛。

Exercises
练习/練習

一、发音练习/發音練習

Pronunciation exercise.

Folk Song: Jasmine Flower

Mòlihuā	茉莉花	茉莉花
Hǎo yì duǒ měilì de mòlihuā,	好一朵美丽的茉莉花，	好一朵美麗的茉莉花，
Hǎo yì duǒ měilì de mòlihuā;	好一朵美丽的茉莉花；	好一朵美麗的茉莉花；
Fēnfāng tǔyàn mǎn zhīyá,	芬芳吐艳满枝芽，	芬芳吐艷滿枝芽，
Yòu bái yòu xiāng rénrén kuā.	又白又香人人夸。	又白又香人人誇。

二、词语练习/詞語練習

Vocabulary exercise.

	Chinese Character	Pinyin	Make a Sentence of Your Own
1		zhuǎnyǎn	
2		cǎisè	
3		míngbai	
4		yuánlái	
5		suǒyǒu	
6		dútè	
7		xíguàn	
8		yǐwéi	

三、根据课文回答问题/根據課文回答問題

Answer the following questions by using complete sentences based on information in the text.

1. 哥哥的邮包里边装的什么？
2. 图片上的人是什么人？
3. 中国一共有多少个民族？
4. 中国哪个民族的人数最多？占中国人口的百分之多少？
5. 中国的少数民族占全国人口的百分之多少？
6. 中国的少数民族中，哪些民族的人数比较多？
7. 中国的五十六个民族都说汉语吗？
8. 每个民族的人穿的服装都一样吗？
9. 每个民族的风俗习惯一样不一样？
10. 现在你知道不知道为什么人们把中文叫做汉语？把中国字叫做汉字？

1. 哥哥的郵包裏邊裝的什麼？
2. 圖片上的人是什麼人？
3. 中國一共有多少個民族？
4. 中國哪個民族的人數最多？占中國人口的百分之多少？
5. 中國的少數民族占全國人口的百分之多少？
6. 中國的少數民族中，哪些民族的人數比較多？
7. 中國的五十六個民族都説漢語嗎？
8. 每個民族的人穿的服裝都一樣嗎？
9. 每個民族的風俗習慣一樣不一樣？
10. 現在你知道不知道爲什麼人們把中文叫做漢語？把中國字叫做漢字？

四、填空

Fill in the blanks.

A. Fill in the blanks based on the text.

1. ______眼感恩节、圣诞节、新年都过______了。
2. 中国是一个______民族的国家，中国______ ______有五十六个民族。
3. 汉族人最______，______全国人口的百分之九十二以______。其他的五十五个民族都被叫______少数民族，占全国人口的百分之八以______。
4. 在五十五个少数民族______，壮族、回族、维吾尔族、蒙古族和藏族的人数______ ______多。
5. 中国的少数民族不但有自己______ ______的风俗______ ______，而且有些民族______有自己的语______和______字。

1. ______眼感恩節、聖誕節、新年都過______了。
2. 中國是一個______民族的國家，中國______ ______有五十六個民族。
3. 漢族人最______，______全國人口的百分之九十二以______。其他的五十五個民族都被叫______少數民族，占全國人口的百分之八以______。
4. 在五十五個少數民族______，壯族、回族、維吾爾族、蒙古族和藏族的人數______ ______多。
5. 中國的少數民族不但有自己______ ______的風俗______ ______，而且有些民族______有自己的語______和______字。

B. Multiple choice.

1. 我们学校的男生比女生少，男生______（a. 占，b. 只，c. 在）全校人数的百分之四十三。
2. 小王不但会说汉语，______（a. 所以，b. 而且，c. 以为）还会说藏语和蒙古语。
3. 新学期快开始了，我得______（a. 就要，b. 赶快，c. 应该）回学校了。
4. 小王三天没来上课了，______（a. 原来，b. 后来，c. 以后）她去北京了。
5. 谢谢你告诉我这个故事，______（a. 要不然，b. 要是，c. 所以）我还得上网查。

1. 我們學校的男生比女生少，男生______（a. 占，b. 只，c. 在）全校人數的百分之四十三。
2. 小王不但會說漢語，______（a. 所以，b. 而且，c. 以爲）還會說藏語和蒙古語。
3. 新學期快開始了，我得______（a. 就要，b. 趕快，c. 應該）回學校了。
4. 小王三天沒來上課了，______（a. 原來，b. 後來，c. 以後）她去北京了。
5. 謝謝你告訴我這個故事，______（a. 要不然，b. 要是，c. 所以）我還得上網查。

五、改写/改寫

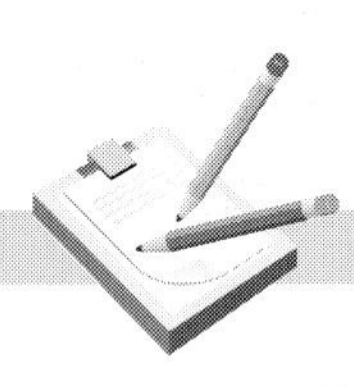

Rewrite the following sentences with "被".

1. 中国把不是汉族的民族叫做少数民族。
2. 每次大家总是把奶奶做的好吃的都吃完了。
3. 我把爷爷、奶奶下飞机的时间忘了。
4. 是谁已经把哥哥寄给我的邮包打开了？
5. 我把奶奶喜欢吃的菜都背下来了。
6. 我很高兴，我已经把五百个常用字都记住了。
7. 大家把我点的菜都吃完了。

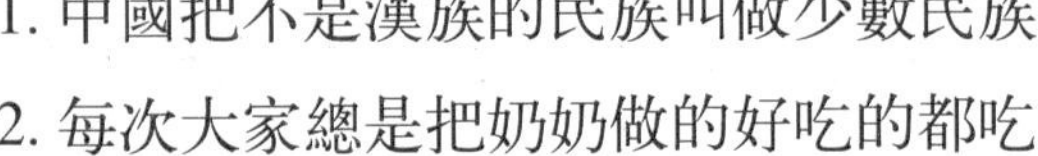

1. 中國把不是漢族的民族叫做少數民族。
2. 每次大家總是把奶奶做的好吃的都吃完了。

3. 我把爺爺、奶奶下飛機的時間忘了。

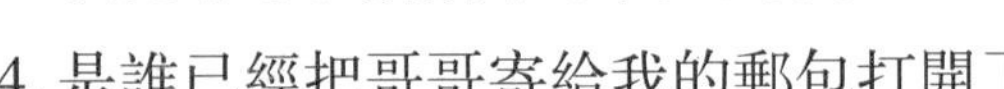

4. 是誰已經把哥哥寄給我的郵包打開了？

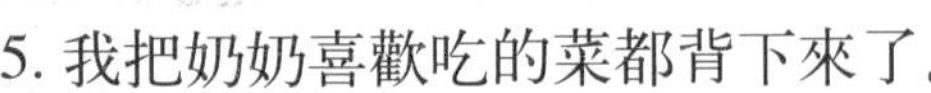

5. 我把奶奶喜歡吃的菜都背下來了。
6. 我很高興，我已經把五百個常用字都記住了。
7. 大家把我點的菜都吃完了。

六、重组/重組

Word order.

1. 五十六个/中国/民族/有/据说/一共

   五十六個/中國/民族/有/據說/一共

   I heard there are altogether fifty-six ethnic groups in China.

2. 从/寄来的/收到/大邮包/奶奶/一个/北京/今天/我

   從/寄來的/收到/大郵包/奶奶/一個/北京/今天/我

   Today I received a big parcel sent by my grandma from Beijing.

3. 朋友/那个人/昨天/我爸爸的/是/打电话的/原来

   朋友/那個人/昨天/我爸爸的/是/打電話的/原來

   It turned out that the person who called yesterday was my father's friend.

4. 不到/全国人口的/中国的/民族/百分之八/据说/少数

   不到/全國人口的/中國的/民族/百分之八/據說/少數

   It is said that China's minority ethnic group constitute less than eight percent of the total population.

5. 少数民族/语言/自己的/许多/而且有/风俗习惯/不但有/不同的

少數民族/語言/自己的/許多/而且有/風俗習慣/不但有/不同的

Many minority ethnic group not only have their own customs but also different languages.

七、翻译/翻譯

Translate the following sentences into Chinese.

1. How time flies! In the twinkling of an eye, Christmas was already over.
2. She can speak not only Mandarin but also Mongolian.
3. Do the minority ethnic group in the US constitute over ten percent of the total population?
4. I originally thought that China has only one ethnic group. Only after I saw the color photos of China's minority ethnic group did I realize that actually there are altogether fifty-six ethnic groups in China and that the customs of the minority ethnic groups are very different from the customs of the Han ethnic group.
5. Last Saturday I went with three of my friends to Chinatown to have dim sum. I had all along been fond of chatting with my friends while eating dim sum. I knew the manager in that restaurant. When I saw him, I also chatted with him. In an instant, all the dim sum on the table had been eaten up by my friends.

八、改错/改錯

Correct mistakes.

1. 时间过真快，转眼我已经三十岁。
2. 你收他寄来的邮包了吗？
3. 你看那本简介完了吗？
4. 我昨天收一个邮包从台北寄的。
5. 那个字被我写了。
6. 我觉得都学生知道中国有很多民族呢。

1. 時間過真快，轉眼我已經三十歲。
2. 你收他寄來的郵包了嗎？
3. 你看那本簡介完了嗎？
4. 我昨天收一個郵包從臺北寄的。
5. 那個字被我寫了。
6. 我覺得都學生知道中國有很多民族呢。

九、课堂活动/課堂活動

In-class activity.

Before starting Lesson 10, go online to find the following information.

1. 中国有多少个民族？
2. 最大的民族是哪个民族？占全国人口的百分之多少？

3. 比较大的少数民族有哪些？他们住在什么地方？这些少数民族有什么特别的风俗习惯？

1. 中國有多少個民族？
2. 最大的民族是哪個民族？占全國人口的百分之多少？
3. 比較大的少數民族有哪些？他們住在什麼地方？這些少數民族有什麼特别的風俗習慣？

十、课外活动/課外活動

After-class activity.

Task: Use the Internet to find the following information on ethnic group in China. Present the information to the class.

藏族、蒙古族、维吾尔族/維吾爾族……

1. What is the population of the ethnic group?
2. What are their special customs and traditional holidays?

十一、写作练习/寫作練習

Writing.

Task: Write an email letter of thanks to someone. The email should contain at least 50 characters and include the following information.

1. Who are you thanking?
2. Why are you thanking this person?

For example:

大明：

你好！

谢谢你邀请[yāoqǐng]我去参加[cānjiā]你的周末晚会[wǎnhuì]，使[shǐ]我能有机会认识几个新朋友，特别是那个长[cháng]头发[tóufa]的女孩子[nǚ háizi]。昨晚我大概是喝多了，觉得你家的地跟我的床一样，软软[ruǎnruǎn]的。如果不是你把我送回家，我今天一定不是在给你写信，而是给警察[jǐngchá]写信了。再一次感谢了！

祝好！

友：小白

十月四号

Suggested words：非常　感谢　帮　为　教　送　礼物　想

大明：

你好！

謝謝你邀請[yāoqǐng]我去參加[cānjiā]你的周末晚會[wǎnhuì]，使[shǐ]我能有機會認識幾個新朋友，特別是那個長[cháng]頭髮[tóufa]的女孩子[nǚ háizi]。昨晚我大概是喝多了，覺得你家的地跟我的床一樣，軟軟[[ruǎnruǎn]的。如果不是你把我送回家，我今天一定不是在給你寫信，而是給警察[jǐngchá]寫信了。再一次感謝了！

祝好！

友：小白

十月四號

Suggested words：非常　感謝　幫　爲　教　送　禮物　想

十二、总结/總結

Summary.

1. Choose 5-10 of your favorite new vocabulary words from the text or reading material.

2. Quote 3-7 of your favorite sentences from the text or reading material here.

	Original sentence	Translation of the sentence (or make a new sentence of your own)
1		
2		
3		
4		
5		

3. From this lesson, you have learned Chinese culture, history, and philosophy. They have helped you to understand,

① 我现在清楚了/我現在清楚了：________________________

② 我现在明白了/我現在明白了：________________________

③ 我现在知道了/我現在知道了：________________________

字词复习（二）/字詞複習（二）

请你找一找，从第六课到第十课，你学过哪些带下列偏旁部首的字。
請你找一找，從第六課到第十課，你學過哪些帶下列偏旁部首的字。
Find characters with the following radicals from Lesson 6 to Lesson 10.

1. 宀
2. 彳
3. 爿丬
4. 口囗
5. 飠饣
6. 言讠
7. 扌
8. 木
9. 糸纟
10. 艹
11. 竹⺮
12. 禾
13. 月
14. 攵

15. 欠

16. 水 氵

17. 辶

18. 廴

19. 阝

20. 刂

21. 米

22. 車 车

23. 耳

24. 广

25. 厂

26. 弓

27. 方

28. 礻

29. 衤

30. 彡

31. 犭

第三单元 第三單元

走进中国 走進中國

Unit Three Approaching China

LESSON 11

第十一课
人山人海

小妹：

你好！

我和另外两个去北京实习的同学，提前一个星期到了中国。我们先飞到香港，然后到广州，经过上海、西安，最后到北京。在这六七天的时间里，中国给我的第一个印象是：中国人真多！

从西安去北京的时候，我们坐的是普通列车。当时正好赶上春节，上了火车我们才知道自己犯了多么大的错误。车厢里，原来一排坐两个人的座位，现在都坐上了四个人；过道里也是人贴着人；而且，人们的脚边还堆满了大包小包。所以，人们要想站得或者坐得舒服一点儿真是难上难。从西安到北京整整十四个小时，一路上我们不敢吃不敢喝，因为厕所里也挤满了人。

小妹，其实到中国以前我就知道中国人多，中国是世界上人口最多的国家，中国的人口占全世界人口的四分之一。但是，只有这次到了中国，我才真的明白了"中国人多"是什么意思。这么说吧，像北京、上海、广州和西安这些大城市，到处都像新年之夜的时代广场——人山人海的！

小妹，这次先写到这儿，祝你狗年万事如意！

哥哥

二月二号

第十一課
人山人海

小妹：

你好！

我和另外兩個去北京實習的同學，提前一個星期到了中國。我們先飛到香港，然後到廣州，經過上海、西安，最後到北京。在這六七天的時間裏，中國給我的第一個印象是：中國人真多！

從西安去北京的時候，我們坐的是普通列車。當時正好趕上春節，上了火車我們纔知道自己犯了多麼大的錯誤。車廂裏，原來一排坐兩個人的座位，現在都坐上了四個人；過道裏也是人貼着人；而且，人們的脚邊還堆滿了大包小包。所以，人們要想站得或者坐得舒服一點兒真是難上難。從西安到北京整整十四個小時，一路上我們不敢吃不敢喝，因爲厠所裏也擠滿了人。

小妹，其實到中國以前我就知道中國人多，中國是世界上人口最多的國家，中國的人口占全世界人口的四分之一。但是，只有這次到了中國，我纔真的明白了“中國人多”是什麼意思。這麼説吧，像北京、上海、廣州和西安這些大城市，到處都像新年之夜的時代廣場——人山人海的！

小妹，這次先寫到這兒，祝你狗年萬事如意！

哥哥

二月二號

New Words
生词表/生詞表

人山人海		rénshān-rénhǎi	*idiom*	hordes of people; huge crowds of people
另外		lìngwài	*pron*	other; another
提前		tíqián	*v*	do sth in advance
先		xiān	*adv*	first
广州	廣州	Guǎngzhōu	*pn*	Guangzhou, the capital of Guangdong Province
西安		Xī'ān	*pn*	Xi'an, the capital of Shaanxi Province
印象		yìnxiàng	*n*	impression
普通列车	普通列車	pǔtōng lièchē		local train
当时	當時	dāngshí	*n*	that time
正好		zhènghǎo	*adv*	just right; coincidentally
赶上	趕上	gǎnshang	*v*	be in time for; overtake
春节	春節	Chūnjié	*n*	Lunar New Year; Spring Festival
火车	火車	huǒchē	*n*	train
犯		fàn	*v*	commit; make (a mistake)
多么	多麼	duōme	*adv*	no matter how; however
错误	錯誤	cuòwù	*n*	mistake; error
车厢	車廂	chēxiāng	*n*	carriage (of a train); railroad car
过道	過道	guòdào	*n*	passageway; corridor
贴	貼	tiē	*v*	keep close to; paste
人们	人們	rénmen	*n*	people
脚		jiǎo	*n*	foot; feet
堆		duī	*v/n*	pile up; heap up; pile; heap
满	滿	mǎn	*adj*	full (of)
包		bāo	*n*	bag; sack; package
所以		suǒyǐ	*conj*	so; therefore; as a result
站		zhàn	*v*	stand
或者		huòzhě	*adv/conj*	perhaps; or; either...or...
舒服		shūfu	*adj*	comfortable
难上难	難上難	nánshàngnán	*idiom*	be extremely difficult
整整		zhěngzhěng	*adv*	wholly; fully
一路上		yīlùshang	*adv*	all the way; throughout the journey
不敢		bùgǎn	*aux*	dare not

因为	因爲	yīnwèi	*conj*	because
厕所	厠所	cèsuǒ	*n*	toilet
挤	擠	jǐ	*v*	crowd; cram
真的		zhēnde	*adv*	truly
意思	意思	yìsi	*n*	meaning
这么说吧	這麽説吧	zhème shuō ba		put it this way
城市		chéngshì	*n*	city; town
到处	到處	dàochù	*n*	everywhere
之		zhī	*particle*	(used between an attribute and the word it modifies)
夜		yè	*n*	night; evening
时代广场	時代廣場	Shídài Guǎngchǎng	*n*	Times Square
这儿	這兒	zhèr	*n*	here
祝		zhù	*v*	wish; express good wishes
狗		gǒu	*n*	dog
万事如意	萬事如意	wànshì-rúyì	*idiom*	everything is as one wishes
二月		èryuè	*n*	February
号	號	hào	*n*	date; number in a series

Grammar Notes
语法简注/語法簡注

1. A给B的印象是……/A給B的印象是……：the impression A gives B is…

中国给我的第一个印象是：中国人真多！

中國給我的第一個印象是：中國人真多！

The first impression that China gave me was that there truly are a great number of Chinese people.

▶ 上海给我的印象是：什么都方便[fāngbiàn]。

上海給我的印象是：什麼都方便[fāngbiàn]。

The impression Shanghai gave me was that everything was convenient there.

▶ 北京给我的印象是：到处人山人海。

北京給我的印象是：到處人山人海。

The impression Beijing gave me was that there were hordes of people everywhere.

Note: An alternative pattern is "B对A的印象是……/B對A的印象是……", the impression B has about A is...

▶ 我对上海的印象是：什么都方便。

我對上海的印象是：什麼都方便。

▶ 我对北京的印象是：到处人山人海。

我對北京的印象是：到處人山人海。

2. 正好：just in time；just right；by chance

① by chance；by good luck

当时正好赶上春节。

當時正好趕上春節。

At that time we met right up with the Lunar New Year.

▶ 我刚要去找我朋友，正好他来了。

我剛要去找我朋友，正好他來了。

I was just about to go to see my friend when he happened to come here.

▶ 上星期我开车回家，正好赶上人们下班，半个小时的路我开了两个小时。

上星期我開車回家，正好趕上人們下班，半個小時的路我開了兩個小時。

When I was driving home last week, I met right up with the congested traffic of the rush hour. It took me two hours—instead of the normal half an hour's driving time—to get home.

② exactly；just right

▶ 我这里不多不少，正好一百块钱。

我這裏不多不少，正好一百塊錢。

I have exactly one hundred dollars.

▶ 现在正好八点。

現在正好八點。

It's exactly eight o'clock now.

3. 满/滿：full

It is an adjective that follows such verbs as 堆 and serves as a complement of result meaning "full".

📖 人们的脚边堆满了大包小包。

人們的脚邊堆滿了大包小包。

Down around people's feet, the floor was piled up with large and small packages.

▶ 他的桌子上堆满了书。

他的桌子上堆滿了書。

His desk is piled up with books.

Other examples：坐满/坐滿、站满/站滿、挤满/擠滿、写满/寫滿、放满/放滿、停满/停滿……

▶ 饭馆儿里坐满了人。

飯館兒裏坐滿了人。

The restaurant is full of people.

▶ 我的作业本[běn]上写满了汉字。

我的作業本[běn]上寫滿了漢字。

My homework notebook is full of Chinese characters.

4. 一路上：all the way；throughout the journey

📖 从西安到北京，一路上我们不敢吃不敢喝。

從西安到北京，一路上我們不敢吃不敢喝。

We neither dared to eat nor to drink throughout the journey from Xi'an to Beijing.

▶ 现在，从北京到上海，火车一路上不停。

現在，從北京到上海，火車一路上不停。

Nowadays the train goes all the way from Beijing to Shanghai without stop.

▶ 我每天坐校车回家，一路上都有人上车、下车。

我每天坐校車回家，一路上都有人上車、下車。

I go home by taking the school bus every day. Throughout the way there are people getting on and off the bus.

5. A占B的……分之……：A constitutes … of B（“NU + 分之 + NU” indicates fraction.)

中国的人口占全世界人口的四分之一。

中國的人口占全世界人口的四分之一。

China's population constitutes a quarter of the whole world's population.

▶ 我们学校有两万人，女学生有一万，这就是说女生占学校人数的二分之一。

我們學校有兩萬人，女學生有一萬，這就是説女生占學校人數的二分之一。

We have twenty thousand people in our school. There are ten thousand female students. This is to say that female students constitute a half of the total population.

▶ 我们学校，中国学生占（学校人数的）三分之二。

我們學校，中國學生占（學校人數的）三分之二。

In our school, Chinese students constitute two thirds of the total population.

6. 只有……， 才……／只有……，纔……：only…(then)…

只有这次到了中国，我才真的明白了“中国人多”是什么意思。

只有這次到了中國，我纔真的明白了“中國人多”是什麽意思。

It was only this time when I went to China that I truly understood what “great number of Chinese people” meant.

▶ 我不常常回家，只有春节的时候，才回家看看。

我不常常回家，只有春節的時候，纔回家看看。

I don't often go home. Only during the Spring Festival do I go home.

▶ 只有学了第十一课，我才知道中国人把中国新年也叫做春节。

只有學了第十一課，我纔知道中國人把中國新年也叫做春節。

Only after learning Lesson 11 did I realize that the Chinese also refer to the Chinese New Year as the Spring Festival.

Reading Passage
阅读/閱讀

几个大学生的经历

春节后坐火车从广州回北京，一跑进站台我们就发现：火车的车厢里，甚至过道上都已经挤满了人，车厢的门口更是挤得人贴着人。看来，从车门挤上去是不可能的了。没办法，只能从车窗爬进去了。我们先爬进去了三个人，然后打算把行李塞进车里。谁知道，这时候跑来一个乘警。那个乘警，不但罚了我们钱，而且还断了我们爬上火车的路。怎么办？车窗爬不上去了，只能从车门挤上去了。人在临近绝望的时候，显得格外顽强！谢天谢地，我们居然从人堆里挤上了车！上了车才发现，我们每个人浑身上下——头发、内衣、外衣、裤子、皮鞋——全都湿透了。

幾個大學生的經歷

春節後坐火車從廣州回北京，一跑進站臺我們就發現：火車的車厢裏，甚至過道上都已經擠滿了人，車厢的門口更是擠得人貼着人。看來，從車門擠上去是不可能的了。没辦法，只能從車窗爬進去了。我們先爬進去了三個人，然後打算把行李塞進車裏。誰知道，這時候跑來一個乘警。那個乘警，不但罰了我們錢，而且還斷了我們爬上火車的路。怎麽辦？車窗爬不上去了，只能從車門擠上去了。人在臨近絶望的時候，顯得格外頑強！謝天謝地，我們居然從人堆裏擠上了車！上了車纔發現，我們每個人渾身上下——頭髮、内衣、外衣、褲子、皮鞋——全都濕透了。

站台	站臺	zhàntái	railway platform
车窗	車窗	chēchuāng	train/car window
打算		dǎsuan	intend; plan
乘警		chéngjǐng	railroad police
罚	罰	fá	fine; punish
断	斷	duàn	break; cut/break off
临近	臨近	línjìn	be close to (certain time point, physical location or state of mind, etc.)
绝望	絶望	juéwàng	despair; desperate
格外		géwài	especially
顽强	頑强	wánqiáng	tenacious; indomitable
居然		jūrán	unexpectedly
湿透	濕透	shītòu	wet through; thoroughly soaked

判断正误/判斷正誤

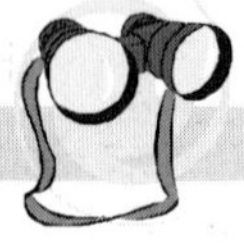

Identify the following statements as true or false based on the reading passage.

1. ___T___ 几个大学生坐火车从广州回北京。
2. ___T___ 这几个大学生最后都上了火车。
3. ___F___ 乘警帮他们上了火车。
4. ___F___ 他们都是从火车的窗户上的火车。
5. ___F___ 他们浑身上下都湿透了，是因为天气太热。

1. _______ 幾個大學生坐火車從廣州回北京。
2. _______ 這幾個大學生最後都上了火車。
3. _______ 乘警幫他們上了火車。
4. _______ 他們都是從火車的窗户上的火車。
5. _______ 他們渾身上下都濕透了，是因爲天氣太熱。

Exercises
练习/練習

一、词语练习/詞語練習

Vocabulary exercise.

	Chinese Character	Pinyin	Make a Sentence of Your Own
1		tíqián	
2		zhènghǎo	
3		yìnxiàng	
4		bù gǎn	
5		dàochù	
6		zhěngzhěng	
7		duī mǎn	
8		jǐ	

二、解释词语/解釋詞語

Define the following terms in your own words.

e.g. 整整：不多不少

1. 一路上：
2. 人贴着人/人貼着人：
3. 人山人海：

三、根据课文回答问题/根據課文回答問題

Answer the following questions using complete sentences based on information in the text.

1. 哥哥和两个同去北京实习的同学，提前多长时间到中国？
2. 他们先飞到哪儿？经过哪儿？最后到哪儿？
3. 中国给哥哥的第一个印象是什么？
4. 从西安去北京的时候，他们坐的是什么火车？
5. 当时是什么时候？
6. 火车上挤不挤？怎么挤？
7. 人们站得、坐得舒服不舒服？

8. 从西安到北京一路上有什么问题？
9. 哥哥去中国以前就知道什么？
10. 这次到了中国，哥哥明白了什么？

1. 哥哥和兩個同去北京實習的同學，提前多長時間到中國？
2. 他們先飛到哪兒？經過哪兒？最後到哪兒？
3. 中國給哥哥的第一個印象是什麼？
4. 從西安去北京的時候，他們坐的是什麼火車？
5. 當時是什麼時候？
6. 火車上擠不擠？怎麼擠？
7. 人們站得、坐得舒服不舒服？
8. 從西安到北京一路上有什麼問題？
9. 哥哥去中國以前就知道什麼？
10. 這次到了中國，哥哥明白了什麼？

四、填空

Fill in the blanks.

1. 我和两个同学一起______北京______ ______。
2. 我们先______到香港，______过上海、西安，最后______北京。
3. 中国______我的第一个印象______：中国人______多！
4. ______了火车我们才______ ______自己______了多么大的______ ______！
5. 原来一______坐两个人的______位，现在都______ ______了四个人。
6. 过道里______是人______着人，而且人们的脚边还堆______了大包小包。
7. 从西安到北京，我们不敢______不敢______，因为厕所里也______满了人。

1. 我和兩個同學一起______北京______ ______。
2. 我們先______到香港，______過上海、西安，最後______北京。
3. 中國______我的第一個印象______：中國人______多！
4. ______了火車我們纔______ ______自己______了多麼大的______ ______！
5. 原來一______坐兩個人的______位，現在都______ ______了四個人。
6. 過道裏______是人______着人，而且人們的脚邊還堆______了大包小包。
7. 從西安到北京，我們不敢______不敢______，因爲厕所裏也______滿了人。

五、改写/改寫

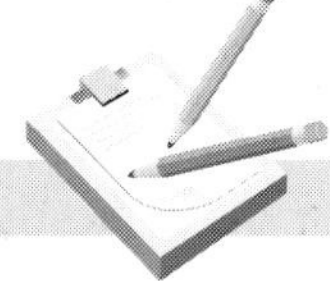

Rewrite the following sentences with the patterns in the parentheses.

1. 我们第一天飞到香港，第二天飞到北京。（先……再……）
2. 新年之夜，时代广场上站满了人。（人贴着人）
3. 听说春节坐火车去北京的人非常多，我就坐飞机去了。（所以）
4. 去中国以前，我不太清楚十三亿人口是什么意思。（才）
5. 中国现在至少有十三亿人口，全世界的人口大约是六十亿，这就是说中国人口大约是世界人口的百分之二十。（占……几分之几）

1. 我們第一天飛到香港，第二天飛到北京。（先……再……）
2. 新年之夜，時代廣場上站滿了人。（人貼着人）
3. 聽説春節坐火車去北京的人非常多，我就坐飛機去了。（所以）
4. 去中國以前，我不太清楚十三億人口是什麼意思。（纔）
5. 中國現在至少有十三億人口，全世界的人口大約是六十億，這就是説中國人口大約是世界人口的百分之二十。（占……幾分之幾）

六、重组/重組

Word order.

1. 的时间里/第一个印象/人山人海/在这五天/上海/都是/给我的/到处

   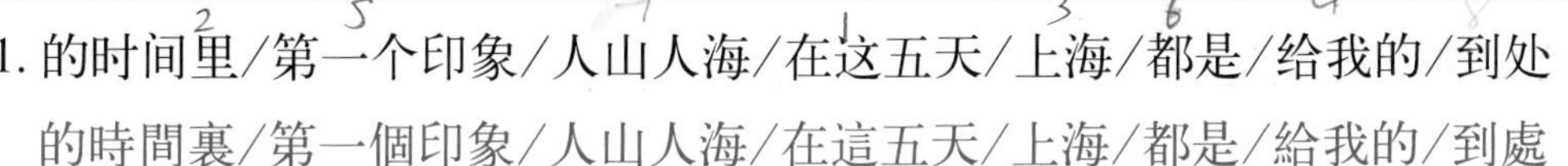

   的時間裏/第一個印象/人山人海/在這五天/上海/都是/給我的/到處

   Within these five days, the first impression that Shanghai gave me was that there were hordes of people everywhere.

   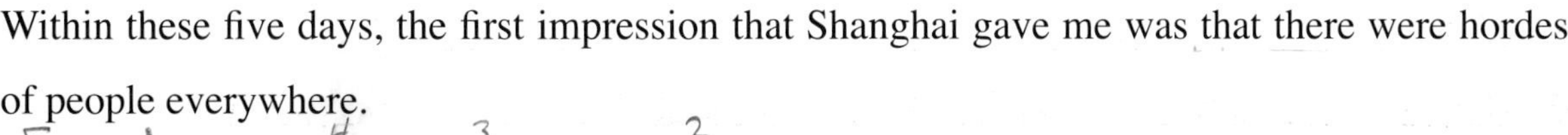

2. 都/新年之夜的/挤得/人山人海的/时代广场

   都/新年之夜的/擠得/人山人海的/時代廣場

   On New Year's Eve, Times Square is crowded with people everywhere.

3. 我有/看看/坐火车/时间/如果/去广州/我就

   我有/看看/坐火車/時間/如果/去廣州/我就

   If I have time, I'll take the train to visit Guangzhou.

4. 上了/有多么长/知道/只有/中国历史/我才/世界历史课

   上了/有多麽長/知道/只有/中國歷史/我纔/世界歷史課

   Only after taking a course on world history did I realize how long the Chinese history is.

5. 四分之一/我就知道/占/到这个学校/全校人数的/中国学生/以前
四分之一/我就知道/占/到這個學校/全校人數的/中國學生/以前
Before coming to this school, I already knew that Chinese students constitute a quarter of the school's population.

七、翻译/翻譯

Translate the following sentences into Chinese.

1. Grandma is coming to the US next month. If I have time, I would take her to New York for a visit.
2. Before going to China, I already knew that China's large cities are crowded with people everywhere.
3. Only after I had an internship at that university did I realize that female students constitute only one fifth of that university's population.
4. Actually, if I had more money, I wouldn't have taken the local train to Xi'an.
5. Every year during the Spring Festival in China, the trains are overcrowded with people. Therefore, it is extremely difficult to get on the train and find a seat.

八、改错/改錯

Correct mistakes.

1. 我们先飞香港，然后到广州，最后北京。
2. 我们是坐普通列车到北京。
3. 其实到中国以前我才知道中国人很多。
4. 只有这次到中国，我就真的明白“中国人多”是什么意思。
5. 中国对我的印象是：中国人真多！
6. 那饭馆里堆满了人。
7. 如果我有钱，我一定去北京、上海、西安去看看。

1. 我們先飛香港，然後到廣州，最後北京。
2. 我們是坐普通列車到北京。
3. 其實到中國以前我纔知道中國人很多。
4. 只有這次到中國，我就真的明白“中國人多”是什麼意思。
5. 中國對我的印象是：中國人真多！
6. 那飯館裏堆滿了人。
7. 如果我有錢，我一定去北京、上海、西安去看看。

九、课堂活动/課堂活動

In-class activity.

How many phrases do you know which are relevant to people?

e.g. 人：好人，大人，……

1. 人人，______，______，______，______，______
2. 人挤人，人贴人 ______，______，______，______
3. 人山人海，______，______

1. 人人，______，______，______，______，______
2. 人擠人，人貼人 ______，______，______，______
3. 人山人海，______，______

十、课外活动/課外活動

After-class activity.

1. Look at the diagram below and find your Chinese zodiac sign.
2. Do you know how old the people are who share your Chinese zodiac sign?

十一、写作练习/寫作練習

Writing.

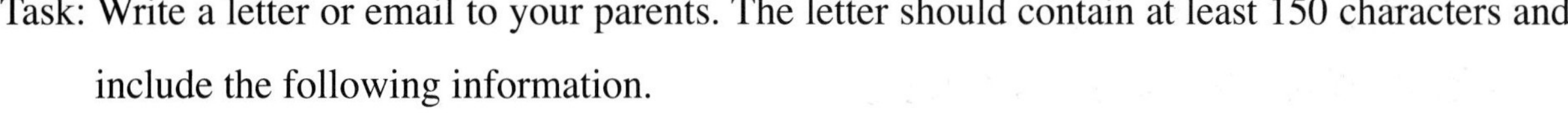

Task: Write a letter or email to your parents. The letter should contain at least 150 characters and include the following information.

1. Ask how your parents are doing.
2. Tell your parents what you have been up to, especially about anything new in your life.
3. Mention anything you may need or want from your parents.

For example:

爸爸、妈妈：

你们好！

爸爸从台湾回来了吗？

我前天收到哥哥从上海发来的一封[fēng]电子邮件。他告诉[gàosù]我，他去看了你们在上海买的房子[fángzi]。他说，房子很大，也很漂亮[piàoliang]。房子里有四个卧室[wòshì]、三个厕所[cèsuǒ]、两个客厅[kètīng]。看样子[yàngzi]，你们不但退休后真的要搬到上海去住了，而且还要把爷爷、奶奶接到上海一起住。哥哥还告诉我，我的卧室里什么东西都是我喜欢的粉色[fěnsè]，很漂亮。

听哥哥这么一说，刚开学我就开始盼着放假[fàngjià]了，到时候好跟你们去上海看看我们未来[wèilái]的新家。

我这学期选[xuǎn]了五门课，每天功课都很多。特别是中文课，每个星期都得用中文写短信[duǎnxìn]，有时候忙得连打电话的时间都没有。

我一切都好，请放心[fàngxīn]，有时间给我打电话吧。

敬祝[jìngzhù]

健康[jiànkāng]

女儿：盼盼

二月五号

爸爸、媽媽：

你們好！

爸爸從臺灣回來了嗎？

我前天收到哥哥從上海發來的一封[fēng]電子郵件。他告訴[gàosù]我，他去看了你們在上海買的房子[fángzi]。他説，房子很大，也很漂亮[piàoliang]。房子裏有四個卧室[wòshì]、三個厕所[cèsuǒ]、兩個客廳[kètīng]。看様子[yàngzi]，你們不但退休後真的要搬到上海去住了，而且還要把爺爺、奶奶接到上海一起住。哥哥還告訴我，我的卧室裏什麼東西都是我喜歡的粉色[fěnsè]，很漂亮。

聽哥哥這麼一説，剛開學我就開始盼着放假[fàngjià]了，到時候好跟你們去上海看看我們未來[wèilái]的新家。

我這學期選[xuǎn]了五門課，每天功課都很多。特别是中文課，每個星期都得用中文寫短信[duǎnxìn]，有時候忙得連打電話的時間都没有。

我一切都好，請放心[fàngxīn]，有時間給我打電話吧。

敬祝[jìngzhù]

健康[jiànkāng]

女兒：盼盼

二月五號

十二、总结/總結

Summary.

1. Choose 5-10 of your favorite new vocabulary words from the text or reading material.

2. Quote 3-7 of your favorite sentences from the text or reading material here.

	Original sentence	**Translation of the sentence** (or make a new sentence of your own)
1		
2		
3		
4		
5		

3. From this lesson, you have learned Chinese culture, history, and philosophy. They have helped you to understand,

① 我现在清楚了为什么中国人/我現在清楚了爲什麼中國人：________________

② 我现在明白了/我現在明白了：________________________

③ 我现在知道了/我現在知道了：________________________

LESSON 12

第十二课
“吃”的文化

小妹：

你好！

到北京实习已经一个多星期了。中国给我的另一个印象是：中国人特别喜欢聚在一起“吃”。

真的，小妹，中国人做什么事都离不开“吃”！

逢年过节，家人、朋友相聚，当然要吃，而且要一连吃上好几天。遇到红白喜事，像结婚、生孩子、过生日什么的，当事人一定会请上所有的亲戚朋友大吃特吃。

如果有谁搬家、升级、毕业或者找到新工作什么的，亲朋好友少不了要庆祝。要庆祝就一定会聚在一起吃。平时有事求人帮忙，事后，求人帮忙的人无论如何都会买上几瓶酒，摆上一桌菜，请帮忙的人吃一顿。

“有朋自远方来，不亦乐乎！”既然“乐乎”，中国人觉得吃饭、干杯当然是表达“乐”的最好方式。

总之，人们有理由要聚在一起吃；没有理由，找个理由，甚至编个理由也要聚在一起吃一顿。当然，现在人们吃饭，已经不单单是为了吃饱肚子了，更重要的是人们借吃饭的机会交流感情，交流信息；借吃饭的机会认识新朋友，享受生活。

小妹，今天晚上我有宴会，我得走了，先写到这儿吧。

祝好！

哥哥

二月十号

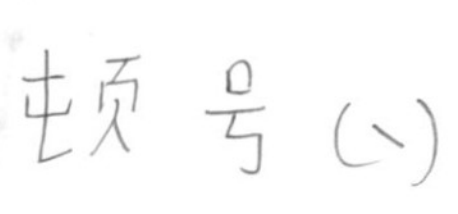

LESSON 12

第十二課
"吃"的文化

小妹:

你好!

到北京實習已經一個多星期了。中國給我的另一個印象是:中國人特別喜歡聚在一起"吃"。

真的，小妹，中國人做什麼事都離不開"吃"!

逢年過節，家人、朋友相聚，當然要吃，而且要一連吃上好幾天。遇到紅白喜事，像結婚、生孩子、過生日什麼的，當事人一定會請上所有的親戚朋友大吃特吃。

如果有誰搬家、陞級、畢業或者找到新工作什麼的，親朋好友少不了要慶祝。要慶祝就一定會聚在一起吃。平時有事求人幫忙，事後，求人幫忙的人無論如何都會買上幾瓶酒，擺上一桌菜，請幫忙的人吃一頓。

"有朋自遠方來，不亦樂乎!"既然"樂乎"，中國人覺得吃飯、乾杯當然是表達"樂"的最好方式。

總之，人們有理由要聚在一起吃；沒有理由，找個理由，甚至編個理由也要聚在一起吃一頓。當然，現在人們吃飯，已經不單單是爲了吃飽肚子了，更重要的是人們借吃飯的機會交流感情，交流信息；借吃飯的機會認識新朋友，享受生活。

小妹，今天晚上我有宴會，我得走了，先寫到這兒吧。

祝好!

哥哥

二月十號

New Words 生词表/生詞表

文化		wénhuà	*n*	culture
聚		jù	*v*	get together; gather
离不开	離不開	lí bu kāi		can't do without
逢年过节	逢年過節	féngnián-guòjié	*idiom*	on New Year's Day and other festivals
相聚		xiāngjù	*v*	meet; gather
一连	一連	yīlián	*adv*	in a row; in succession
遇		yù	*v*	meet; encounter
红白喜事	紅白喜事	hóng-bái xǐshì	*idiom*	weddings and funerals
生孩子		shēng háizi		give birth to a baby
过生日	過生日	guò shēngrì		celebrate one's birthday
当事人	當事人	dāngshìrén	*n*	party (to a lawsuit); person involved
所有		suǒyǒu	*adj*	all
亲戚	親戚	qīnqi	*n*	relative
谁	誰	shéi	*pron*	who; someone; anyone
搬家		bānjiā	*vo*	move (house); relocate
升级	陞級	shēngjí	*vo*	go up one grade; promote to a higher grade
毕业	畢業	bìyè	*v*	graduate; finish school
找		zhǎo	*vc*	look for; try to find
工作		gōngzuò	*n*	work; job
什么的	什麼的	shénmede	*pron*	and so on; thing like that
亲朋好友	親朋好友	qīnpéng-hǎoyǒu	*idiom*	relatives and friends
少不了		shǎobuliǎo	*idiom*	can't do without; be indispensable
庆祝	慶祝	qìngzhù	*v*	celebrate
求人		qiúrén	*vo*	ask for help
帮忙	幫忙	bāngmáng	*v/n*	help
事后	事後	shìhòu	*n*	after the event; afterwards
无论如何	無論如何	wúlùn-rúhé	*idiom*	in any case; anyway
买	買	mǎi	*v*	buy
瓶		píng	*n/m*	bottle
酒		jiǔ	*n*	wine; liquor
摆	擺	bǎi	*v*	arrange; lay; put
顿	頓	dùn	*m*	(measure word for meals)

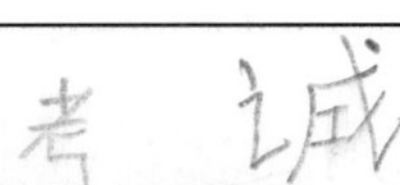

朋		péng	*n*	friend
自		zì	*prep*	from
远方	遠方	yuǎnfāng	*n*	distant place
不亦乐乎	不亦樂乎	bù yì lè hū	*idiom*	Isn't it a pleasure?
既然		jìrán	*conj*	since; now that
乐	樂	lè	*adj*	happy
干杯	乾杯	gānbēi	*vo*	drink a toast; cheers
表达	表達	biǎodá	*v*	express
方式		fāngshì	*n*	way; mode
总之	總之	zǒngzhī	*conj*	in short
理由		lǐyóu	*n*	reason; excuse
甚至		shènzhì	*conj*	even; so much so that
编	編	biān	*v*	make up; fabricate
单单	單單	dāndān	*adv*	alone; only
饱	飽	bǎo	*adj*	full
肚子		dùzi	*n*	belly; abdomen
重要		zhòngyào	*adj*	important; significant
借		jiè	*v*	borrow; lend; make use of
机会	機會	jīhuì	*n*	opportunity
交流		jiāoliú	*v*	exchange
信息		xìnxī	*n*	information
感情		gǎnqíng	*n*	feeling; emotion; affection
享受		xiǎngshòu	*v*	enjoy
今晚		jīn wǎn		this evening; tonight
宴会	宴會	yànhuì	*n*	banquet; dinner party

Grammar Notes
语法简注/語法簡注

1. 离不开/離不開：can't do without

中国人做什么事都离不开"吃"！

中國人做什麼事都離不開"吃"！

The Chinese can't do without eating.

▶ 鱼儿离不开水。

魚兒離不開水。

Fish can't live without water.

▶ 我的中文还不够好，写中文信的时候总是离不开字典。

我的中文還不够好，寫中文信的時候總是離不開字典。

My Chinese is still not good enough. When I write letters in Chinese, I can't do without a dictionary.

2. 一连/一連：in a row; in succession (an action that occurs in succession)

逢年过节，家人、朋友相聚，当然要吃，而且要一连吃好几天。

逢年過節，家人、朋友相聚，當然要吃，而且要一連吃好幾天。

On New Year's Day or other festivals when family members and friends gather together, they would eat, and furthermore, they would eat for quite a few days in succession.

▶ 上个星期天我一连打了八个电话。

上個星期天我一連打了八個電話。

I made eight phone calls in a row last Sunday.

▶ 不知道怎么了，他一连两个星期没来上课了。

不知道怎麼了，他一連兩個星期没來上課了。

Somehow he hasn't come to class for two weeks.

3. 什么的/什麼的：and what not; and so on; etc.

遇到红白喜事，像结婚、生孩子、过生日什么的……

遇到紅白喜事，像結婚、生孩子、過生日什麼的……

when encountering such events as weddings, births, birthdays, and so forth…

▶ 我喜欢打球、跑步什么的。

我喜歡打球、跑步什麽的。

I like such sports as playing balls, running, and so forth.

▶ 如果有谁搬家、找到工作、毕业什么的，亲朋好友少不了要庆祝。

如果有誰搬家、找到工作、畢業什麽的，親朋好友少不了要慶祝。

If someone moves, finds a job, graduates from school, and so forth, (his or her) relatives and friends would want to celebrate.

4. 无论如何／無論如何：in any case; invariably; whatever happens; at any rate

📖 求人帮忙的人无论如何都会买上几瓶酒，请帮忙的人吃一顿。

求人幫忙的人無論如何都會買上幾瓶酒，請幫忙的人吃一頓。

The person who has requested help from others would invariably buy a few bottles of spirit and treat those who offer help to a dinner.

▶ 明年我无论如何要到中国去看看。

明年我無論如何要到中國去看看。

In any case, I'd go to China for a visit next year.

▶ 今天是我好朋友的生日，晚上我无论如何得给他打个电话。

今天是我好朋友的生日，晚上我無論如何得給他打個電話。

It's my good friend's birthday today. I must give him a call tonight, no matter what.

5. V(请、吃、买、摆) ＋上／V(請、吃、買、擺) ＋上

① V＋上：used after a verb indicating the attainment of an object

📖 遇到红白喜事，当事人一定会请上所有的亲戚朋友大吃特吃。

遇到紅白喜事，當事人一定會請上所有的親戚朋友大吃特吃。

When encountering weddings and funerals, the party concerned would surely treat all the relatives and friends to a big dinner.

▶ 事后，求人帮忙的人一定会买上几瓶酒，摆上一桌菜，请帮忙的人吃一顿。

事後，求人幫忙的人一定會買上幾瓶酒，擺上一桌菜，請幫忙的人吃一頓。

After the event, the person who has requested help from others would surely buy a few bottles of wine, serve many dishes on the table, and treat those who helped.

▶ 我的飞机是十点的，现在九点半，不知道我还能不能赶上。

我的飛機是十點的，現在九點半，不知道我還能不能趕上。

My plane leaves at ten o'clock. Right now it's half past nine o'clock. I don't know whether I'm still able to catch the plane!

② V+上：indicating the beginning and continuation of an action

▶ 逢年过节，人们要一连吃上好几天。

逢年過節，人們要一連吃上好幾天。

On New Year's Day or other festivals people would eat for quite a few days in succession.

▶ 我整整两天没睡觉了，今天我要睡上二十个小时。

我整整兩天沒睡覺了，今天我要睡上二十個小時。

I haven't slept for two whole days. I'm going to sleep for twenty hours today.

6. 表达……的方式/表達……的方式：the way to express… (feelings or emotions)

📖 吃饭、干杯自然是表达“乐”的最好方式了。

吃飯、乾杯自然是表達“樂”的最好方式了。

Eating and drinking a toast is naturally the best way to express “pleasure”.

▶ 唠叨常常是中国妈妈表达“爱”的方式。

嘮叨常常是中國媽媽表達“愛”的方式。

Being garrulous is often the way Chinese mothers express their love.

▶ 做好吃的是奶奶表达“爱”的方式。

做好吃的是奶奶表達“愛”的方式。

Making delicious food is the way Grandma expresses her love.

7. 单单/單單：only; merely

📖 现在人们吃饭已经不单单是为了吃饱肚子了。

現在人們吃飯已經不單單是爲了吃飽肚子了。

Nowadays eating is no longer done merely for the sake of filling up the stomach.

▶ 我不单单选了中文课，还选了日文课。

我不單單選了中文課，還選了日文課。

I took not only Chinese class but also Japanese class.

▶ 单单做中文作业，我每星期就得花两个小时的时间。

單單做中文作業，我每星期就得花兩個小時的時間。

I have to spend two hours per week merely in doing Chinese homework.

8. 借……机会，……/借……機會，……：take opportunity to…

📖 更重要的是人们借吃饭的机会交流感情。

更重要的是人們借吃飯的機會交流感情。

What's more important is that people take the opportunity of eating to communicate.

▶ 人们借吃饭的机会，交流信息，认识新朋友。

人們借吃飯的機會，交流信息，認識新朋友。

People take the opportunity of eating to exchange information and make new friends.

▶ 我想借今天的机会谢谢您。

我想借今天的機會謝謝您。

I'd like to take today's opportunity to thank you.

满汉全席

满汉全席兴于清代。过去官府中举办满汉全席时，首先要奏乐、鸣炮、行礼迎接宾客入座。客人入座后，先上进门点心。进门点心有甜、咸两种。进门点心以后是三道茶：清茶、香茶、炒米茶。然后才正式入席。满汉全席上的菜分冷菜、头菜、炒菜、甜菜、点心和水果。据说满汉全席一共有六道一百零八样菜，“全席”要三天才能吃完。

滿漢全席

滿漢全席興於清代。過去官府中舉辦滿漢全席時，首先要奏樂、鳴炮、行禮迎接賓客入座。客人入座後，先上進門點心。進門點心有甜、鹹兩種。進門點心以後是三道茶：清茶、香茶、炒米茶。然後纔正式入席。滿漢全席上的菜分冷菜、頭菜、炒菜、甜菜、點心和水果。據説滿漢全席一共有六道一百零八樣菜，“全席”要三天纔能吃完。

满汉全席	滿漢全席	Mǎnhàn Quánxí	Feast of Complete Manchu-Han Courses
兴于	興於	xīngyú	start from
官府		guānfǔ	local authorities
奏乐	奏樂	zòuyuè	strike up a tune; play music
鸣炮	鳴炮	míngpào	fire gun/cannons (in salute)

判断正误/判斷正誤

Identify the following statements as true or false based on the reading passage.

1. _______ 满汉全席兴于清代。
2. _______ 满汉全席有八十样菜。
3. _______ 吃满汉全席时要奏乐。
4. _______ 满汉全席要吃一天才能吃完。

1. _______ 滿漢全席興於清代。
2. _______ 滿漢全席有八十樣菜。
3. _______ 吃滿漢全席時要奏樂。
4. _______ 滿漢全席要吃一天纔能吃完。

Exercises 练习/練習

一、词语练习/詞語練習

Vocabulary exercise.

	Chinese Character	Pinyin	Make a Sentence of Your Own
1		tèbié	
2		lí bu kāi	
3		yīlián	
4		suǒyǒude	
5		děi	
6		píngshí	
7		bāngmáng	
8		jīhuì	

二、解释词语/解釋詞語

Define the following terms in your own words.

e.g. 逢年过节：每到过年、过节（的时候）

1. 有朋自远方来，不亦乐乎：
2. 亲朋好友：
3. 少不了：

e.g. 逢年過節：每到過年、過節（的時候）

1. 有朋自遠方來，不亦樂乎：
2. 親朋好友：
3. 少不了：

三、根据课文回答问题/根據課文回答問題

Answer the following questions using complete sentences based on information in the text.

1. 中国给哥哥的另一个印象是什么？
2. 哥哥为什么这么说？
3. 中国人都什么时候聚在一起吃？逢年过节，怎么吃？遇到红白喜事，怎么吃？搬家以后呢？求人帮忙以后呢？"有朋自远方来"呢？
4. 中国人现在吃饭只是为了吃饱肚子吗？那是为了什么呢？
5. 中国人为什么那么喜欢聚在一起吃呢？
6. 你也喜欢跟朋友聚在一起吃饭吗？你们什么时候聚在一起吃？

1. 中國給哥哥的另一個印象是什麽？
2. 哥哥爲什麽這麽説？
3. 中國人都什麽時候聚在一起吃？逢年過節，怎麽吃？遇到紅白喜事，怎麽吃？搬家以後呢？求人幫忙以後呢？"有朋自遠方來"呢？
4. 中國人現在吃飯只是爲了吃飽肚子嗎？那是爲了什麽呢？
5. 中國人爲什麽那麽喜歡聚在一起吃呢？
6. 你也喜歡跟朋友聚在一起吃飯嗎？你們什麽時候聚在一起吃？

四、填空

Fill in the blanks.

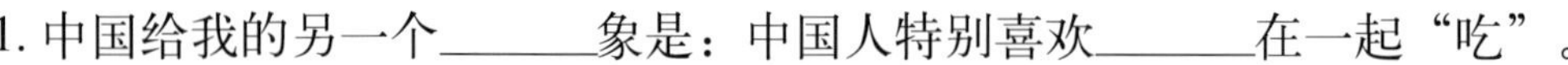

A. Fill in the blanks based on the text.

1. 中国给我的另一个______象是：中国人特别喜欢______在一起“吃”。
2. 真的，中国人做什么事都______不______“吃”！
3. ______年过节，家人、朋友______在一起，当然要吃。
4. 遇上______ ______喜事，当事人一定会请上所有的亲______朋友，______吃______吃。
5. 总______，人们有理由要聚在一起吃；没有理由，找个理由，______ ______编个理由，也要聚______一起吃一______。
6. 现在人们吃饭是借吃饭的______会，交流______ ______，交流______ ______，______ ______新朋友。

1. 中國給我的另一個______象是：中國人特別喜歡______在一起“吃”。
2. 真的，中國人做什麼事都______不______“吃”！
3. ______年過節，家人、朋友______在一起，當然要吃。
4. 遇上______ ______喜事，當事人一定會請上所有的親______朋友，______吃______吃。
5. 總______，人們有理由要聚在一起吃；沒有理由，找個理由，______ ______編個理由，也要聚______一起吃一______。
6. 現在人們吃飯是借吃飯的______會，交流______ ______，交流______ ______，______ ______新朋友。

B. Insert the words from the left in appropriate place in the sentence, and translate them into English.

e.g. 当然　去北京的人，↓都要去看看长城。

1. 而且　中国人过春节的时候一定要跟亲朋好友聚在一起吃饭，一吃就要吃上好几天。

   Translation：

2. 如果　遇上结婚、生孩子这样的事，中国人一定会吃饭庆祝。

   Translation：

3. 甚至　人们有理由要聚在一起吃；没有理由，找个理由，编个理由也要聚在一起吃一顿。

   Translation：

4. 既然　吃饭的时候可以交流信息，所以很多商人都喜欢请人吃饭。

   Translation：

5. 像　　饭馆、茶馆、酒吧这些地方，都是人们最爱去的地方。

Translation：

e.g. 當然　去北京的人，↓都要去看看長城。

1. 而且　中國人過春節的時候一定要跟親朋好友聚在一起吃飯，一吃就要吃上好幾天。

Translation：

2. 如果　遇上結婚、生孩子這樣的事，中國人一定會吃飯慶祝。

Translation：

3. 甚至　人們有理由要聚在一起吃；没有理由，找個理由，編個理由也要聚在一起吃一頓。

Translation：

4. 既然　吃飯的時候可以交流信息，所以很多商人都喜歡請人吃飯。

Translation：

5. 像　　飯館、茶館、酒吧這些地方，都是人們最愛去的地方。

Translation：

五、改写/改寫

Rewrite the following sentences with the patterns in the parentheses.

1. 要是你不想跟她去吃饭，你就早一点儿告诉她。（如果……）
2. 以前总是你请我吃饭，今天的饭钱一定要我来付。（无论如何）
3. 每次去奶奶家，奶奶一定给我做我最爱吃的红烧鱼。（少不了）
4. 周末的时候，我常在家看看书、听听音乐或出去买买东西。（什么的）
5. 我认识小王二十多年了，她结婚的时候，我一定要去。（当然）

1. 要是你不想跟她去吃飯，你就早一點兒告訴她。（如果……）
2. 以前總是你請我吃飯，今天的飯錢一定要我來付。（無論如何）
3. 每次去奶奶家，奶奶一定給我做我最愛吃的紅燒魚。（少不了）
4. 周末的時候，我常在家看看書、聽聽音樂或出去買買東西。（什麼的）
5. 我認識小王二十多年了，她結婚的時候，我一定要去。（當然）

六、重组/重組

Word order.

1. 是/好吃的饭/我妈妈/的方式/给我/表达“爱”/做一顿/一种
   是/好吃的飯/我媽媽/的方式/給我/表達“愛”/做一頓/一種

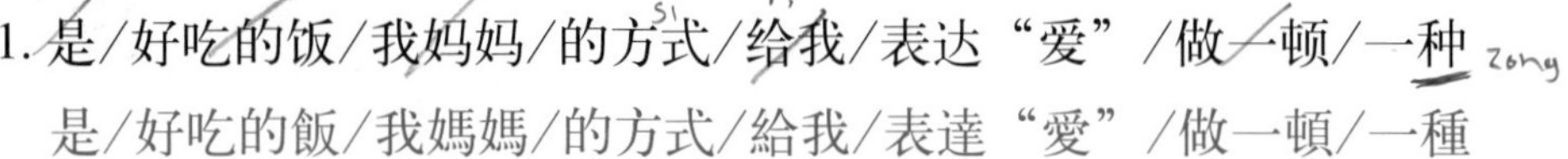

   Cooking a delicious meal for me is a way Mom expresses her love.

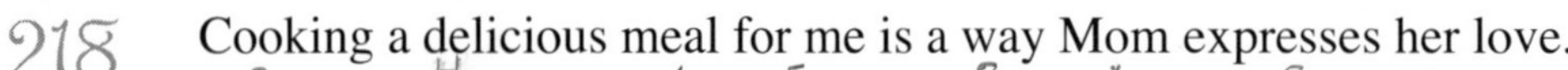

2. 北京人/找个理由/一起/就聚在/一顿/这几年/常常/吃
   北京人/找個理由/一起/就聚在/一頓/這幾年/常常/吃
   In recent years people in Beijing would often find an excuse for gathering and eating.
3. 请他/帮我/吃顿饭/我无论如何/既然/得/我朋友/搬家
   請他/幫我/吃頓飯/我無論如何/既然/得/我朋友/搬家
   Since my friend helped me move, I must treat him to a meal in any case.
4. 而且/春节/吃上/要吃/好几天/相聚/一定/要一连/家人
   而且/春節/吃上/要吃/好幾天/相聚/一定/要一連/家人
   When family members gather together during the Spring Festival, certainly they would eat, and furthermore, they would eat for quite a few days in succession.
5. 所有的/当事人/遇到/等喜事/亲戚朋友/生孩子/一定会/结婚/请上/大吃特吃
   所有的/當事人/遇到/等喜事/親戚朋友/生孩子/一定會/結婚/請上/大吃特吃
   When encountering such happy events as weddings, births, and so forth, the party concerned would surely treat all the relatives and friends to a big dinner.

七、翻译/翻譯

Translate the following sentences into Chinese.

1. In order to master Chinese, I often consult my Chinese language teacher. This is because if you want to master Chinese, you can't do without your teacher's help.
2. Because I must hand in my homework tomorrow, I have to search and find *The Book of China's Family Names* online today, no matter what.
3. If someone graduates from school, gets married, and so forth, his or her relatives and friends would want to celebrate. In order to celebrate, they would get together and eat.
4. People feel that nowadays eating is no longer merely for the sake of filling up the stomach. What's more important is that people can take the opportunity of eating to enjoy life.
5. If a person asks other people for help, after the event, the person who has requested help from others would invariably treat those who has helped to a meal.

八、改错/改錯

Correct mistakes.

1. 到北京实习已经一星期多。
2. 真的，中国人做什么事不离开“吃”！
3. 如果有人搬家、毕业，亲朋好友一定要庆祝。
4. 人们有理由要聚一起吃；没有理由，找理由，甚至编理由，也要聚一起吃。
5. 当然，现在人们吃饭好像已经不单单是因为吃饱肚子。
6. 如果有人找到新工作，亲朋好友离不开要庆祝。
7. 那个小妹妹刚刚一岁，还少不了她妈妈。

1. 到北京實習已經一星期多。
2. 真的，中國人做什麼事不離開“吃”！
3. 如果有人搬家、畢業，親朋好友一定要慶祝。
4. 人們有理由要聚一起吃；沒有理由，找理由，甚至編理由，也要聚一起吃。
5. 當然，現在人們吃飯好像已經不單單是因爲吃飽肚子。
6. 如果有人找到新工作，親朋好友離不開要慶祝。
7. 那個小妹妹剛剛一歲，還少不了她媽媽。

九、课堂活动/課堂活動

In-class activity.

A. All of the following terms contain the character “吃”, yet their meanings have nothing to do with eating. Please write down their Pinyin. Do you know what they mean?

1. 吃醋
2. 吃惊
3. 吃豆腐
4. 吃软饭
5. 吃闲饭

1. 吃醋
2. 吃驚
3. 吃豆腐
4. 吃軟飯
5. 吃閑飯

B. How many Chinese idioms containing the character “吃” do you know?

1. 吃喝玩乐

2. 好吃懒做

1. 吃喝玩樂

2. 好吃懶做

十、课外活动/課外活動

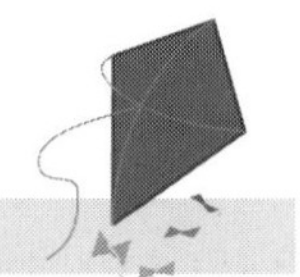

After-class activity.

Confucius was one of the most famous philosophers in Chinese history. Go online to find the following information about Confucius (http://www.greatdreams.com/masters/Confucius.htm).

- Confucius was born in ___________, in ___________ Province in China.
- The Metaphysics of Confucius are ____
- The Ethics of Confucius are ____

Confucius' teachings:

- 孔子曰：有朋自远方来，不亦乐乎！/孔子曰：有朋自遠方來，不亦樂乎！

  Translation：____

十一、写作练习/寫作練習

Writing.

Task: Write a letter to your grandparents. The letter should contain at least 150 characters and include the following information.

1. Inquire about your grandparent's health.
2. Tell them how you have been doing, such as your school or personal life.

For example：

亲爱的爷爷、奶奶：

你们好吗？

现在天气冷了，你们还常到公园去散步吗？

我听爸爸说，最近他给你们买了一台[tái]电脑，爷爷也已经开始学习怎么用电脑了。真是太好了！今年我的中文老师每星期都让我们用中文写一篇[piān]短信，等爷爷学会了用电脑发邮件，我一定要常常向爷爷请教。另外，我记得小时候，爷爷常常给我讲故事。爷爷，您能把那些故事用电子邮件发给我吗？以后，上中文课时，老师再让我们用中文讲故事，我就不用费[fèi]时间上网查了。谢谢爷爷。

我常常想你们，想奶奶做的饭。

敬祝

健康

孙子：懒懒

二月四号

親愛的爺爺、奶奶：

你們好嗎？

現在天氣冷了，你們還常到公園去散步嗎？

我聽爸爸説，最近他給你們買了一臺[tái]電腦，爺爺也已經開始學習怎麼用電腦了。真是太好了！今年我的中文老師每星期都讓我們用中文寫一篇[piān]短信，等爺爺學會了用電腦發郵件，我一定要常常向爺爺請教。另外，我記得小時候，爺爺常常給我講故事。爺爺，您能把那些故事用電子郵件發給我嗎？以後，上中文課時，老師再讓我們用中文講故事，我就不用費[fèi]時間上網查了。謝謝爺爺。

我常常想你們，想奶奶做的飯。

敬祝

健康

孫子：懶懶

二月四號

十二、总结/總結

Summary.

1. Choose 5-10 of your favorite new vocabulary words from the text or reading material.

2. Quote 3-7 of your favorite sentences from the text or reading material here.

	Original sentence	**Translation of the sentence** (or make a new sentence of your own)
1		
2		
3		
4		
5		

3. From this lesson, you have learned Chinese culture, history, and philosophy. They have helped you to understand,

① 我现在清楚了为什么中国人/我現在清楚了爲什麽中國人：____________________

② 我现在明白了/我現在明白了：____

③ 我现在知道了/我現在知道了：____

LESSON 13

第十三课

中国人怎么打招呼

小妹：

你好！

这次到中国，学校除了为我们安排了一些商业实习活动以外，还为我们安排了中文课和中国文化课。今天的文化课我们学的是中国人怎么打招呼。

文化课的老师说，在中国，不认识的人之间一般是不打招呼的。所以，无论是在路上，还是在公园里，两个人相遇，只要互相不认识，通常谁也不用跟谁打招呼。但是，熟人相遇，是一定要打招呼的，就是两个人离得老远，双方也都会主动走过去打招呼。

打招呼的时候，有时候人们使用语言，有时候不使用语言。不用语言的时候，人们用招手、点头和微笑来打招呼。

招手打招呼就是：打招呼的人举起手，晃一晃，算是打招呼了。

点头打招呼就是：打招呼的人看着对方，点点头，算是打招呼了。

微笑打招呼就是：打招呼的人看着对方，笑一笑，算是打招呼了。

使用语言打招呼有这么几种方式：

称谓式，如：称呼对方老张、钱老师、马大夫，等等。

祝愿式，如：新年快乐！恭喜发财！万事如意！等等。

关心式，如：吃了吗？病好点儿了吗？儿子回来了吗？等等。

文化课的老师特别强调，中国人上下级相遇，一般下级会主动先跟上级打招呼，而且还会称呼上级的头衔；而上级叫一声下级的名字就可以了。晚辈和长辈相遇，晚辈应该主动先跟长辈打招呼；而长辈只要答应一声，就算是向晚辈打招呼了。

小妹，有人敲门。这次先写到这儿。祝你情人节愉快！

哥哥

二月十四号

LESSON 13

第十三課
中國人怎麽打招呼

小妹:

你好!

這次到中國，學校除了爲我們安排了一些商業實習活動以外，還爲我們安排了中文課和中國文化課。今天的文化課我們學的是中國人怎麽打招呼。

文化課的老師説，在中國，不認識的人之間一般是不打招呼的。所以，無論是在路上，還是在公園裏，兩個人相遇，只要互相不認識，通常誰也不用跟誰打招呼。但是，熟人相遇，是一定要打招呼的，就是兩個人離得老遠，雙方也都會主動走過去打招呼。

打招呼的時候，有時候人們使用語言,有時候不使用語言。不用語言的時候，人們用招手、點頭和微笑來打招呼。

招手打招呼就是：打招呼的人舉起手，晃一晃，算是打招呼了。

點頭打招呼就是：打招呼的人看着對方，點點頭，算是打招呼了。

微笑打招呼就是：打招呼的人看着對方，笑一笑，算是打招呼了。

使用語言打招呼有這麽幾種方式:

稱謂式，如：稱呼對方老張、錢老師、馬大夫，等等。

祝願式，如：新年快樂！恭喜發財！萬事如意！等等。

關心式，如：吃了嗎？病好點兒了嗎？兒子回來了嗎？等等。

文化課的老師特别强調，中國人上下級相遇，一般下級會主動先跟上級打招呼，而且還會稱呼上級的頭銜；而上級叫一聲下級的名字就可以了。晚輩和長輩相遇，晚輩應該主動先跟長輩打招呼；而長輩只要答應一聲，就算是向晚輩打招呼了。

小妹，有人敲門。這次先寫到這兒。祝你情人節愉快!

哥哥

二月十四號

New Words
生词表／生詞表

打招呼		dǎ zhāohu		greet; say hello to
招呼		zhāohu	*v*	greet; say hello to
除了……以外		chúle yǐwài		except; besides
安排		ānpái	*v*	arrange; plan
一些		yīxiē	*m*	a few; some
商业	商業	shāngyè	*n*	business; commerce
活动	活動	huódòng	*n*	activity
文化课	文化課	wénhuàkè	*n*	culture course
无论	無論	wúlùn	*conj*	whatever; however
路上		lùshang	*n*	road; way
相遇		xiāngyù	*v*	meet
只要		zhǐyào	*conj*	if only; as long as
互相		hùxiāng	*adv*	each other; mutually
通常		tōngcháng	*adv*	generally
熟人		shúrén	*n*	acquaintance
老远	老遠	lǎoyuǎn	*adv*	far away
双方	雙方	shuāngfāng	*n*	both sides
主动	主動	zhǔdòng	*adj*	on one's own initiative
过去	過去	guòqu	*v*	pass (by); go over; (used after a verb to indicate motion away from the speaker)
使用		shǐyòng	*v*	use; make use of
招手		zhāoshǒu	*vo*	beckon; wave one's hand
微笑		wēixiào	*v/n*	smile
举	舉	jǔ	*v*	raise; lift
晃		huàng	*v*	shake; sway
算是		suànshì	*v*	count as; be considered as
种	種	zhǒng	*n*	type; kind
称谓	稱謂	chēngwèi	*n*	form of address
式		shì	*n*	form; style
如		rú	*v*	such as; for example
马	馬	Mǎ	*pn*	(a surname)
大夫		dàifu	*n*	physician; doctor
祝愿	祝願	zhùyuàn	*n/v*	wish
恭喜		gōngxǐ	*v*	congratulate

恭喜发财	恭喜發財	gōngxǐ-fācái	*idiom*	May you be prosperous!
关心	關心	guānxīn	*v*	be concerned about
病		bìng	*n*	illness
儿子	兒子	érzi	*n*	son
强调	強調	qiángdiào	*v*	stress; emphasize
下级	下級	xiàjí	*n*	subordinate
上级	上級	shàngjí	*n*	higher level; higher authority
称呼	稱呼	chēnghu	*n*	form of address
头衔	頭銜	tóuxián	*n*	title
而		ér	*conj*	and; as well as
声	聲	shēng	*n/m*	sound; (used for sounds)
可以		kěyǐ	*v*	can; may; be able to
晚辈	晚輩	wǎnbèi	*n*	younger generation; one's junior
长辈	長輩	zhǎngbèi	*n*	elder generation; one's senior
答应	答應	dāying	*v*	answer; respond
敲门	敲門	qiāomén	*vo*	knock the door
情人节	情人節	Qíngrénjié	*n*	Valentine's Day
愉快		yúkuài	*adj*	happy; joyful

Grammar Notes
语法简注/語法簡注

1. 除了A以外，还B/除了A以外，還B：in addition to A, (also) B; apart from A, (also) B

学校除了为我们安排了一些商业实习以外，还为我们安排了中文课和中国文化课。

學校除了爲我們安排了一些商業實習以外，還爲我們安排了中文課和中國文化課。

In addition to some business internship activities for us, the school also arranged classes on Chinese language and culture.

▶ 明年除了去北京以外，我还要去台北。

明年除了去北京以外，我還要去臺北。

Apart from going to Beijing, I'm going to Taipei next year.

▶ 饮茶的时候，除了可以跟朋友聊天儿，还可以跟服务员聊天儿。

飲茶的時候，除了可以跟朋友聊天兒，還可以跟服務員聊天兒。

While eating dim sum at a restaurant, one can chat with waiters apart from chatting with one's friends.

2. 无论是……，还是……/無論是……，還是……：no matter… or…

无论是在路上，还是在公园里，两人相遇，只要互相不认识，通常谁也不用跟谁打招呼。

無論是在路上，還是在公園裏，兩人相遇，只要互相不認識，通常誰也不用跟誰打招呼。

No matter on the road or in the park, when two strangers meet, they don't need to greet each other generally.

▶ 无论是老师，还是学生，都喜欢现在的中文书。

無論是老師，還是學生，都喜歡現在的中文書。

No matter teachers or students, they like the current Chinese textbook.

▶ 在美国，无论是熟人还是生人，见面都会互相打招呼。

在美國，無論是熟人還是生人，見面都會互相打招呼。

In the US, no matter acquaintances or strangers, they would greet each other when they meet.

3. 有时候……，有时候……/有時候……，有時候……：sometimes … (and/yet) sometimes…

打招呼的时候，人们有时候使用语言，有时候不使用语言。

打招呼的時候，人們有時候使用語言，有時候不使用語言。

In greeting, people sometimes speak, yet sometimes they don't speak.

▶ 我有时候觉得中文很难，有时候觉得不太难。

我有時候覺得中文很難，有時候覺得不太難。

Sometimes I feel Chinese is very difficult, yet sometimes I feel it is not too difficult.

▶ 在家里，我有时候跟爸爸、妈妈说中文，有时候跟他们说英文，有时候一句话里既有中文又有英文。

在家裏，我有時候跟爸爸、媽媽説中文，有時候跟他們説英文，有時候一句話裏既有中文又有英文。

At home I sometimes speak Chinese with my mom and dad, and sometimes speak English with them. Sometimes I use both Chinese and English in one sentence.

4. ……式：... style

📖 关心式/關心式：concern-style；称谓式/稱謂式：address-style

▶ 她的这件衣服是中国式的。

她的這件衣服是中國式的。

This dress of hers is Chinese-style.

▶ 请你告诉我，怎么打招呼算是美国式的？

請你告訴我，怎麼打招呼算是美國式的？

Please tell me, what kind of greeting is considered to be American-style greeting?

5. 算是：count as; be considered as

📖 笑一笑，算是打招呼了。

Smiling counts as greeting.

▶ 举起手，晃一晃，算是打招呼了。

舉起手，晃一晃，算是打招呼了。

Raising and waving your hand counts as greeting.

▶ 今天我请我朋友吃了顿饭，算是给他过生日了。

今天我請我朋友吃了頓飯，算是給他過生日了。

Giving my friend a treat today counts as celebrating his birthday.

6. 只要……，就……：as long as...; provided that..., ...would...; if only...

📖 上级只要叫一声下级的名字就可以了。

上級只要叫一聲下級的名字就可以了。

Provided that the superior calls the subordinate's name, that would be fine.

▶ 我只要说中文，妈妈就高兴。

我只要説中文，媽媽就高興。

So long as I speak Chinese, Mom would be happy.

▶ 长辈只要答应一声，就算是向晚辈打招呼了。

長輩只要答應一聲，就算是向晚輩打招呼了。

So long as the person of the older generation replies, that would count as greeting the person of the younger generation.

7. 而：and yet; but

It is a conjunction that connects opposite elements.

📖 而上级只要叫一声下级的名字就可以了。

而上級只要叫一聲下級的名字就可以了。

And yet the superior only needs to call the subordinate's name once.

▶ 去中国而不坐普通列车，你还是不能明白“挤”是什么意思。

去中國而不坐普通列車，你還是不能明白“擠”是什麼意思。

In China, if you didn't take the local train, you still wouldn't understand what “being crowded” means.

▶ 上中文课而不天天记汉字，你还是学不好中文。

上中文課而不天天記漢字，你還是學不好中文。

If you take Chinese course yet don't memorize Chinese characters every day, you still won't be able to learn Chinese well.

中国人的名字是怎么来的

汉字“名”上面是个“夕”字，下面是个“口”字。“夕”指的是太阳下山的时候，也就是傍晚的时候，泛指晚上。“口”就是人们用来吃饭、说话的“嘴”。“夕”字下边放个“口”字，意思大概是晚上天黑看不见了，就用“嘴”说话、打招呼。

古代的时候，人们没有名字，见面点点头，或者做个手势，算是打招呼了。这样做在白天问题不大，可是到了傍晚或者晚上，谁也看不清谁，点头和做手势就都有问题了，人们必须开口才能打招呼，于是人们就慢慢地有了名字。

中國人的名字是怎麼來的

漢字“名”上面是個“夕”字，下面是個“口”字。“夕”指的是太陽下山的時候，也就是傍晚的時候，泛指晚上。“口”就是人們用來吃飯、説話的“嘴”。“夕”字下邊放個“口”字，意思大概是晚上天黑看不見了，就用“嘴”説話、打招呼。

古代的時候，人們没有名字，見面點點頭，或者做個手勢，算是打招呼了。這樣做在白天問題不大，可是到了傍晚或者晚上，誰也看不清誰，點頭和做手勢就都有問題了，人們必須開口纔能打招呼，於是人們就慢慢地有了名字。

太阳	太陽	tàiyáng	sun
傍晚		bàngwǎn	night fall; dusk
泛指		fànzhǐ	generally refer to; be used in a general sense
嘴		zǔi	mouth
手势	手勢	shǒushì	gesture

判断正误/判斷正誤

Identify the following statements as true or false based on the reading passage.

1. ______ “夕”是晚上的意思。
2. ______ 古时候，人们没有名字。
3. ______ 晚上的时候，因为谁也看不清谁，就不用打招呼了。
4. ______ 只有白天的时候，人们才打招呼。
5. ______ 因为人们要打招呼，所以人们有了名字。

1. ______ “夕”是晚上的意思。
2. ______ 古時候，人們没有名字。
3. ______ 晚上的時候，因爲誰也看不清誰，就不用打招呼了。
4. ______ 只有白天的時候，人們纔打招呼。
5. ______ 因爲人們要打招呼，所以人們有了名字。

Exercises 练习/練習

一、词语练习/詞語練習

Vocabulary exercise.

	Chinese Character	Pinyin	Make a Sentence of Your Own
1		huódòng	
2		bìng	
3		gàosu	
4		zhǔdòng	
5		shóu rén	
6		yīnggāi	
7		chēnghu	
8		guānxīn	

二、解释词语/解釋詞語

Define the following terms in your own words.

e.g. 恭喜发财：祝你有很多钱。

1. 熟人：
2. 生人：
3. 长辈：
4. 晚辈：

e.g. 恭喜發財：祝你有很多錢。

1. 熟人：
2. 生人：
3. 長輩：
4. 晚輩：

三、根据课文回答问题/根據課文回答問題

Answer the following questions using complete sentences based on information in the text.

1. 这次到中国，哥哥的学校为他们安排了什么活动？
2. 今天的文化课讲的什么？
3. 在中国，不认识的人之间打不打招呼？熟人之间呢？
4. 用语言打招呼有什么方式？
5. 不用语言的时候，人们怎么打招呼？
6. 在中国，上下级相遇，下级怎么跟上级打招呼？上级跟下级呢？
7. 晚辈和长辈相遇，晚辈怎么跟长辈打招呼？长辈跟晚辈呢？

1. 這次到中國，哥哥的學校爲他們安排了什麽活動？

2. 今天的文化課講的什麽？

3. 在中國，不認識的人之間打不打招呼？熟人之間呢？

4. 用語言打招呼有什麽方式？

5. 不用語言的時候，人們怎麽打招呼？

6. 在中國，上下級相遇，下級怎麽跟上級打招呼？上級跟下級呢？

7. 晚輩和長輩相遇，晚輩怎麽跟長輩打招呼？長輩跟晚輩呢？

四、填空

Fill in the blanks.

A. Fill in the blanks based on the text.

1. 在中国，不______ ______的人之间一般是______打招呼的。无论是在路______，还是在公园______，两人相______，只要互相不______ ______，谁也不______跟谁打招呼。
2. 但是，______人相见，是一定要______招呼的，就______两个人______得老远，双方也都会主______走______去打招呼。
3. 招手打招呼：打招呼的人举______手，______一______，算______打招呼了。
4. 点头打招呼：打招呼的人看着对方，______点头，______是打招呼了。
5. 微笑打招呼：打招呼的人看______对方，______一______，算______打招呼了。
6. 上下级相遇，______级一定会主动先______上级打招呼，而且还一定会______呼上级的头______。
7. 晚辈和长辈相遇，______辈应该主动______跟长辈打招呼，长辈只要答______一声，就可以了。

1. 在中國，不______ ______的人之間一般是______打招呼的。無論是在路______，還是在公園______，兩人相______，只要互相不______ ______，誰也不______跟誰打招呼。
2. 但是，______人相見，是一定要______招呼的，就______兩個人______得老遠，雙方也都會主______ 走______去打招呼。
3. 招手打招呼：打招呼的人舉______手，______ 一 ______，算______打招呼了。
4. 點頭打招呼：打招呼的人看着對方，______點頭，______是打招呼了。
5. 微笑打招呼：打招呼的人看______對方，______一______，算______打招呼了。
6. 上下級相遇，______級一定會主動先______上級打招呼，而且還一定會______呼上級的頭______。
7. 晚輩和長輩相遇，______輩應該主動______跟長輩打招呼，長輩只要答______一聲，就可以了。

B. Insert the words on the left to the sentences on the right, and translate them into English.

e.g. 来 对不认识的人，人们可以用微笑↓打招呼。

1. 以外 除了中国，老王没有去过别的国家。

Translation:

2. 只要 在中国，上级不用跟下级打招呼，笑一笑或点一点头就可以了。

Translation:

3. 就是 在美国，不认识的人相遇也会互相说一声"你好！"

Translation:

4. 无论 在中国，走到哪儿，都会看到很多人。

Translation:

5. 算是 路上有个人跟我打招呼，我笑了笑，跟他打招呼了。

Translation:

e.g. 來 對不認識的人，人們可以用微笑↓打招呼。

1. 以外 除了中國，老王没有去過别的國家。

Translation:

2. 只要 在中國，上級不用跟下級打招呼，笑一笑或點一點頭就可以了。

Translation:

3. 就是 在美國，不認識的人相遇也會互相說一聲"你好！"

Translation:

4. 無論 在中國，走到哪兒，都會看到很多人。

Translation:

5. 算是 路上有個人跟我打招呼，我笑了笑，跟他打招呼了。

Translation:

C. Choose the most appropriate greeting for each of the following situations.

a. 点点头 b. 笑一笑 c. 招招手

d. 说声"你好！" e. 说："好一点儿了？" f. 说："生病了？"

（小王是你的同学。）

1. 你在图书馆[túshūguǎn]看书，小王在你对面坐下，你会________。
2. 你刚买完东西，两手拿着大包小包，看到小王，你会________。
3. 你正在跟马老师聊天儿，看到小王走过来，你会________。
4. 你在路上走，看到小王跟她男朋友说着话走过来，你会________。
5. 小王昨天生病[bìng]没来上课，今天你看到她的时候，你会________。

a. 點點頭　　b. 笑一笑　　c. 招招手

d. 説聲“你好！”　　e. 説：“好一點兒了？”　　f. 説：“生病了？”

（小王是你的同學。）

1. 你在圖書館[túshūguǎn]看書，小王在你對面坐下，你會________。

2. 你剛買完東西，兩手拿着大包小包，看到小王，你會________。

3. 你正在跟馬老師聊天兒，看到小王走過來，你會________。

4. 你在路上走，看到小王跟她男朋友説着話走過來，你會________。

5. 小王昨天生病[bìng]没來上課，今天你看到她的時候，你會________。

五、改写／改寫

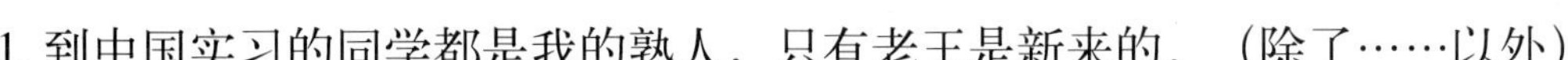

Rewrite the following sentences with the patterns in the parentheses.

1. 到中国实习的同学都是我的熟人，只有老王是新来的。（除了……以外）
2. 小王最喜欢吃不花钱的饭，哪儿有不花钱的聚会，哪儿就有她。（只要）
3. 小王说我爸爸是她的老板，我从来没见过她。（可是）
4. 老王跟谁都不打招呼，校长来了也不说一声“您好”。（就是）
5. 我们是平辈，所以我先跟你打招呼，或者你先跟我打招呼都可以。（谁……谁）

1. 到中國實習的同學都是我的熟人，只有老王是新來的。（除了……以外）
2. 小王最喜歡吃不花錢的飯，哪兒有不花錢的聚會，哪兒就有她。（只要）
3. 小王説我爸爸是她的老闆，我從來没見過她。（可是）
4. 老王跟誰都不打招呼，校長來了也不説一聲“您好”。（就是）
5. 我們是平輩，所以我先跟你打招呼，或者你先跟我打招呼都可以。（誰……誰）

六、重组／重組

Word order.

1. 以外／明年／还要／去西安／去上海／除了／我

   以外／明年／還要／去西安／去上海／除了／我

   In addition to going to Shanghai, I'm going to Xi'an next year.

2. 就／我／我的老师／写作业／只要／高兴／每天

   就／我／我的老師／寫作業／只要／高興／每天

   So long as I do my homework every day, my teacher would be happy.

3. 可是又不／毛笔字／写不好／天天练习／学写／你还是／你要／要是

   可是又不／毛筆字／寫不好／天天練習／學寫／你還是／你要／要是

   If you are learning to write characters with a brush, and yet you don't practice every day, you still won't be able to write the characters well.

4. 先向/打招呼/下级/一定要/上级/相遇/上下级
先向/打招呼/下級/一定要/上級/相遇/上下級
When a subordinate meets a superior, the person of lower rank must greet the person of upper rank first.

5. 还是/无论是/跟谁/在公园里/谁也/在路上/不用/生人相遇/打招呼
還是/無論是/跟誰/在公園裏/誰也/在路上/不用/生人相遇/打招呼
When two strangers meet, no matter on the road or in the park, neither of them needs to greet the other.

七、翻译/翻譯

Translate the following sentences into Chinese.

1. As long as I have time, I would like to go to visit China.
2. Dad said if Elder Brother could write letters to Grandpa in Chinese, Grandpa would be extremely happy.
3. In Beijing, when two acquaintances meet, even if they are far away from each other, both would walk over and greet each other.
4. In our school, no matter teachers or students, they all like the current textbook.
5. In the US, even if two strangers meet in the park, they would greet each other.
6. In China, when a teacher and a student meet, the student should take the initiative to greet the teacher first.
7. In addition to going to work every day, Dr. Ma also has to teach his son how to write Chinese characters on weekends.

八、改错/改錯

Correcte mistakes.

1. 学校为我们安排了商业实习活动以外，为我们安排了中国文化课。
2. 在中国，生人之间是不打招呼。
3. 熟人相遇，就是两个人离老远，双方会主动走过去打招呼。
4. 文化课的老师告诉我们：在中国，上、下级相遇，下级一定要先打招呼上级。
5. 我看见我朋友，我向他笑一笑，是打招呼。

1. 學校爲我們安排了商業實習活動以外，爲我們安排了中國文化課。

2. 在中國，生人之間是不打招呼。

3. 熟人相遇，就是兩個人離老遠，雙方會主動走過去打招呼。

4. 文化課的老師告訴我們：在中國，上、下級相遇，下級一定要先打招呼上級。

5. 我看見我朋友，我向他笑一笑，是打招呼。

九、课堂活动/課堂活動

In-class activity.

Distinguish different ways of greeting for each picture.

A: 小王，好久不见。/小王，好久不見。 A: ______ A: ______

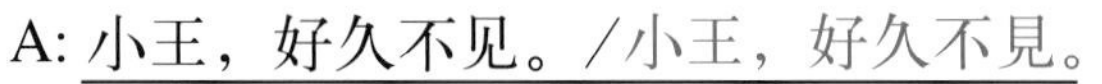

B: 老张，你好吗？/老張，你好嗎？ B: ______ B: ______

A: ______ A: ______

B: ______ B: ______

十、课外活动/課外活動

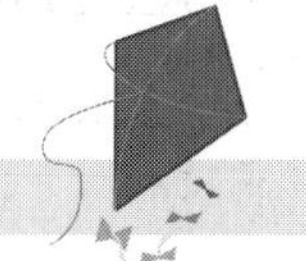

After-class activity.

A. Go online to find information about Chinese Valentine's Day and answer the quesitons below.

http://www.chinesefortunecalendar.com/77.htm

1. 中国的情人节是几月几日？
2. 相爱的人们在那一天常去哪儿？做什么？
3. 故事里有谁？他们一年能见几次？为什么？

1. 中國的情人節是幾月幾日？
2. 相愛的人們在那一天常去哪兒？做什麼？
3. 故事裏有誰？他們一年能見幾次？爲什麼？

B. 歇后语/歇後語, *Xiehouyu*, an allegorical saying, is made up of two parts, with the former part as a riddle and the latter part as the answer to the riddle. Usually people only say the former part with the implied meaning, omitting the latter part. For instance, "When he sees other people, Little Wang is like 'a rabbit seeing people—with red eyes'". In Chinese, "兔子看人——眼红/兔子看人——眼紅" means "someone is green with envy".

Use the following websites to fill in the table below.

http://www.epig.idv.tw/x1.htm

http://home.kimo.com.tw/skyknowbood/o2.html

	1st half of the sentence	2nd half of the sentence	Implied meaning
1	王小二过年/王小二過年		
2	老王卖瓜/老王賣瓜	自卖自夸/自賣自誇	
3	肉包子打狗		
4	狗熊掰棒子		

十一、写作练习/寫作練習

Writing.

Task: Write an email to a friend talking about a new crush you have. The email should contain at least 200 characters and include the following information.

1. Tell your friend about your new crush.
2. What do you like about this person.
3. Describe your affection for this person.
4. Ask your friend for advice about your new crush.

For example:

聪聪：

你怎么样？

还记得上次晚会上我认识的那个高个儿、长头发、大眼睛的女孩子吗？她叫什么来着？晚会上我紧张得连她的名字都没问。不知道怎么了，就从那次晚会以后，我老是想到她，她的眼睛、她的笑容[xiàoróng]、她的……有时候，连上课的时候都想到她。昨天，我去上课的时候在路上碰[pèng]到了她，可是我脑子一下子就空[kōng]了，什么都说不出来了，只是看着人家傻[shǎ]笑……

聪聪，我该怎么办？你知道我从来没交过女朋友，帮帮我吧，谢了。

盼回音！

友：笨笨

二月二十号

聽聽：

你怎麽樣？

還記得上次晚會上我認識的那個高個兒、長頭髮、大眼睛的女孩子嗎？她叫什麽來着？晚會上我緊張得連她的名字都没問。不知道怎麽了，就從那次晚會以後，我老是想到她，她的眼睛、她的笑容[xiàoróng]、她的……有時候，連上課的時候都想到她。昨天，我去上課的時候在路上碰[pèng]到了她，可是我腦子一下子就空[kōng]了，什麽都説不出來了，只是看着人家傻[shǎ]笑……

聽聽，我該怎麽辦？你知道我從來没交過女朋友，幫幫我吧，謝了。

盼回音！

友：笨笨

二月二十號

十二、总结/總結

Summary.

1. Choose 5-10 of your favorite new vocabulary words from the text or reading material.

2. Quote 3-7 of your favorite sentences from the text or reading material here.

	Original sentence	Translation of the sentence (or make a new sentence of your own)
1		
2		
3		
4		
5		

3. From this lesson, you have learned Chinese culture, history, and philosophy. They have helped you to understand,

① 我现在清楚了为什么中国人/我現在清楚了爲什麽中國人：________________

② 我现在明白了/我現在明白了：________________

③ 我现在知道了/我現在知道了：________________

LESSON 14

第十四课
中国人的称谓

小妹：

你好！

这个星期的文化课，我们学的是“中国人的称谓”。

文化课的老师说，中国人传统的想法是：“名不正，则言不顺。”这就是说，人们无论做什么事，如问路、买东西或者跟别人说话，都要先得体地称呼对方。所以，知道怎么得体地称呼他人是非常重要的。

文化课的老师告诉我们，平辈人之间，像同学、同事、朋友等，一般互相称呼姓名，甚至小名，比如：宋宜凡、凡凡；或者在姓前边加上“老”或“小”，像老宋、小宋等。

长辈称呼晚辈、年长的称呼年轻的，长辈、年长的只要叫晚辈、年轻的名字就可以了。但是，晚辈对长辈，年轻的对年长的，可千万不能叫对方的名字，否则会被认为没有礼貌、没有教养。

文化课的老师还说，在中国，对上级或者有地位的人，不管这些人年长还是年轻，人们都一定会称呼这些人的姓再加上他们的头衔，比如：刘总、白经理、江老板、简律师、史大夫、王教授等。

另外，在社交中，人们还常常用称呼亲属的方式称呼不是亲属的人，比如：把父母的同事或朋友叫做“叔叔”、“阿姨”；把比父母长一辈的人叫做“爷爷”、“奶奶”。甚至对第一次遇到的生人，人们也会叫他们“老爷爷”、“老奶奶”、“叔叔”、“阿姨”、“大哥”、“大姐”等。

小妹，明天早上六点我们要去爬长城，今天我得早点儿休息。过两天再给你写信。

祝好！

哥哥

二月二十号

第十四課
中國人的稱謂

小妹：

你好！

這個星期的文化課，我們學的是“中國人的稱謂”。

文化課的老師說，中國人傳統的想法是：“名不正，則言不順。”這就是說，人們無論做什麼事，如問路、買東西或者跟別人說話，都要先得體地稱呼對方。所以，知道怎麼得體地稱呼他人是非常重要的。

文化課的老師告訴我們，平輩人之間，像同學、同事、朋友等，一般互相稱呼姓名，甚至小名，比如：宋宜凡、凡凡；或者在姓前邊加上“老”或“小”，像老宋、小宋等。

長輩稱呼晚輩、年長的稱呼年輕的，長輩、年長的只要叫晚輩、年輕的名字就可以了。但是，晚輩對長輩，年輕的對年長的，可千萬不能叫對方的名字，否則會被認爲沒有禮貌、沒有教養。

文化課的老師還說，在中國，對上級或者有地位的人，不管這些人年長還是年輕，人們都一定會稱呼這些人的姓再加上他們的頭銜，比如：劉總、白經理、江老闆、簡律師、史大夫、王教授等。

另外，在社交中，人們還常常用稱呼親屬的方式稱呼不是親屬的人，比如：把父母的同事或朋友叫做“叔叔”、“阿姨”；把比父母長一輩的人叫做“爺爺”、“奶奶”。甚至對第一次遇到的生人，人們也會叫他們“老爺爺”、“老奶奶”、“叔叔”、“阿姨”、“大哥”、“大姐”等。

小妹，明天早上六點我們要去爬長城，今天我得早點兒休息。過兩天再給你寫信。

祝好！

哥哥

二月二十號

New Words
生词表/生詞表

Simplified	Traditional	Pinyin	Part of speech	English
传统	傳統	chuántǒng	*n*	tradition
想法		xiǎngfǎ	*n*	idea; opinion
名不正，则言不顺	名不正，則言不順	míng bù zhèng, zé yán bù shùn	*idiom*	If names be not correct, language is not in accordance with the truth of things.
问路	問路	wènlù	*vo*	ask the way
别人		biérén	*pron*	other people; others
得体	得體	détǐ	*adj*	appropriate
他人		tārén	*pron*	other people
平辈	平輩	píngbèi	*n*	persons of the same generation
同事		tóngshì	*n*	colleague; fellow worker
姓名		xìngmíng	*n*	name
小名		xiǎomíng	*n*	pet name for child
前边	前邊	qiánbian	*n*	front
加		jiā	*v*	add
年长	年長	niánzhǎng	*adj*	senior; older in age
年轻	年輕	niánqīng	*adj*	young
千万	千萬	qiānwàn	*adv/nu*	be sure to; must; ten million
否则	否則	fǒuzé	*conj*	otherwise
认为	認爲	rènwéi	*v*	think; consider
礼貌	禮貌	lǐmào	*n*	politeness; manners
教养	教養	jiàoyǎng	*n*	education; upbringing
姐姐		jiějie	*n*	elder sister
弟弟		dìdi	*n*	younger brother
妹妹		mèimei	*n*	younger sister
地位		dìwèi	*n*	status; position
不管		bùguǎn	*conj*	no matter (what, who, when, where, how)
刘	劉	Liú	*pn*	(a surname)
总	總	zǒng	*n*	chief; president (of a company)
白		Bái	*pn/n*	(a surname); white
江		Jiāng	*pn*	(a surname)
老板	老闆	lǎobǎn	*n*	boss
简	簡	Jiǎn	*pn*	(a surname)
律师	律師	lǜshī	*n*	lawyer
史		Shǐ	*pn*	(a surname)
教授		jiàoshòu	*n*	professor

社交		shèjiāo	*n*	social exchanges
亲属	親屬	qīnshǔ	*n*	relatives
叔叔		shūshu	*n*	uncle; father's younger brother; (used as a form of address for a man of one's father's generation but younger than one's father)
阿姨		āyí	*n*	aunt; mother's sister; (a form of address for a woman of one's mother's generation)
辈	輩	bèi	*n*	generation in the family
生人		shēngrén	*n*	stranger
老爷爷	老爺爺	lǎoyéye	*n*	grandpa; great grandfather; (used by children in addressing an old man)
老奶奶		lǎonǎinai	*n*	granny; great grandmother; (used by children in addressing an old woman)
大哥		dà gē		eldest brother
大姐		dà jiě		eldest sister
明天		míngtiān	*n*	tomorrow
爬		pá	*v*	climb
长城	長城	Chángchéng	*pn*	Great Wall
休息		xiūxi	*v*	rest

原则

V. 得 得体

无论 QW+都/也 + V.P.

Grammar Notes
语法简注/語法簡注

1. 无论+question words，都/也……
   無論+question words，都/也…… — no matter who/what/where…

人们无论做什么事，都一定得先得体地称呼对方。
人們無論做什麼事，都一定得先得體地稱呼對方。
No matter what people do, they must first address the other party appropriately.

▶ 在北京、上海， 无论哪儿都是人。
在北京、上海， 無論哪兒都是人。
In Beijing and Shanghai it is full of people no matter where it is.

▶ 春节的时候，普通列车上挤满了人，无论坐着还是站着都不舒服。
春節的時候，普通列車上擠滿了人，無論坐着還是站着都不舒服。
During the Spring Festival, the local trains are crowded with people. No matter whether you are sitting or standing, you wouldn't feel comfortable.

2. 甚至：even

甚至对第一次遇见的生人，人们也会叫他们“老爷爷”、“老奶奶”。
甚至對第一次遇見的生人，人們也會叫他們“老爺爺”、“老奶奶”。
Even for a stranger whom one has met for the first time, one would address the other party with terms such as “elder grandpa”or “elder grandma” .

▶ 在中国，同事之间一般互相称呼姓名，甚至小名。
在中國，同事之間一般互相稱呼姓名，甚至小名。
In China, among colleagues, they generally address one another by full name, or even by childhood name.

▶ 我爸爸天天守着电脑，甚至星期天也守着。
我爸爸天天守着電腦，甚至星期天也守着。
My dad hangs around the computer every day, even on Sundays.

3. A对B/A對B：A to B; A towards B

晚辈对长辈，可千万不能叫对方的名字。
晚輩對長輩，可千萬不能叫對方的名字。
The younger generation absolutely must not address the older generation by name.

▶ 在中国，下级对上级一定要称呼他们的姓，再加上他们的头衔。

在中國，下級對上級一定要稱呼他們的姓，再加上他們的頭銜。

In China, the subordinates must address the higher-ups by their surname along with their title.

▶ 妈妈常对我说："对老师一定要有礼貌。"

媽媽常對我說："對老師一定要有禮貌。"

Mom often tells me, "You must be polite to your teachers."

4. 千万/千萬：be sure to; must

① 千万+ affirmative sentence/千萬+affirmative sentence: must be sure to

▶ 到了广州，千万给我打个电话。

到了廣州，千萬給我打個電話。

When you arrive in Guangzhou, be sure to give me a call.

▶ 哥哥对我说，到了北京，千万要到长城去看看。

哥哥對我說，到了北京，千萬要到長城去看看。

Elder Brother told me that I should by all means go to the Great Wall when I am in Beijing.

② 千万+不能/千萬+不能：absolutely must not; must never; by no means

📖 晚辈称呼长辈，下级称呼上级，年轻的称呼年长的，千万不能叫对方的名字。

晚輩稱呼長輩，下級稱呼上級，年輕的稱呼年長的，千萬不能叫對方的名字。

When the younger generation addresses the older generation, the subordinates address the higher-ups, or the younger persons address their elder, they absolutely must not address the other party by name.

▶ 去一个国家，入境的时候，千万不能带水果。

去一個國家，入境的時候，千萬不能帶水果。

When you go to another country, you must never take any fruit at the time of entry.

▶ 哥哥告诉我，春节的时候，千万不能坐普通列车。

哥哥告訴我，春節的時候，千萬不能坐普通列車。

Elder Brother told me that during the Spring Festival I absolutely must not take a local train.

③ 千万+别/千萬+别：must not; by no means

▶ 晚上，你千万别一个人出去。

晚上，你千萬别一個人出去。

You must not go out alone at night.

▶ 在中国，你千万别跟生人打招呼。

在中國，你千萬别跟生人打招呼。

In China, generally you must not greet strangers.

▶ 爸爸常对哥哥说：“你喝酒以后千万别开车。”
爸爸常對哥哥說：“你喝酒以後千萬別開車。”
Dad often says to Elder Brother, “You absolutely must not drive after drinking.”

④ 千万不能/千万别……，否则……
千萬不能/千萬別……，否則…… 〉absolutely must not…otherwise…

📖 晚辈称呼长辈，下级称呼上级，年轻的称呼年长的，千万不能叫对方的名字，否则会被认为没有礼貌、没有教养。
晚輩稱呼長輩，下級稱呼上級，年輕的稱呼年長的，千萬不能叫對方的名字，否則會被認爲没有禮貌、没有教養。
When the younger generation addresses the older generation, the subordinates address the higher-ups, or the younger persons address their elder, they absolutely must not address the other party by name. Otherwise, they would be considered to have had no proper education or upbringing.

▶ 上李老师的课，千万别睡觉，否则他会让你站起来唱歌。
上李老師的課，千萬別睡覺，否則他會讓你站起來唱歌。
When you attend Mr. Li’s class, you absolutely must not fall asleep. Otherwise he would make you stand up and sing.

5. 不管S1……，S1/S2一定……：no matter (whether) S1…, S1 / S2 would definitely…

📖 下级对上级，或者是对有地位的人，不管这些人年长还是年轻，人们一定会称呼他们的姓，再加上他们的头衔。
下級對上級，或者是對有地位的人，不管這些人年長還是年輕，人們一定會稱呼他們的姓，再加上他們的頭銜。
When addressing the higher-ups or people of high status and position, no matter whether they are old or young, people would definitely address them by their surname along with their title.

▶ 明年不管你去不去中国，我一定去。
明年不管你去不去中國，我一定去。
No matter whether you go to China or not next year, I’ll definitely go.

▶ 遇到你的上级，不管他跟你打不打招呼，你一定要跟他打招呼。
遇到你的上級，不管他跟你打不打招呼，你一定要跟他打招呼。
When meeting your boss, no matter whether he greets you or not, you must definitely greet him.

▶ 不管我明天高兴不高兴，我都得去上课。

不管我明天高興不高興，我都得去上課。

No matter whether I'm happy or not tomorrow, I have to attend my class.

6. 在……中：in…; in the midst of…

📖 在社交中，人们常常用称呼亲属的方式来称呼不是亲属的人。

在社交中，人們常常用稱呼親屬的方式來稱呼不是親屬的人。

In social activities, people often address non-relatives in the same manner as used for relatives.

▶ 在工作中，我学到了很多在学校里学不到的东西。

在工作中，我學到了很多在學校裏學不到的東西。

During work I learned many things which I couldn't have learned in school.

7. 把……叫做：refer to someone as…; call someone…

📖 把父母的同事或朋友叫做"叔叔"、"阿姨"。

Call your parents' colleagues or friends "uncle" and "aunt".

▶ 把比父母长一辈的人叫做"爷爷"、"奶奶"。

把比父母長一輩的人叫做"爺爺"、"奶奶"。

Call those who are one generation older than your parents "grandpa" and "grandma".

▶ 有些人习惯把自己的爸爸、妈妈叫做"老爸"、"老妈"。

有些人習慣把自己的爸爸、媽媽叫做"老爸"、"老媽"。

Some people are used to calling their own dads and moms "old pa" and "old ma".

Reading Passage 阅读/閱讀

师傅　先生　老师　同志　小姐

二三十年以前，中国人不分男女老少，统统互相称呼“同志”。现在，除了公共汽车上的售票员还把乘客称作“同志”以外，“师傅”、“先生”、“老师”、“小姐”等称呼已经取代了“同志”。

一般情况下，人们把“蓝领”模样的人，如出租汽车司机叫做“师傅”；把“白领”模样的人，如生意人、坐办公室的人称为“先生”。

“老师”本来是人们对在学校教书的人的称呼。现在，对那些年龄大一点儿又有些学问的人，人们统统尊称他们为“老师”，特别是在报社、电台和文艺界，“老师”的称呼更流行。

師傅　先生　老師　同志　小姐

二三十年以前，中國人不分男女老少，統統互相稱呼“同志”。現在，除了公共汽車上的售票員還把乘客稱作“同志”以外，“師傅”、“先生”、“老師”、“小姐”等稱呼已經取代了“同志”。

一般情況下，人們把“藍領”模樣的人，如出租汽車司機叫做“師傅”；把“白領”模樣的人，如生意人、坐辦公室的人稱爲“先生”。

“老師”本來是人們對在學校教書的人的稱呼。現在，對那些年齡大一點兒又有些學問的人，人們統統尊稱他們爲“老師”，特別是在報社、電臺和文藝界，“老師”的稱呼更流行。

师傅	師傅	shīfu	master (colloquial term of address for service workers); master worker
同志		tóngzhì	comrade
售票员	售票員	shòupiàoyuán	ticket seller
取代		qǔdài	replace
蓝领	藍領	lánlǐng	blue-collar worker
模样	模樣	múyàng	appearance
出租汽车	出租汽車	chūzū qìchē	taxi
司机	司機	sījī	driver
教书	教書	jiāoshū	teach

学问	學問	xuéwèn	learning; knowledge
统统	統統	tǒngtǒng	all; completely
尊称	尊稱	zūnchēng	address somebody respectfully
文艺界	文藝界	wényìjiè	literary and art circles
电台	電臺	diàntái	radio station

判断正误/判斷正誤

Identify the following statements as true or false based on the reading passage.

1. _______ 二三十年前，中国人都互相称同志。
2. _______ 现在因为有了不同的称呼，“同志”已经没人用了。
3. _______ 现在人们互相称先生。
4. _______ “老师”是人们对学校教书人的称呼。
5. _______ 公共汽车上人们互相称“师傅”。
6. _______ 只要是有学问的人都可以叫“老师”。

1. _______ 二三十年前，中國人都互相稱同志。
2. _______ 現在因爲有了不同的稱呼，“同志”已經没人用了。
3. _______ 現在人們互相稱先生。
4. _______ “老師”是人們對學校教書的人的稱呼。
5. _______ 公共汽車上人們互相稱“師傅”。
6. _______ 只要是有學問的人都可以叫“老師”。

Exercises
练习/練習

一、词语练习/詞語練習

Vocabulary exercise.

	Chinese Character	Pinyin	Make a Sentence of Your Own
1		qiānwàn	
2		hùxiāng	
3		chēnghu	
4		shèjiāo	
5		lǐmào	

	Chinese Character	Pinyin	Make a Sentence of Your Own
6		zǎodiǎnr	
7		zhíjiē	
8		xiūxi	

二、解释词语/解釋詞語

Define the following terms in your own words.

e.g. 同事：一起工作的人。

1. 同学：
2. 同屋 [wū]：
3. 得体：
4. 休息：

e.g. 同事：一起工作的人。

1. 同學：
2. 同屋 [wū]：
3. 得體：
4. 休息：

三、根据课文回答问题/根據課文回答問題

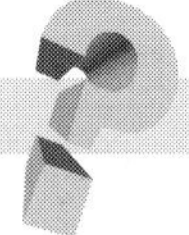

Answer the following questions using complete sentences based on information in the text.

1. 这个星期的文化课，哥哥学的什么？
2. 为什么知道怎么称呼他人非常重要？
3. 中国人平辈之间一般相互怎么称呼？
4. 哥哥、姐姐怎么叫弟弟、妹妹？弟弟、妹妹怎么叫哥哥、姐姐？
5. 长辈怎么称呼晚辈？
6. 晚辈怎么称呼长辈？
7. 上级怎么称呼下级？
8. 下级怎么称呼上级？
9. 中国人怎么用称呼亲属的方式来称呼不是亲属的人？

1. 這個星期的文化課，哥哥學的什麼？
2. 爲什麼知道怎麼稱呼他人非常重要？
3. 中國人平輩之間一般相互怎麼稱呼？
4. 哥哥、姐姐怎麼叫弟弟、妹妹？弟弟、妹妹怎麼叫哥哥、姐姐？
5. 長輩怎麼稱呼晚輩？
6. 晚輩怎麼稱呼長輩？
7. 上級怎麼稱呼下級？
8. 下級怎麼稱呼上級？
9. 中國人怎麼用稱呼親屬的方式來稱呼不是親屬的人？

四、填空

Fill in the blanks.

A. Fill in the blanks based on the text.

1. 中国人传统的想法是______ ______ ______，______ ______ ______ ______。
2. ______辈人之间，一般______ ______称呼姓名，甚______小名。
3. 长辈称呼______辈、上级称呼______级、年长的称呼年______的，只要______对方的名字______可以了。
4. 晚辈对______辈，下级对______级，年轻的对年______的，千______不能______对方的名字，否______会______认为没有礼______。
5. 在中国，有地______的人，不管这些人年长______ ______年轻，人们都会称呼他们的姓______加上他们的______衔。
6. 在______交中，人们常用称呼亲属的方式______称呼______是亲属的人。

1. 中國人傳統的想法是______ ______ ______，______ ______ ______ ______。
2. ______輩人之間，一般______ ______稱呼姓名，甚______小名。
3. 長輩稱呼______輩、上級稱呼______級、年長的稱呼年______的，只要______對方的名字______可以了。
4. 晚輩對______輩，下級對______級，年輕的對年______的，千______不能______對方的名字，否______會______認爲没有禮______。
5. 在中國，有地______的人，不管這些人年長______ ______年輕，人們都會稱呼他們的姓______加上他們的______銜。
6. 在______交中，人們常用稱呼親屬的方式______稱呼______是親屬的人。

B. Please fill in the blanks with proper titles based on the text.

1. 我在公司工作的时候，小王让我做什么我就得做什么，因为他是我们公司的_______。
2. 小王是我哥哥，我是小王的_______。
3. 小王是老张的学生，老张是小王的_______。
4. 王太太是我妈妈的朋友，我叫她王_______。
5. 我给江先生工作，他就是我的_______。
6. 我们都在刘先生的公司工作，我们叫他刘_______。
7. 我生病的时候常常去找王_______看病。

1. 我在公司工作的時候，小王讓我做什麼我就得做什麼，因爲他是我們公司的_______。
2. 小王是我哥哥，我是小王的_______。
3. 小王是老張的學生，老張是小王的_______。
4. 王太太是我媽媽的朋友，我叫她王_______。

5. 我給江先生工作，他就是我的______。

6. 我們都在劉先生的公司工作，我們叫他劉______。

7. 我生病的時候常常去找王______看病。

五、改写/改寫

Rewrite the following sentences with the patterns in the parentheses.

1. 中国人跟长辈和跟平辈的人说话的时候，说的话是不一样的。（对……不同的）
2. 平辈人之间不用特别的称呼。（只要……，就……）
3. 如果跟长辈说话不客气，别人会说你没礼貌。（否则）
4. 小王只是我的朋友，不是我的男朋友！（而）
5. 对有地位的人，就是他比你年轻，你也不能直接叫他的名字。（不管）

1. 中國人跟長輩和跟平輩的人說話的時候，說的話是不一樣的。（對……不同的）
2. 平輩人之間不用特別的稱呼。（只要……，就……）
3. 如果跟長輩說話不客氣，別人會說你沒禮貌。（否則）
4. 小王只是我的朋友，不是我的男朋友！（而）
5. 對有地位的人，就是他比你年輕，你也不能直接叫他的名字。（不管）

六、重组/重組

Word order.

1. 称呼生人/用/一定不会/的方式/美国人/称呼亲属
   稱呼生人/用/一定不會/的方式/美國人/稱呼親屬
   The Americans would definitely not address strangers in the same manner as used for relatives.
2. 会把/或者朋友/叔叔或阿姨/父母的同事/中国人/叫做
   會把/或者朋友/叔叔或阿姨/父母的同事/中國人/叫做
   The Chinese would call their parents' colleagues or friends "uncle" or "aunt".
3. 所以/要上班/休息/明天/今天得/早上五点/早点儿/我
   所以/要上班/休息/明天/今天得/早上五點/早點兒/我
   I have to go to work at 5 o'clock tomorrow morning, and therefore must sleep earlier today.
4. 怎么/还是在美国/称呼他人/在中国/都一定要/不管是/知道
   怎麼/還是在美國/稱呼他人/在中國/都一定要/不管是/知道
   No matter whether you are in China or in the US, you must definitely know how to address other people.

5. 你千万不能/他的头衔/在中国/叫他的名字/自己的上级/称呼/你遇到/而要/如果
你千萬不能/他的頭銜/在中國/叫他的名字/自己的上級/稱呼/你遇到/而要/如果
In China, if you meet your boss, you must never hail him by name. Rather, you should address him by his title.

七、翻译/翻譯

Translate the following sentences into Chinese.

1. Mom said to me, "You absolutely must not go out alone at night."
2. As one can find everything by searching online, nowadays no matter whether you are a student or a teacher, you would have a computer.
3. In social activities, Americans generally address the other party by name. Sometimes, they even address the higher-ups by name.
4. Because Manager Li is a person of status, no matter whether he is old or young, people would hail him by his surname along with his title.
5. In the US, the younger generation can hail the older generation by name. However, in China, the younger generation must never hail the older generation by name. Otherwise, they would be considered to have had no proper education.

八、改错/改錯

Correcte mistakes.

1. 平辈人，一般互相称呼姓名，甚至小名。
2. 长辈称呼晚辈，只要叫对方的名字可以了。
3. 千万不能叫自己的父母的名字，会认为没有教养。
4. 在社交中，人们常称呼亲属的方式来称呼不是亲属的人。
5. 晚辈叫父母的同事或朋友“叔叔”、“阿姨”、“伯伯”等。
6. 我们要去爬长城明天早上六点，今天我得休息早点儿。
7. 在中国，人们也叫生人“大哥、大姐”。

1. 平輩人，一般互相稱呼姓名，甚至小名。
2. 長輩稱呼晚輩，只要叫對方的名字可以了。
3. 千萬不能叫自己的父母的名字，會認爲没有教養。
4. 在社交中，人們常稱呼親屬的方式來稱呼不是親屬的人。
5. 晚輩叫父母的同事或朋友“叔叔”、“阿姨”、“伯伯”等。
6. 我們要去爬長城明天早上六點，今天我得休息早點兒。
7. 在中國，人們也叫生人“大哥、大姐”。

九、课堂活动/課堂活動

In-class activity.

Matching game: draw lines between the proper titles to the pictures below.

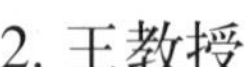

1. 小张/小張
2. 王教授
3. 李大哥
4. 刘经理/劉經理
5. 马律师/馬律師
6. 江大夫
7. 姐姐
8. 妈妈/媽媽

a

b

c

d

e

f
g
h

i

j

十、课外活动/課外活動

After-class activity.

"同志" is a very unique title used in China in the past twenty years. Today, this title has been replaced by "先生"、"小姐" in China's interior and has been adopted in China's Taiwan, Hong Kong and many other overseas places with a transformed meaning. Do a research on this title, its history, original meaning, and the transformed meaning. Present it in class.

十一、写作练习/寫作練習

Writing.

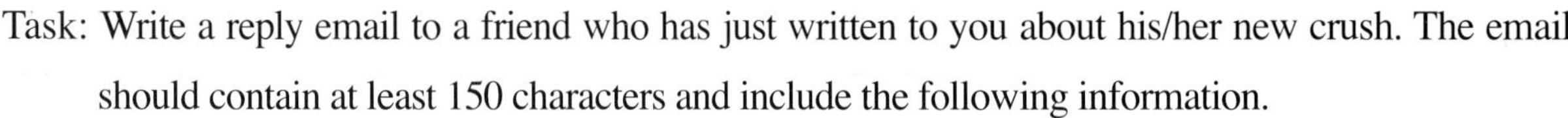

Task: Write a reply email to a friend who has just written to you about his/her new crush. The email should contain at least 150 characters and include the following information.

1. Tell your friend whether or not you know his/her new crush.
2. If you know the person, then say what you think of him/her. If you don't know the person, then respond to your friend's description of his/her new crush.
3. Suggest how your friend should court his/her new crush.

For example:

笨笨：

你好！

来信收到。看来你是喜欢上她了。那个女孩子真的很不错，又聪明[cōngming]又漂亮，学习又好，很多男[nán]生都追[zhuī]她。

这么着吧，期中[qīzhōng]考试[kǎoshì]以后，你搞[gǎo]个晚会，我出面[chūmiàn]请她和我一起帮你准备晚会。这样，你就有机会了解她是不是也喜欢你了。祝你好运[hǎoyùn]。

好了，定好了时间告诉我。

祝好！

友：聪聪

二月二十五号

笨笨：

你好！

來信收到。看來你是喜歡上她了。那個女孩子真的很不錯，又聰明[cōngming]又漂亮，學習又好，很多男[nán]生都追[zhuī]她。

這麼着吧，期中[qīzhōng]考試[kǎoshì]以後，你搞[gǎo]個晚會，我出面[chūmiàn]請她和我一起幫你准備晚會。這樣，你就有機會瞭解她是不是也喜歡你了。祝你好運[hǎoyùn]。

好了，定好了時間告訴我。

祝好！

友：聰聰

二月二十五號

十二、 总结/總結

Summary.

1. Choose 5-10 of your favorite new vocabulary words from the text or reading material.

2. Quote 3-7 of your favorite sentences from the text or reading material here.

	Original sentence	Translation of the sentence (or make a new sentence of your own)
1		
2		
3		
4		
5		

3. From this lesson, you have learned Chinese culture, history, and philosophy. They have helped you to understand,

① 我现在清楚了为什么中国人/我現在清楚了爲什麽中國人：________________

② 我现在明白了/我現在明白了：________________

③ 我现在知道了/我現在知道了：________________

LESSON 15

第十五课
中国人的谦虚

小妹：

你好！

这个星期的文化课，老师讲的是“中国人的谦虚”。

老师在课上讲到：中国人认为谦虚是一种美德，谦虚的人受人尊敬。相反，自高自大、自以为了不起，是不受欢迎的。所以，从古到今，中国人无论说话还是做事都表现得很谦虚。

比如说，有人夸一个人中文说得好，被夸的人常常会说“哪里，哪里，还差得远呢”，“您过奖了”。

还比如一个人夸另一个人长得漂亮，被夸的人常常会说“您真会说话”，“您真会开玩笑”等。

如果一个人赞美另一个人的衣服好看，被赞美的人会说“这是减价的时候买的”，“是朋友送的”或者“已经穿了好几年了”等。

中国人送礼的时候，送礼的人一般会说“这是一点儿小意思”，“东西不好，真不好意思拿出手”。接受礼物的人就会说：“真是的，人来了就好，还买什么礼物呀”等。

另外，中国人在讲话、作报告前后也都会说“我对这个问题研究得还很不够”，“我的报告中免不了有错误，请大家多多批评”等。其实，中国人这么说这么做，并不一定是他们真的觉得自己或自己的礼物不够好，而只是表示“谦虚”。就连大思想家孔子都谦虚地说：“三人行，必有我师。”

小妹，今晚有个朋友带我去“酒吧一条街”，先写到这儿吧。

祝好！

哥哥

二月二十五号

LESSON 15

第十五課
中國人的謙虛

小妹：

你好！

這個星期的文化課，老師講的是“中國人的謙虛”。

老師在課上講到：中國人認爲謙虛是一種美德，謙虛的人受人尊敬。相反，自高自大、自以爲了不起，是不受歡迎的。所以，從古到今，中國人無論說話還是做事都表現得很謙虛。

比如說，有人誇一個人中文說得好，被誇的人常常會說“哪裏，哪裏，還差得遠呢”，“您過獎了”。

還比如一個人誇另一個人長得漂亮，被誇的人常常會說“您真會說話”，“您真會開玩笑”等。

如果一個人贊美另一個人的衣服好看，被贊美的人會說“這是減價的時候買的”，“是朋友送的”或者“已經穿了好幾年了”等。

中國人送禮的時候，送禮的人一般會說“這是一點兒小意思”，“東西不好，真不好意思拿出手”。接受禮物的人就會說：“真是的，人來了就好，還買什么禮物呀”等。

另外，中國人在講話、作報告前後也都會說“我對這個問題研究得還很不夠”，“我的報告中免不了有錯誤，請大家多多批評”等。其實，中國人這么說這么做，并不一定是他們真的覺得自己或自己的禮物不夠好，而只是表示“謙虛”。就連大思想家孔子都謙虛地說：“三人行，必有我師。”

小妹，今晚有個朋友帶我去“酒吧一條街”，先寫到這兒吧。

祝好！

哥哥

二月二十五號

New Words
生词表/生詞表

谦虚	謙虛	qiānxū	*n*	modest
美德		měidé	*n*	virtue
受		shòu	*v*	receive
尊敬		zūnjìng	*v*	respect; honor
相反		xiāngfǎn	*adj/adv*	opposite; contrary; on the contrary
自高自大		zìgāo-zìdà	*idiom*	arrogant
以为	以爲	yǐwéi	*v*	consider; think
了不起		liǎobuqǐ	*idiom*	amazing; terrific; wonderful
欢迎	歡迎	huānyíng	*v*	welcome
从古到今	從古到今	cónggǔ-dàojīn	*idiom*	from ancient times to the present
表现	表現	biǎoxiàn	*v*	show; display; behave
比如		bǐrú	*v*	for example
夸	誇	kuā	*v*	praise; boast
哪里	哪裏	nǎli	*pron*	(a polite response to a compliment)
差		chà	*adj*	differ from
过奖	過獎	guòjiǎng	*v*	overpraise
漂亮		piàoliang	*adj*	beautiful
开玩笑	開玩笑	kāi wánxiào		joke; make a joke
赞美	贊美	zànměi	*v*	praise
衣服		yīfu	*n*	clothing; clothes
好看		hǎokàn	*adj*	good-looking
减价	減價	jiǎnjià	*vo*	reduce the price; mark down
送礼	送禮	sònglǐ	*vo*	give as a present
礼物	禮物	lǐwù	*n*	gift; present
小意思		xiǎoyìsi	*n*	small gift; keepsake
不好意思		bù hǎoyìsi	*idiom*	feel embarrassed; feel sorry
拿		ná	*v*	present; show; hold; take
出手		chūshǒu	*vo*	give out; dispose of
接受		jiēshòu	*v*	accept
真是的		zhēnshìde	*idiom*	(expressing gentle displeasure or annoyance)
另外		lìngwài	*conj*	in addition; besides
讲话	講話	jiǎnghuà	*vo*	speak; talk
报告	報告	bàogào	*n/v*	report
问题	問題	wèntí	*n*	question; problem

研究		yánjiū	*v/n*	research
够	夠	gòu	*v*	be enough; reach (a standard)
免不了		miǎnbuliǎo	*idiom*	be unavoidable; be bound to be
批评	批評	pīpíng	*v/n*	criticize; criticism
表示		biǎoshì	*v*	express; show
思想家		sīxiǎngjiā	*n*	thinker
孔子		Kǒngzǐ	*pn*	Confucius
三人行，必有我师	三人行，必有我師	sān rén xíng, bì yǒu wǒ shī	*idiom*	Where there are three people walking together, one of them must be qualified to be my teacher.
酒吧		jiǔbā	*n*	(wine) bar
街		jiē	*n*	street

Grammar Notes
语法简注/語法簡注

1. 受：receive; accept; suffer

📖 谦虚的人受人尊敬。

谦虛的人受人尊敬。

A modest person is respected by people.

▶ 六十年代，黑人在美国非常受歧视[qíshì]。

六十年代，黑人在美國非常受歧視[qíshì]。

During the 1960's, African-Americans were very much discriminated against in the US.

▶ 教师是一个受人尊敬的职业。

教師是一個受人尊敬的職業。

Teaching is a respectable profession.

2. 自以为/自以爲：consider oneself…

📖 自以为了不起，是不受欢迎的。

自以爲了不起，是不受歡迎的。

A person who is too proud of himself is unwelcome.

▶ 那个人自以为什么都懂， 其实他什么都不懂。

那個人自以爲什麼都懂， 其實他什麼都不懂。

That person considers himself knowledgeable about everything. Actually he knows nothing.

▶ 我妹妹自以为长得很漂亮。

我妹妹自以爲長得很漂亮。

My younger sister considers herself very pretty.

3. 从……到……/從……到……：from... to...

📖 从古到今，中国人无论说话还是做事都表现得很谦虚。

從古到今，中國人無論説話還是做事都表現得很謙虛。

From ancient times to today, the Chinese have shown modesty in words and deeds.

▶ 从上个周末到这个周末我们都在忙着搬家。

從上個周末到這個周末我們都在忙着搬家。

We've been busy moving from last weekend to this weekend.

▶ 从学校到我家，开车要开半个小时。

從學校到我家，開車要開半個小時。

It takes half an hour's drive from the school to my house.

4. 会/會：be good at

📖 您真会说话。

您真會説話。

You are truly good at speaking. (You have a glib tongue.)

▶ 您真会开玩笑。

您真會開玩笑。

You are truly good at joking.

▶ 那个美国人很会做中国菜。

那個美國人很會做中國菜。

That American is very good at making Chinese food.

5. 好+儿/好+幾：quite a few; several

📖 我的衣服已经穿了好儿年了。

我的衣服已經穿了好幾年了。

I've already been wearing the same clothes for quite a few years.

▶ 今天好儿个同学都没来上课。

今天好幾個同學都没來上課。

Quite a few classmates didn't come to class today.

▶ 这个故事我已经听了好儿遍了。

這個故事我已經聽了好幾遍了。

I've heard this story several times.

6. 真是的：why bother; really (used to express displeasure or annoyance)

📖 真是的，人来了就好，还买什么礼物呀？

真是的，人來了就好，還買什麽禮物呀？

It's good enough that you come. What need for buying the gift?

Note: Here the speaker pretends to be gently blaming the other party for bringing him/her a present.

▶ 真是的，你何必客气呢？

真是的，你何必客氣呢？

Why do you have to be so polite?

▶ 真是的，你怎么老是不听你爸爸的话？

真是的，你怎麽老是不聽你爸爸的話？

Really, why do you always disobey your dad? (It's too bad that he always disobeys his dad.)

7. 还买什么礼物呀？/還買什麼禮物呀？

This is a rhetorical question that implies blame or reproach, and often indicates the speaker feels that the other party should not have taken the action referred to in the question.

📖 还买什么礼物呀？

還買什麼禮物呀？

What need is there for buying the gift?

▶ 还吃什么饭呀？赶快走吧，我们已经晚了。

還吃什麼飯呀？趕快走吧，我們已經晚了。

What need is there for eating? Hurry up, we're already late.

▶ 还开什么车呀？走路只要十分钟就到了。

還開什麼車呀？走路只要十分鐘就到了。

What need is there for driving? It's only ten minutes' walk.

8. 免不了：unavoidable; be bound to be; can't avoid (mistakes, accidents, and other kinds of negative consequences)

📖 我的报告免不了有很多错误。

我的報告免不了有很多錯誤。

My report unavoidably would contain many mistakes.

▶ 他写字写得太快，所以免不了有错误。

他寫字寫得太快，所以免不了有錯誤。

He wrote too fast. So unavoidably there were some mistakes.

▶ 喝酒以后开车，免不了会出事。

喝酒以後開車，免不了會出事。

If you drive after drinking, you are bound to have an accident.

▶ 春节的时候坐火车，免不了挤。

春節的時候坐火車，免不了擠。

When traveling by train during the Spring Festival, you can't avoid crowds of people.

9. 多多 ＋V：多多 is an adverb meaning "many" or "a great deal".

📖 请大家多多批评。

請大家多多批評。

Your criticism is welcome.

▶ 请你们多多帮忙。

請你們多多幫忙。

Please offer me your kind help.

▶ 请多多关照。[guānzhào]

請多多關照。[guānzhào]

Please offer me your kind help.

10. 并：an adverb emphasizing the negative phrase or statement that follows

📖 中国人这么说这么做，并不一定真的觉得自己不够好，而只是为了表示谦虚。

中國人這麽説這麽做，并不一定真的覺得自己不夠好，而只是爲了表示謙虛。

In saying and doing these, the Chinese don't necessarily feel that they themselves aren't good enough. They are merely showing modesty.

▶ 她每天都在学校的餐厅吃饭。这并不是因为她有钱，而只是为了方便。

她每天都在學校的餐廳吃飯。這并不是因爲她有錢，而只是爲了方便。

She eats at her school's cafeteria every day. This is not because she is rich. It is merely for convenience.

▶ 我发现如果不是春节的时候，火车上并不挤。

我發現如果不是春節的時候，火車上并不擠。

I find that it is actually not crowded on the train except the Spring Festival.

▶ 如果有人夸王大夫英文说得好，她一定会说："您过奖了。"她这么说并不是因为她觉得自己英文说得不好，而只是为了表示谦虚。

如果有人誇王大夫英文説得好，她一定會説："您過獎了。"她這麽説并不是因爲她覺得自己英文説得不好，而只是爲了表示謙虛。

If someone praises Dr. Wang for her English, she would surely reply, "I am flattered." This is not because she feels that she is not good at English. In saying this, she is merely showing modesty.

Reading Passage
阅读/閱讀

中国人送礼的讲究

中国人跟全世界的人一样，常常要送礼。中国人送礼喜欢用红色的和彩色的纸包装，而不用白色的和黑色的。中国人觉得红色代表吉利，而白色和黑色代表不吉利。

中国人送礼绝对不送男人"绿色的帽子"，也不能送别人特别是老人"钟"。

中国人送礼时说的客气话，真正的意思是在赞扬接受礼物的人。而接受礼物的人说的话，也不表示接受礼物的人不喜欢所收的礼物或是不想接受礼物，而只是表示客气。

另外，中国人收了礼物后，一般不会当着送礼人的面，把礼物打开，而是等送礼人走后再打开。

中國人送禮的講究

中國人跟全世界的人一樣，常常要送禮。中國人送禮喜歡用紅色的和彩色的紙包裝，而不用白色的和黑色的。中國人覺得紅色代表吉利，而白色和黑色代表不吉利。

中國人送禮絕對不送男人“綠色的帽子”，也不能送别人特别是老人“鐘”。

中國人送禮時說的客氣話，真正的意思是在贊揚接受禮物的人。而接受禮物的人說的話，也不表示接受禮物的人不喜歡所收的禮物或是不想接受禮物，而只是表示客氣。

另外，中國人收了禮物後，一般不會當着送禮人的面，把禮物打開，而是等送禮人走後再打開。

送礼	送禮	sònglǐ	present a gift (to sb.)
讲究	講究	jiǎngjiu	be particular about; care especially about
红色	紅色	hóngsè	red
黑色		hēisè	black
吉利		jílì	auspicious
绿色	綠色	lǜsè	green
帽子		màozi	hat
钟	鐘	zhōng	clock
当……面	當……面	dāng...miàn	in (someone's) presence; in/to one's face

判断正误/判斷正誤

Identify the following statements as true or false based on the reading passage.

1. ________ 中国人很喜欢送礼。
2. ________ 中国人喜欢用红纸包礼物。
3. ________ 中国人不送男人“绿色的帽子”，是因为绿色不吉利。
4. ________ 中国人不送老人“钟”，是因为老人一般不用钟。
5. ________ 中国人当着送礼物人的面打开礼物。

1. ________ 中國人很喜歡送禮。

2. ________ 中國人喜歡用紅紙包禮物。

3. ________ 中國人不送男人“綠色的帽子”，是因爲綠色不吉利。

4. ________ 中國人不送老人“鐘”，是因爲老人一般不用鐘。

5. ________ 中國人當着送禮物人的面打開禮物。

Exercises
练习/練習

一、词语练习/詞語練習

Vocabulary exercise.

	Chinese Character	Pinyin	Make a Sentence of Your Own
1		qiānxū	
2		kuā	
3		miǎnbuliǎo	
4		hǎokàn	
5		kāi wánxiào	
6		zànměi	
7		bù hǎoyìsi	

二、解释词语/解釋詞語

Define the following terms in your own words.

e.g. 赞美：说别人的好话。

1. 自高自大：

2. 三人行，必有我师：

3. 会说话：

e.g. 贊美：説别人的好話。

1. 自高自大：

2. 三人行，必有我師：

3. 會説話：

三、根据课文回答问题/根據課文回答問題

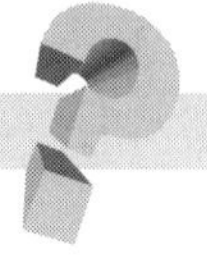

Answer the following questions using complete sentences based on information in the text.

1. 这个星期的文化课，老师讲的是什么？
2. 为什么中国人说话、做事处处都表现得很谦虚？
3. 如果有人夸一个人的中文说得好，被夸的人说什么？
4. 有人夸一个人长得漂亮，被夸的人说什么？
5. 如果有人赞美一个人的衣服好看，被赞美的人会说什么？
6. 中国人送礼的时候，送礼的人一般会说什么？接受礼物的人说什么？
7. 中国人在讲话、作报告以前或者以后会说什么？
8. 中国人无论说话还是做事一定要表现得怎么样？为什么？
9. 中国的大思想家孔子是怎么表示谦虚的？

1. 這個星期的文化課，老師講的是什麽？
2. 爲什麽中國人説話、做事處處都表現得很謙虚？
3. 如果有人誇一個人的中文説得好，被誇的人説什麽？
4. 有人誇一個人長得漂亮，被誇的人説什麽？
5. 如果有人贊美一個人的衣服好看，被贊美的人會説什麽？
6. 中國人送禮的時候，送禮的人一般會説什麽？接受禮物的人説什麽？
7. 中國人在講話、作報告以前或者以後會説什麽？
8. 中國人無論説話還是做事一定要表現得怎麽樣？爲什麽？
9. 中國的大思想家孔子是怎麽表示謙虚的？

四、填空

Fill in the blanks.

A. Fill in the blanks based on the text.

1. 中国人认为谦虚是一种美______，谦虚的人______人尊______。______高______大的人，是不______欢迎的。
2. 一个人______你长得漂亮，你可以说："您真______说话。"
3. 如果一个人赞______你的衣服好看，你可以说："这是减______的时候买的。"
4. 别人在送给你______ ______的时候，一______会说"东西不好，真不好意思______出手"。你应该说："______是的，人来了就好，还买什么______物呀？"

5. 中国人在讲话、作报告前后会说：“我的报告中______ ______ ______有很多错______，请大家______ ______批评。”

6. 其______，中国人这么______这么______，只是为了表示______ ______。

1. 中國人認爲謙虛是一種美______，謙虛的人______人尊______。______高______大的人，是不______歡迎的。

2. 一個人______你長得漂亮，你可以說：“您真______說話。”

3. 如果一個人贊______你的衣服好看，你可以說：“這是減______的時候買的。”

4. 別人在送給你______ ______的時候，一______會說“東西不好，真不好意思______出手”。你應該說：“______是的，人來了就好，還買什麼______物呀？”

5. 中國人在講話、作報告前後會說：“我的報告中______ ______ ______有很多錯______，請大家______ ______批評。”

6. 其______，中國人這麼______ 這麼______，只是爲了表示______ ______。

B. Insert the words on the left to the sentences on the right, and translate them into English.

e.g. 所以　　中国人很客气，↓说话、做事总是表现得很谦虚。

1. 连　　谦虚是中国人的美德，大思想家孔子都说自己要向别人学习。

Translation:

2. 其实　　中国人送礼时常说：“东西不好，真不好意思拿出手。”他的礼物并不一定真的不好，而是他在说客气话。

Translation:

3. 就　　以前，如果家里有人去世，有些中国人会一个月不吃肉[ròu]。

Translation:

4. 另外　　中国人说话有时候有别的意思。

Translation:

5. 免不了　　在美国出生的中国孩子，如果爸爸、妈妈在家不跟他们说中文，他们长大以后就不会说中文。

Translation:

e.g. 所以　　中國人很客氣，↓說話、做事總是表現得很謙虛。

1. 連　　謙虛是中國人的美德，大思想家孔子都說自己要向別人學習。

Translation:

2. 其實　　中國人送禮時常說：“東西不好，真不好意思拿出手。”他的禮物并不一定真的不好，而是他在說客氣話。

Translation:

3. 就　　以前，如果家裏有人去世，有些中國人會一個月不吃肉[ròu]。

Translation:

4. 另外　　中國人說話有時候有別的意思。

Translation:

5. 免不了　　在美國出生的中國孩子，如果爸爸、媽媽在家不跟他們說中文，他們長大以後就不會說中文。

Translation:

五、改写/改寫

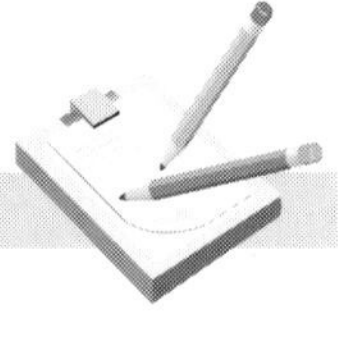

Rewrite the following sentences with the patterns in the parentheses.

1. 十五六岁的孩子常常喜欢做父母不让他们做的事。（相反……）
2. 小王是个很客气的人，她一天要说十几次“对不起”。（比如）
3. 中国人喜欢吃，不管天上飞的还是地上走的，他们都吃。（总之）
4. 在中国，当你听到别人说他自己不好的时候，他并不是觉得自己不好。（其实）
5. 在美国，小孩子事情没做好，父母不会批评他们，会说他已经不错了。（而）

1. 十五六歲的孩子常常喜歡做父母不讓他們做的事。（相反……）
2. 小王是個很客氣的人，她一天要說十幾次“對不起”。（比如）
3. 中國人喜歡吃，不管天上飛的還是地上走的，他們都吃。（總之）
4. 在中國，當你聽到別人說他自己不好的時候，他并不是覺得自己不好。（其實）
5. 在美國，小孩子事情没做好，父母不會批評他們，會說他已經不錯了。（而）

六、重组/重組

Word order.

1. 那就/在中国/坐普通列车/会挤/春节的时候/免不了/要是

   那就/在中國/坐普通列車/會擠/春節的時候/免不了/要是

   In China, if you take local trains during the Spring Festival, you can't avoid the crowd of people.

2. 到/上个星期/写报告/这个星期/江教授/从/一直忙着

   到/上個星期/寫報告/這個星期/江教授/從/一直忙着

   Professor Jiang has been busy writing a paper from last week to this week.

3. 相反/不受欢迎的/谦虚的人/自高自大的人/受人尊敬/是/在中国

   相反/不受歡迎的/謙虛的人/自高自大的人/受人尊敬/是/在中國

   A modest person is respected by people in China. In contrast, an arrogant person is unwelcome.

4. 几句/都会说上/在作报告/谦虚的话/中国人/以前或者以后

幾句/都會説上/在作報告/謙虚的話/中國人/以前或者以後

Either before or after making a report, the Chinese would say several sentences expressing modesty.

5. 都/所以/谦虚是/表现得很谦虚/认为/还是做事/因为中国人/无论说话/一种美德/他们

都/所以/謙虚是/表現得很謙虚/認爲/還是做事/因爲中國人/無論説話/一種美德/他們

Because the Chinese regard modesty as a virtue, the Chinese show modesty in words and deeds.

七、翻译/翻譯

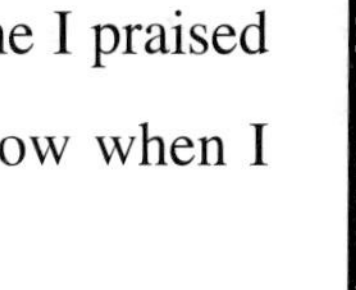

Translate the following sentences into Chinese.

1. That female student considers herself ugly. Actually everybody thinks she is very pretty.
2. I went to Uncle Shi's house for dinner on his birthday. As soon as he saw me present a gift to him, he said, "Why the bother? It's good enough that you come. What need is there for giving me a gift?"
3. The Chinese regard modesty as a virtue. The Americans regard self-confidence as a virtue. Then is it that a modest person is necessarily not self-confident, while a self-confident person is necessarily not modest?
4. You have just studied Chinese for a year. Therefore, if you write Chinese characters too fast, you can't avoid making mistakes in writing.
5. I have a good friend who was from Xi'an. When she first came to the US, each time I praised her clothes, she would say, "These were purchased by my mother for me." But now when I praise her clothes again, she says, "Thanks. Your clothes are good-looking as well."

八、改错/改錯

Correct mistakes.

1. 老师在课上讲：中国人以为谦虚是一种美德。
2. 从古到今，中国人说话、做事表现很谦虚处处。
3. 还比如一个人夸另一个人长漂亮，被夸人一定会说："您别开我玩笑了。"
4. 中国人送礼的时候，也常常会说许多客气话谦虚。
5. 我的报告免不了有很多错误，请大家批评多多。
6. 中国人这么说这么做，并不一定是他们真的觉得自己不够好或者不如别人，而只是谦虚。

1. 老師在課上講：中國人以爲謙虚是一種美德。
2. 從古到今，中國人説話、做事表現很謙虚處處。

3. 還比如一個人誇另一個人長漂亮，被誇人一定會說："您別開我玩笑了。"
4. 中國人送禮的時候，也常常會說許多客氣話謙虛。
5. 我的報告免不了有很多錯誤，請大家批評多多。
6. 中國人這麼說這麼做，并不一定是他們真的覺得自己不夠好或者不如別人，而只是謙虛。

九、课堂活动/課堂活動

In-class activity.

Role playing: fill in the following table based on the principles mentioned in the text. Pay attention to the relationships between A and Yifan and how they address each other.

	Relationship	A	宜凡
1	同学跟宜凡 同學跟宜凡	小凡，你的中文说得真好！ 小凡，你的中文說得真好！	
2	哥哥跟宜凡		哥，你快别拿我开玩笑了！我的中文哪能跟你比？ 哥，你快別拿我開玩笑了！我的中文哪能跟你比？
3	爷爷跟宜凡 爺爺跟宜凡	凡凡啊，你的毛笔字现在比以前写得好多了。 凡凡啊，你的毛筆字現在比以前寫得好多了。	
4	王老师跟宜凡 王老師跟宜凡		王老师，您可别这么说。我中文学得好，都是您教得好。 王老師，您可別這麼說。我中文學得好，都是您教得好。
5	宜凡作报告 宜凡作報告	欢迎宋宜凡小姐给我们讲话。 歡迎宋宜凡小姐給我們講話。	
6	陌生人跟宜凡	小姐，你真漂亮。	
7	王太太（妈妈的朋友）跟宜凡 王太太（媽媽的朋友）跟宜凡	小凡啊，才两年不见，又长漂亮了。 小凡啊，纔兩年不見，又長漂亮了。	

十、课外活动/課外活動

After-class activity.

Same as people across the world, Chinese people like sending gifts to others. However, Chinese people are very dainty about what to send and whom to send. One must take care not to make mistakes in sending gifts.

Fill in the following table based on your knowledge and research did online.

	Present	Yes/No	Reason
1	伞/傘		
2	钟/鐘		
3	刀子		
4	鞋		
5	书（打牌时）/書（打牌時）		
6	绿帽子/綠帽子		
7	梨		
8			
9			

十一、写作练习/寫作練習

Writing.

Task: Write a comic exchange based on the example below.

Comic Dialogue: The Chinese are no longer modest!

For example:

中：皮特，这趟去中国，有什么感想[gǎnxiǎng]?

外：中国变化真大！

中：举个例子。

外：中国人很谦虚，是不是？

中：是呀，我们中国人一向很谦虚。

外：可是，这趟我到中国一看，中国人不谦虚了。

中：不可能！

外：真的，我到处[dàochù]都看到“中国很行[xíng]”、“中国人民很行”和“北京很行”。

中：不会吧！？

外：你连我都不信[xìn]了，不信你看看，我把那些字都抄下来了。

中：嗨，那是“中国银行[háng]”、“中国人民银行”和“北京银行”。

外：啊？

中：皮特，這趟去中國，有什麼感想[gǎnxiǎng]？

外：中國變化真大！

中：舉個例子。

外：中國人很謙虛，是不是？

中：是呀，我們中國人一向很謙虛。

外：可是，這趟我到中國一看，中國人不謙虛了。

中：不可能！

外：真的，我到處[dàochù]都看到"中國很行[xíng]、""中國人民很行"和"北京很行"。

中：不會吧！？

外：你連我都不信[xìn]了，不信你看看，我把那些字都抄下來了。

中：嗨，那是"中國銀行[háng]"、"中國人民銀行"和"北京銀行"。

外：啊？

十二、总结/總結

Summary

1. Choose 5-10 of your favorite new vocabulary words from the text or reading material.

2. Quote 3-7 of your favorite sentences from the text or reading material here.

	Original sentence	**Translation of the sentence** (or make a new sentence of your own)
1		
2		
3		
4		
5		

3. From this lesson, you have learned Chinese culture, history, and philosophy. They have helped you to understand,

① 我现在清楚了为什么中国人/我現在清楚了爲什麼中國人：______________________

② 我现在明白了/我現在明白了：____

③ 我现在知道了/我現在知道了：____

LESSON 16

第十六课
中国在变化中

小妹：

你好！

时间过得真快，再过两三天，我们的实习就要结束了。这大概也是我从中国发给你的最后一封电子邮件了。四五个星期的时间，我对中国总的印象是：中国在变化中。

中国不但城市、农村在变，而且中国人也在变。不但中国人的生活方式在变，而且中国人的心理、观念也在变。二十多年来，中国在政治、经济、文化、社会等各个方面的变化，不但让外国人跌破眼镜，就连中国人自己也惊叹不已。下面是我在"谷歌"和"雅虎"上看到的一些报道：

* 2001年12月11日，中国成为世界贸易组织成员。

* 2004年奥运会，中国获得32枚金牌，成为世界上获金牌第二多的国家。

* 过"洋节"的中国人越来越多。2004年调查发现：北京、上海、重庆、哈尔滨等城市，在1800名被调查的年轻人中，过圣诞节的占68.5%，过情人节的占61.8%，过母亲节的占59.4%，过父亲节的占52.7%。

* 中国的家庭已经从"三代同堂"的大家庭变成"小三口"的小家庭。

* 中国各种消费都超过了美国，正在变成经济大国。

* 全球500强跨国公司九成登陆中国。

* 迪士尼乐园将登陆上海。

……

小妹，想告诉你的太多了。回美国以后，我一交了实习报告就回家去看你和爸爸、妈妈。那时候，我再好好地给你们讲我在中国的所见所闻。

祝好！

哥哥

三月十号

LESSON 16

第十六課
中國在變化中

小妹：

你好！

時間過得真快，再過兩三天，我們的實習就要結束了。這大概也是我從中國發給你的最後一封電子郵件了。四五個星期的時間，我對中國總的印象是：中國在變化中。

中國不但城市、農村在變，而且中國人也在變。不但中國人的生活方式在變，而且中國人的心理、觀念也在變。二十多年來，中國在政治、經濟、文化、社會等各個方面的變化，不但讓外國人跌破眼鏡，就連中國人自己也驚嘆不已。下面是我在“谷歌”和“雅虎”上看到的一些報道：

＊ 2001年12月11日，中國成爲世界貿易組織成員。

＊ 2004年奥運會，中國獲得32枚金牌，成爲世界上獲金牌第二多的國家。

＊ 過“洋節”的中國人越來越多。2004年調查發現：北京、上海、重慶、哈爾濱等城市，在1800名被調查的年輕人中，過聖誕節的占68.5%，過情人節的占61.8%，過母親節的占59.4%，過父親節的占52.7%。

＊ 中國的家庭已經從“三代同堂”的大家庭變成“小三口”的小家庭。

＊ 中國各種消費都超過了美國，正在變成經濟大國。

＊ 全球500强跨國公司九成登陸中國。

＊ 迪士尼樂園將登陸上海。

……

小妹，想告訴你的太多了。回美國以後，我一交了實習報告就回家去看你和爸爸、媽媽。那時候，我再好好地給你們講我在中國的所見所聞。

祝好！

哥哥

三月十號

New Words
生词表/生詞表

变化	變化	biànhuà	*v*	change
大概		dàgài	*adv*	probably
封		fēng	*m*	(for sth enveloped)
农村	農村	nóngcūn	*n*	rural area; the countryside
心理		xīnlǐ	*n*	mentality; psychology
观念	觀念	guānniàn	*n*	concept; idea
政治		zhèngzhì	*n*	politics
经济	經濟	jīngjì	*n*	economy
社会	社會	shèhuì	*n*	society
各个	各個	gègè	*pron*	each; every; all
方面		fāngmiàn	*n*	aspect
外国	外國	wàiguó	*n*	foreign country
跌破眼镜	跌破眼鏡	diēpò-yǎnjìng	*idiom*	come as a surprise
惊叹不已	驚嘆不已	jīngtàn bùyǐ	*idom*	wonder at sth greatly
下面		xiàmian	*n*	next
谷歌		Gǔgē	*pn*	Google
雅虎		Yǎhǔ	*pn*	Yahoo
报道	報道	bàodào	*n/v*	news report; report (on)
成为	成爲	chéngwéi	*v*	become; turn into
世界贸易组织	世界貿易組織	Shìjiè Màoyì Zǔzhī	*pn*	World Trade Organization
成员	成員	chéngyuán	*n*	member
奥运会	奥運會	Àoyùnhuì	*n*	Olympic Games (abbreviation for Àolínpǐkè Yùndònghuì)
获	獲	huò	*v*	obtain; win
枚		méi	*m*	(used in connection with coins, stamps, bombs, etc.)
金牌		jīnpái	*n*	gold medal
洋节	洋節	yáng jié		foreign festival/holiday
越来越	越來越	yuèláiyuè	*idiom*	more and more
调查	調查	diàochá	*v*	survey; investigate
重庆	重慶	Chóngqìng	*pn*	Chongqing (city)
哈尔滨	哈爾濱	Hā'ěrbīn	*pn*	Harbin (city)
母亲节	母親節	Mǔqīnjié	*pn*	Mother's Day
父亲节	父親節	Fùqīnjié	*pn*	Father's Day

三代同堂		sān dài tóng táng	*idiom*	three generations living under the same roof
家庭		jiātíng	*n*	family
小三口		xiǎo sān kǒu	*idiom*	small family with two parents and one child
消费	消費	xiāofèi	*v*	consume
超过	超過	chāoguò	*v*	surpass; exceed
经济大国	經濟大國	jīngjì dàguó		economic power
全球		quán qiú		whole world; globe
跨国公司	跨國公司	kuàguó gōngsī	*n*	multinational corporation
成		chéng	*n*	one-tenth
登陆	登陸	dēnglù	*vo*	land; disembark
迪士尼		Díshìní	*pn*	Disney
乐园	樂園	lèyuán	*n*	amusement park
将	將	jiāng	*adv*	about to
所见所闻	所見所聞	suǒjiàn-suǒwén	*idiom*	what one sees and hears

Grammar Notes
语法简注/語法簡注

1. 在……中：amidst; in the midst of

📖 中国在变化中。
中國在變化中。
China is in the midst of changes.

▶ 世界在变化中。
世界在變化中。
The world is in the midst of changes.

▶ 中国人的消费习惯在变化中。
中國人的消費習慣在變化中。
Chinese people's consumption habits are changing.

2. ……来/……來：It means "ever since" and is used after a time expression, indicating a period of time that extends from the past to this moment.

📖 二十多年来，中国的变化，连中国人自己也惊叹不已。
二十多年來，中國的變化，連中國人自己也驚嘆不已。
Even the Chinese people marvel at the great changes in the last twenty-plus years in China.

▶ 几年来他一直没回家过春节。
幾年來他一直沒回家過春節。
He hasn't gone home for the Spring Festival for the past a couple of years.

▶ 三天来，我一直忙得没时间打电话。
三天來，我一直忙得沒時間打電話。
For the last three days, I've been too busy to make any phone call.

3. 越来越/越來越：more and more + adjective/verb（多、好、高、大、挤/擠、漂亮、不客气/不客氣、没礼貌/沒禮貌、有钱/有錢、爱/愛、喜欢/喜歡）

📖 过"洋节"的中国人越来越多。
過"洋節"的中國人越來越多。
More and more Chinese people celebrate western holidays.

▶ 喜欢吃中国菜的美国人越来越多。
喜歡吃中國菜的美國人越來越多。
More and more Americans like Chinese food.

▶ 北京变得越来越挤。

北京變得越來越擠。

Beijing has become more and more crowded.

▶ 我越来越喜欢我的中文课。

我越來越喜歡我的中文課。

I like my Chinese class more and more.

4. 变成/變成：change to

📖 中国的家庭已经从“三代同堂”的大家庭变成“小三口”的小家庭。

中國的家庭已經從“三代同堂”的大家庭變成“小三口”的小家庭。

Chinese families have already changed from a big family with “three generations living under the same roof ” to a small family “with two parents and one child”.

▶ 她已经从小女孩变成大人了。

她已經從小女孩變成大人了。

She has already changed from a little girl to an adult.

▶ 中国正在变成经济大国。

中國正在變成經濟大國。

China is changing into an economic power.

5. NU+成：成 means “one-tenth” or “ten percent”.

📖 全球500强跨国公司，九成登陆。

全球500強跨國公司，九成登陸。

Ninty percent of the 500 top transnational corporations in the whole world have come to operate [in China].

▶ 大概七成的学生都喜欢我们的新课本。

大概七成的學生都喜歡我們的新課本。

About senventy percent of the students like our new textbook.

▶ 这个学校，四成的学生是中国人。

這個學校，四成的學生是中國人。

About fourty percent of the students in this school are Chinese.

6. 将/將：will

📖 迪士尼乐园将登陆上海。

迪士尼樂園將登陸上海。

The Disneyland will come to operate in Shanghai.

▶ 因为经济问题，明年美国人的消费将减少。

因爲經濟問題，明年美國人的消費將減少。

Because of economic problems, Americans' consumption will decrease next year.

▶ 中国将主办2008年的奥运会。

中國將主辦2008年的奥運會。

China will host the Olympic Games in 2008.

7. 那时候/那時候：at that time

📖 那时候，我再好好地给你们讲我在中国的所见所闻。

那時候，我再好好地給你們講我在中國的所見所聞。

At that time, I'll tell you thoroughly what I've seen and heard in China.

▶ 今晚我有宴会。那时候，我要和朋友们大吃特吃。

今晚我有宴會。那時候，我要和朋友們大吃特吃。

I'm having a banquet tonight. At that time, my friends and I will have a hearty meal.

▶ 下个月弟弟要去上海。那时候，他要给妈妈买很多东西。

下個月弟弟要去上海。那時候，他要給媽媽買很多東西。

Next month my younger brother is going to Shanghai. At that time, he'll buy a lot of things for Mom.

8. 再：After first doing one thing, the subject will then do another.

(S1)+ verb phrase + (以后/以後)，(S1) 再+ verb phrase

📖 回美国以后，我再给你们讲我在中国的见闻。

回美國以後，我再給你們講我在中國的見聞。

After going back to America, I'll tell you what I've seen and heard in China.

▶ 我想学完两年中文以后，再去中国。

我想學完兩年中文以後，再去中國。

I want to go to China after finishing two years' study of Chinese.

▶ 大学毕业以后，我想先工作两年再结婚。

大學畢業以後，我想先工作兩年再結婚。

After graduating from college, I want to work for two years before getting married.

9. 好好(儿)地/好好(兒)地 [hǎohāo(r) de]：to one's heart's content; all out

📖 好好(儿)地给你们讲我在中国的所见所闻。

好好(兒)地給你們講我在中國的所見所聞。

I'll tell you thoroughly what I've seen and heard in China.

▶ 这个星期天，我要好好儿地睡一天。

這個星期天，我要好好兒地睡一天。

I'm going to sleep (to my heart's content) for a whole day this Sunday.

▶ 奶奶拉着我的手说："让奶奶好好儿地看看你。"

奶奶拉着我的手說："讓奶奶好好兒地看看你。"

Holding my hand, Grandma said, "Let me take a good look at you."

▶ 她对你那么好，你得好好地谢谢她。

她對你那麼好，你得好好地謝謝她。

She's been so kind to you. You must thank her indeed.

▶ 王叔叔要开始讲故事了，请你们好好儿地听。

王叔叔要開始講故事了，請你們好好兒地聽。

Uncle Wang is starting to tell a story. Please listen attentively.

Note: Other examples of the reduplication of adjectives include: 慢慢(儿)/慢慢（兒）[mànmānr]，早早(儿)/早早（兒）[zǎozāor]，etc.

▶ 爷爷散步的时候总喜欢慢慢（儿）地走。

爺爺散步的時候總喜歡慢慢（兒）地走。

When he takes a walk, Grandpa always likes to walk slowly.

▶ 他今天不舒服，早早（儿）地就回家了。

他今天不舒服，早早（兒）地就回家了。

He didn't feel well today, so he went back home very early.

Reading Passage
阅读/閱讀

"玩儿了吗？"成为长春人最流行的问候语

细心人早已发现，中国人的见面问候语正在发生变化。以前，人们常说的"吃了吗"正在被"玩了吗"、"去哪儿玩"所代替。长春市一位姓苏的女士说："十一"放假，她和她丈夫接到的短信以及朋友见面时的问候语都是"玩了吗"，"去哪儿玩"。

一位姓王的老大爷说：他小时候，就盼着过年过节能吃顿好的。后来有了儿女，每到过年过节，他和老伴儿总要摆上一大桌，让一家人欢聚一堂，好好地吃一顿。但是现在不同了，好吃好喝已经一点儿也不新鲜了。他和老伴儿希望到北京、上海去看看。几年来，他们老两口儿几乎走遍了整个中国。今后，他们还打算到国外去看看。

“玩兒了嗎？”成爲長春人最流行的問候語

細心人早已發現，中國人的見面問候語正在發生變化。以前，人們常説的“吃了嗎”正在被“玩了嗎”、“去哪兒玩”所代替。長春市一位姓蘇的女士説：“十一”放假，她和她丈夫接到的短信以及朋友見面時的問候語都是“玩了嗎”，“去哪兒玩”。

一位姓王的老大爺説：他小時候，就盼着過年過節能吃頓好的。後來有了兒女，每到過年過節，他和老伴兒總要擺上一大桌，讓一家人歡聚一堂，好好地吃一頓。但是現在不同了，好吃好喝已經一點兒也不新鮮了。他和老伴兒希望到北京、上海去看看。幾年來，他們老兩口兒幾乎走遍了整個中國。今後，他們還打算到國外去看看。

细心	細心	xìxīn	careful; attentive
问候语	問候語	wènhòuyǔ	words of greeting
代替		dàitì	replace
放假期间	放假期間	fàngjià qījiān	during vacation
老伴儿	老伴兒	lǎobànr	(of an old couple) husband or wife
欢聚一堂	歡聚一堂	huānjù-yìtáng	happily gather under the same roof
新鲜	新鮮	xīnxiān	new; fresh; novel
老两口儿	老兩口兒	lǎo liǎng kǒur	old couple
几乎	幾乎	jīhū	almost
走遍		zǒubiàn	travel all over

判断正误/判斷正誤

Identify the following statements as true or false based on the reading passage.

1. _______ 以前，中国人见面问“吃了吗”。
2. _______ 现在中国人见面问“玩了吗”。
3. _______ 以前，中国人过年过节盼着吃顿好的。
4. _______ 现在中国人希望去旅游。

1. _______ 以前，中國人見面問“吃了嗎”。
2. _______ 現在中國人見面問“玩了嗎”。
3. _______ 以前，中國人過年過節盼着吃頓好的。
4. _______ 現在中國人希望去旅游。

Exercises
练习/練習

一、词语练习/詞語練習

Vocabulary exercise.

	Chinese Character	Pinyin	Make a Sentence of Your Own
1		dàgài	
2		zuìhòu	
3		jiéshù	
4		biànhuà	
5		guānniàn	
6		hǎohāo de	
7		yuèláiyuè	
8		suǒjiàn-suǒwén	

二、相关词语/相關詞語

Word analogy.

	Item	Synonym	Antonym
1	农村/農村		
2	开始/開始		
3	母亲节/母親節		
4	观念/觀念		
5	社会/社會		
6	中国节/中國節		

三、根据课文回答问题/根據課文回答問題

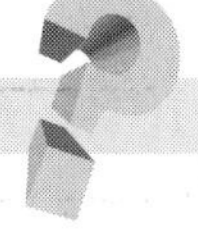

Answer the following questions using complete sentences based on information in the text.

1. 哥哥的实习什么时候结束？
2. 四五个星期的时间，哥哥对中国总的印象是什么？
3. 中国什么方面在变化？中国人对这些变化是怎么想的？
4. 中国是什么时候正式成为世界贸易组织成员的？
5. 2004年奥运会中国获得了多少块金牌，排名第几？

6. 中国人过不过“洋节”？有百分之几的人过洋节？
7. 中国的家庭从“三代同堂”变成了什么样的家庭？
8. 世界500强跨国公司有多少已经登陆中国了？
1. 哥哥的實習什麽時候結束？
2. 四五個星期的時間，哥哥對中國總的印象是什麽？

3. 中國什麽方面在變化？中國人對這些變化是怎麽想的？
4. 中國是什麽時候正式成爲世界貿易組織成員的？
5. 2004年奥運會中國獲得了多少塊金牌，排名第幾？
6. 中國人過不過“洋節”？有百分之幾的人過洋節？
7. 中國的家庭從“三代同堂”變成了什麽樣的家庭？
8. 世界500强跨國公司有多少已經登陸中國了？

四、填空

Fill in the blanks.

A. Fill in the blanks based on the text.

1. 时间过得真______，还有两三天我们四个星期的实习就要结______了。这大______也是我在中国发给你的最后一封电子邮______了。
2. 我对中国总的印______是：中国在变______中，中国人在变；不但中国人的生______方式在变，而且中国人的心______、观______也在变。
3. 二十多年来，中国的变化，就连中国人自己也 ______ ______不已。
1. 時間過得真______，還有兩三天我們四個星期的實習就要結______了。這大______也是我在中國發給你的最後一封電子郵______了。
2. 我對中國總的印______是：中國在變______中，中國人在變；不但中國人的生______方式在變，而且中國人的心______、觀______也在變。
3. 二十多年來，中國的變化，就連中國人自己也 ______ ______不已。

B. Complete the sentence based on the text.

1. 中国在______上获得32枚金牌。
2. 中国人现在过的节很多， 比如：______，______，______。
3. 现在除了看报，人们还能在______，______上看到报道。
4. 中国的家庭已经从“三代同堂”的大家庭变成“小______”的小家庭。
1. 中國在______上獲得32枚金牌。
2. 中國人現在過的節很多， 比如：______，______，______。
3. 現在除了看報，人們還能在______，______上看到報道。
4. 中國的家庭已經從“三代同堂”的大家庭變成“小______”的小家庭。

五、连线/連綫

Draw lines between two columns to match the information below.

1. 中国的农村在变：　现在中国人觉得生女儿跟生儿子一样好。
2. 中国人的观念在变：　现在很多中国年轻人不想结婚也不想要孩子。
3. 中国的城市在变：　现在很多农民[nóngmín]到城市找工作。
4. 中国的经济在变：　过年的时候，越来越多的中国家庭到饭馆儿去吃年饭了。
5. 中国的文化在变：　中国的私人公司越来越多，越来越大。
6. 中国的社会在变：　现在中国越来越多的家庭有汽车了。
7. 中国人的生活方式在变：现在年轻人活得越来越自我了。
8. 中国人的心理在变：　大城市里新的高楼越来越多。

1. 中國的農村在變：　現在中國人覺得生女兒跟生兒子一樣好。
2. 中國人的觀念在變：　現在很多中國年輕人不想結婚也不想要孩子。
3. 中國的城市在變　現在很多農民[nóngmín]到城市找工作。
4. 中國的經濟在變：　過年的時候，越來越多的中國家庭到飯館兒去吃年飯了。
5. 中國的文化在變：　中國的私人公司越來越多，越來越大。
6. 中國的社會在變：　現在中國越來越多的家庭有汽車了。
7. 中國人的生活方式在變：現在年輕人活得越來越自我了。
8. 中國人的心理在變：　大城市裏新的高樓越來越多。

六、改写/改寫

Rewrite the following sentences with the patterns in the parentheses.

1. 中国的农村在变，城市也在变。（不但……而且）
2. 宋宜凡的哥哥到中国两个星期以后，他告诉宋宜凡，中国人真多。（对……的印象）
3. 现在中国人觉得单身不是什么大问题了。（被……接受）
4. 现在不少农民到城里去找工作。（越来越……）
5. 在十个中国人中，有七个人是农民。（七成）

1. 中國的農村在變，城市也在變。（不但……而且）
2. 宋宜凡的哥哥到中國兩個星期以後，他告訴宋宜凡，中國人真多。（對……的印象）
3. 現在中國人覺得單身不是什麼大問題了。（被……接受）
4. 現在不少農民到城裏去找工作。（越來越……）
5. 在十個中國人中，有七個人是農民。（七成）

七、重组/重組

Word order.

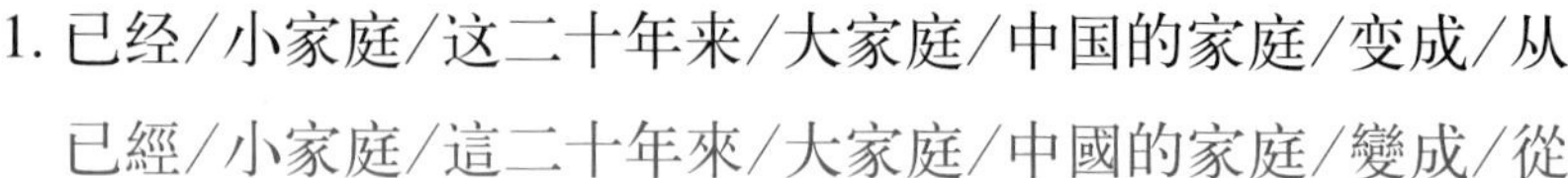

1. 已经/小家庭/这二十年来/大家庭/中国的家庭/变成/从
   已經/小家庭/這二十年來/大家庭/中國的家庭/變成/從
   Chinese families have changed from big families to small families during the past twenty years.

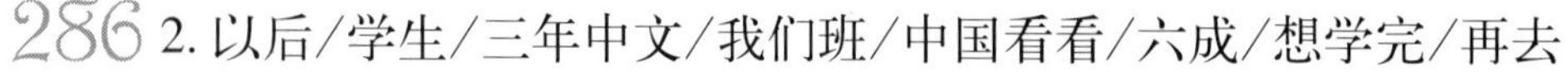

2. 以后/学生/三年中文/我们班/中国看看/六成/想学完/再去
   以後/學生/三年中文/我們班/中國看看/六成/想學完/再去
   Sixty percent of the students in our class want to study Chinese for three years, and then visit China.
3. 中国人/因为/的变化/据报道/中国各种消费/美国/消费习惯/已超过了
   中國人/因爲/的變化/據報導/中國各種消費/美國/消費習慣/已超過了
   It was reported that due to changes in Chinese people's habits in consumption, China has surpassed the US in every kind of consumption.
4. 不但/年轻人中/过情人节/被调查的/有八成/过圣诞节 /而且/在1500个
   不但/年輕人中/過情人節/被調查的/有八成/過聖誕節 /而且/在1500個
   Among the 1500 young people who have been surveyed, eighty percent of them celebrate not only Christmas but also Valentine's Day.
5. 金牌/让外国人/获得/2004年奥运会/惊叹不已/中国/那么多枚
   金牌/讓外國人/獲得/2004年奥運會/驚嘆不已/中國/那麼多枚
   Foreigners couldn't help marveling at the fact that China won so many gold medals in the Olympic Games 2004.

八、翻译/翻譯

Translate the following sentences into Chinese.

1. No matter which Chinese city you visit, you will discover that it has become more and more crowded in recent years.
2. I heard that China will become an economic power in two or three years. (use "jiāng")
3. After my internship in Beijing comes to an end, upon going back to the US, I will then tell my parents thoroughly my overall impression of China.
4. As discovered through a survey, western holidays have become more and more popular among young Chinese people.
5. Because the average Chinese people have become more and more wealthy, nowadays more

and more Chinese people would like to visit other countries.

6. For the last one to two decades not only Chinese people's ways of life are changing but also the mentality and concepts of the Chinese are changing.

九、改错/改錯

Correct mistakes.

1. 这大概是我在中国最后一封电子邮件发给你的了。
2. 四五星期的时间，我给中国的印象是：中国变化中。
3. 中国城市不但变，农村而且也变。
4. 不但中国人的生活方式在变，中国人的心理、观念也在变。
5. 下面是我从“谷歌”和 “雅虎”看的一些报道。
6. “洋节”被中国人接受越来越多。
7. 中国正在变经济大国。

1. 這大概是我在中國最後一封電子郵件發給你的了。
2. 四五星期的時間，我給中國的印象是：中國變化中。
3. 中國城市不但變，農村而且也變。
4. 不但中國人的生活方式在變，中國人的心理、觀念也在變。
5. 下面是我從“谷歌”和“雅虎”看的一些報道。
6. “洋節”被中國人接受越來越多。
7. 中國正在變經濟大國。

十、课堂活动/課堂活動

In-class activity.

Find relevant information online and give a presentation about one or two changes in China.

十一、课外活动/課外活動

After-class activity.

Give a presentation about some changes in Chinese people's habits that you hear about or find online.

十二、写作练习／寫作練習

Writing.

Task: Write an invitation email to all of your friends. The invitation should contain at least 200 characters and include the following information.

1. Who you are inviting.
2. The event, venue, time and your contact information.
3. Directions to the party.
4. What you have prepared for the party, such as food or activities.

For example:

亲爱的朋友们：

你们好！

特邀请各位三月五日（星期六）十二点来我家，一起观看[guānkàn]“湖人队[Húrénduì]”和“热浪队[Rèlàngduì]”的比赛[bǐsài]。

我将为大家提供[tígòng]六十四寸电视[diànshì]、各种[gèzhǒng]饮料[yǐnliào]和点心。

方向和路线[lùxiàn]：

1. 从学校出发[chūfā]，从四号出口下五号高速公路[gāosù gōnglù]；
2. 下了高速公路后往[wàng]北[běi]拐[guǎi]，也就是往左[zuǒ]拐；
3. 过三个红绿灯[hónglǜdēng]，再后往西[xī]拐，也就是往右[yòu]拐；
4. 右拐以后，往前开五分钟，你就会看到一个红房子，房号是1688。那就是我家。

有问题请打我的手机[shǒujī]：1-888-888-8888

星期六见！

你们忠实的朋友：笨笨

二月二十八号

親愛的朋友們：

你們好！

特邀請各位三月五日（星期六）十二點來我家，一起觀看[guānkàn]“湖人隊[Húrénduì]”和“熱浪隊[Rèlàngduì]”的比賽[bǐsài]。

我將爲大家提供[tígòng]六十四寸電視[diànshì]、各種[gèzhǒng]飲料[yǐnliào]和點心。

方向和路綫[lùxiàn]：

1. 從學校出發[chūfā]，從四號出口下五號高速公路[gāosù gōnglù]；
2. 下了高速公路後往[wàng]北[běi]拐[guǎi]，也就是往左[zuǒ]拐；

3. 過三個紅緑燈[hónglǜdēng]，再後往西[xī]拐，也就是往右[yòu]拐；

4. 右拐以後，往前開五分鐘，你就會看到一個紅房子，房號是1688。那就是我家。

有問題請打我的手機[shǒujī]：1-888-888-8888

星期六見！

你們忠實的朋友：笨笨

二月二十八號

十三、总结/總結

Summary.

1. Choose 5-10 of your favorite new vocabulary words from the text or reading material.

2. Quote 3-7 of your favorite sentences from the text or reading material here.

	Original sentence	Translation of the sentence (or make a new sentence of your own)
1		
2		
3		
4		
5		

3. From this lesson, you have learned Chinese culture, history, and philosophy. They have helped you to understand,

① 我现在清楚了/我現在清楚了：__________

② 我现在明白了/我現在明白了：__________

③ 我现在知道了/我現在知道了：__________

字词复习（三）/字詞複習（三）

请你找一找，从十一课到十六课，你学过的带下列偏旁部首的字。

請你找一找，從十一課到十六課，你學過的帶下列偏旁部首的字。

Find characters with the following radicals from Lesson 11 to Lesson 16.

1. 禾 ____________________

2. 足⻊ ____________________

3. 金钅 ____________________

4. 寸 ____________________

5. ⺍ ____________________

6. 耂 ____________________

7. 夂 ____________________

8. 長长 ____________________

9. 食饣 ____________________

10. 辶 ____________________

11. 冖 ____________________

12. 冫 ____________________

13. 衤 ____________________

14. 阝 ____________________

15. 夂

16. 灬

17. 刂

18. 求

19. 車车

20. 頁页

21. 氣气

22. 黑

23. 又

24. 今

25. 只

26. 斤

27. 弓

28. 毛

29. 少

30. 户

31. 欠

32. 廴

生词索引 VOCABULARY INDEX 生詞索引

A

阿姨		āyí	*n*	aunt; mother's sister; (a form of address for a woman of one's mother's generation)	L 14
啊		a	*particle*	(used after forms of address or at the end of interrogative sentences)	L 2
矮		ǎi	*adj*	short (in stature); low (in height)	L 2
爱	愛	ài	*v*	love; like; be apt (to do)	L 2
安排		ānpái	*v*	arrange; plan	L 13
按		àn	*prep*	according to; in accordance with	L 6
奥运会	奧運會	Àoyùnhuì	*n*	Olympic Games (abbreviation for Àolínpǐkè Yùndònghuì)	L 16

B

八点	八點	bādiǎn	*nu*	eight o'clock	L 1
把		bǎ	*prep*	(used to advance the object of a verb to the position before it)	L 5
爸爸		bàba	*n*	dad; pa	L 2
吧		ba	*particle*	(used at the end of a declarative sentence to indicate uncertainty)	L 2
白		bái	*pn/n*	(a surname); white	L 14
百分之		bǎifēn zhī		percentage	L 8
百家姓		Bǎijiāxìng	*pn*	*Book of China's Family Names* (literally, "a hundred surnames")	L 9
摆	擺	bǎi	*v*	arrange; lay; put	L 12
搬		bān	*v*	move; remove	L 3
搬家		bānjiā	*vo*	move (house); relocate	L 12

办法	辦法	bànfǎ	*n*	way; means	L 1
帮忙	幫忙	bāngmáng	*v/n*	help	L 12
包		bāo	*n*	bag; sack; package	L 11
饱	飽	bǎo	*adj*	full	L 12
报道	報道	bàodào	*n/v*	news report; report (on)	L 16
报告	報告	bàogào	*n/v*	report	L 15
报纸	報紙	bàozhǐ	*n*	newspaper	L 8
北京		Běijīng	*pn*	Beijing	L 10
背		bèi	*v*	recite from memory; learn by heart	L 5
倍		bèi	*m*	time; fold	L 6
被		bèi	*prep*	by (used in the passive voice to introduce the doer of the action)	L 10
辈	輩	bèi	*n*	generation in the family	L 14
比		bǐ	*v/prep*	compare; contrast; than	L 4
比较	比較	bǐjiào	*adv/v*	relatively; compare	L 7
比如		bǐrú	*v*	for example	L 15
毕业	畢業	bìyè	*v*	graduate; finish school	L 12
编	編	biān	*v*	make up; fabricate	L 12
遍		biàn	*m*	(for actions) once through; one time	L 5
变化	變化	biànhuà	*v*	change	L 16
表达	表達	biǎodá	*v*	express	L 12
表示		biǎoshì	*v*	express; show	L 15
表现	表現	biǎoxiàn	*v*	show; display; behave	L 15
别		bié	*pron*	other; another	L 8
别人		biérén	*pron*	other people; others	L 14
并		bìng	*conj*	and; furthermore	L 5
病		bìng	*n*	illness	L 13
不		bù	*adv*	not; no	L 1
不错	不錯	bùcuò	*adj*	correct; right; not bad; pretty good	L 8
不但		bùdàn	*conj*	not only... (but also...)	L 10
不断	不斷	bùduàn	*adv*	constantly; continuously	L 7
不敢		bùgǎn	*aux*	dare not	L 11
不管		bùguǎn	*conj*	no matter (what, who, when, where, how)	L 14
不过	不過	bùguò	*adv*	only; merely; no more than	L 8
不好意思		bù hǎoyìsi	*idiom*	feel embarrassed; feel sorry	L 15

不同		bùtóng	*adj*	different; distinct	L 10
不亦乐乎	不亦樂乎	bù yì lè hū	*idiom*	Isn't it a pleasure?	L 12
不用		bùyòng	*adv*	need not	L 4

C

才	纔	cái	*adv*	only; just	L 1
彩色		cǎisè	*n*	multicolor; color	L 10
菜		cài	*n*	dish; course; vegetable	L 4
菜名		cài míng		name of a dish	L 5
餐厅	餐廳	cāntīng	*n*	dining hall; restaurant	L 4
厕所	厠所	cèsuǒ	*n*	toilet	L 11
茶		chá	*n*	tea	L 9
查		chá	*v*	check; examine; look up	L 9
差		chà	*adj*	differ from	L 15
差不多		chàbuduō	*adj*	similar	L 6
常常		chángcháng	*adv*	often	L 3
常见	常見	cháng jiàn		common; be commonly seen	L 9
常用		cháng yòng		often used; in common use	L 8
长城	長城	Chángchéng	*pn*	Great Wall	L 14
长江	長江	Chángjiāng	*pn*	Yangtze River	L 7
超过	超過	chāoguò	*v*	surpass; exceed	L 16
朝代		cháodài	*n*	dynasty	L 7
车厢	車廂	chēxiāng	*n*	carriage (of a train); railroad car	L 11
称呼	稱呼	chēnghu	*n*	form of address	L 13
称谓	稱謂	chēngwèi	*n*	form of address	L 13
成		chéng	*v*	become; turn into	L 5
			n	one-tenth	L 16
成立		chénglì	*v*	found; establish	L 7
成为	成爲	chéngwéi	*v*	become; turn into	L 16
成员	成員	chéngyuán	*n*	member	L 16
城市		chéngshì	*n*	city; town	L 11
吃		chī	*v*	eat; have	L 2
重庆	重慶	Chóngqìng	*pn*	Chongqing (city)	L 16

出来	出來	chūlai	*vc*	come out; (used as a complement after a verb to indicate an outward movement or result)	L 5
出生		chūshēng	*v*	be born	L 1
出手		chūshǒu	*vo*	give out; dispose of	L 15
除了……以外		chúle yǐwài		except; besides	L 13
穿		chuān	*v*	wear; put on (clothes, shoes, etc.)	L 10
传统	傳統	chuántǒng	*n*	tradition	L 14
春节	春節	Chūnjié	*n*	Lunar New Year; Spring Festival	L 11
次		cì	*m*	time; occurrence	L 3
从	從	cóng	*prep*	from	L 1
从古到今	從古到今	cónggǔ-dàojīn	*idiom*	from ancient times to the present	L 15
从小	從小	cóng xiǎo		since childhood	L 9
错误	錯誤	cuòwù	*n*	mistake; error	L 11

D

答应	答應	dāying	*v*	answer; respond	L 13
打		dǎ	*v*	make (a phone call); hit	L 3
打(印)		dǎ(yìn)	*v*	print	L 5
打开	打開	dǎkāi	*vc*	open; uncover	L 10
打仗		dǎzhàng	*vo*	fight a battle; wage war	L 7
打招呼		dǎ zhāohu		greet; say hello to	L 13
大概		dàgài	*adv*	probably	L 16
大哥		dà gē		eldest brother	L 14
大家		dàjiā	*pron*	all of us; everybody	L 5
大姐		dà jiě		eldest sister	L 14
大开眼界	大開眼界	dàkāi-yǎnjiè	*idiom*	open a new horizon (to sb)	L 10
大拇指		dàmǔzhǐ	*n*	thumb	L 5
大学	大學	dàxué	*n*	college; university	L 1
大学生	大學生	dàxuéshēng	*n*	college or university student	L 1
大约	大約	dàyuē	*adv*	approximately; about	L 6
大夫		dàifu	*n*	physician; doctor	L 13
代表		dàibiǎo	*n/v*	representative; represent	L 10

带	帶	dài	*v*	take; bring	L 7
戴		dài	*v*	wear; put on (hats, gloves, glasses, etc.)	L 10
单单	單單	dāndān	*adv*	alone; only	L 12
但是		dànshì	*conj*	but; however	L 3
当时	當時	dāngshí	*n*	that time	L 11
当事人	當事人	dāngshìrén	*n*	party (to a lawsuit); person involved	L 12
到		dào	*v*	arrive; reach; (a directional preposition or a resultative verb complement)	L 3
到处	到處	dàochù	*n*	everywhere	L 11
到底		dàodǐ	*adv*	at last; on earth (used in question for emphasis)	L 6
得体	得體	détǐ	*adj*	appropriate	L 14
得		děi de	*aux* *particle*	must; have to (structural particle used after a verb or adjective to introduce a complement)	L 1 L 4
地		de	*particle*	(an adverbial particle)	L 5
的		de	*particle*	(a particle indicating possession or modification)	L 1
登陆	登陸	dēnglù	*vo*	land; disembark	L 16
等		děng	*particle*	and so on; and so forth; etc.	L 7
迪士尼		Díshìní	*pn*	Disney	L 16
第		dì	*pref*	(a prefix for ordinal number)	L 1
弟弟		dìdi	*n*	younger brother	L 14
地位		dìwèi	*n*	status; position	L 14
第一		dì-yī		the first	L 1
点	點	diǎn	*v* *n*	select; choose decimal point	L 5 L 8
点菜	點菜	diǎn cài		order dishes	L 5
点头	點頭	diǎntóu	*vo*	nod one's head	L 5
点心	點心	diǎnxin	*n*	dim sum; pastry; dessert	L 9
电话	電話	diànhuà	*n*	telephone; phone call	L 2
电脑	電腦	diànnǎo	*n*	computer	L 2
电子邮件	電子郵件	diànzǐ yóujiàn		email	L 5
调查	調查	diàochá	*v*	survey; investigate	L 16
跌破眼镜	跌破眼鏡	diēpò-yǎnjìng	*idiom*	come as a surprise	L 16
订	訂	dìng	*v*	reserve; order; book	L 5
东西	東西	dōngxi	*n*	thing; stuff	L 4

都		dōu	*adv*	all; both; every	L 2
独特	獨特	dútè	*adj*	unique; distinctive	L 10
肚子		dùzi	*n*	belly; abdomen	L 12
段		duàn	*m*	period (of time); section	L 3
堆		duī	*v/n*	pile up; heap up; pile; heap	L 11
对	對	duì	*prep*	to; towards	L 8
顿	頓	dùn	*m*	(measure word for meals)	L 12
多		duō	*adj*	many; much; more	L 1
多么	多麼	duōme	*adv*	no matter how; however	L 11
多少		duōshao	*pron*	how many; how much	L 8
多谢	多謝	duō xiè		thanks a lot	L 9

E

儿子	兒子	érzi	*n*	son	L 13
而		ér	*conj*	and; as well as	L 13
而且		érqiě	*conj*	and; but also	L 10
二月		èryuè	*n*	February	L 11

F

发	發	fā	*v*	deliver; send out	L 5
发音	發音	fāyīn	*n/vo*	pronunciation; pronounce	L 5
凡凡		Fánfan	*pn*	(a given name)	L 1
犯		fàn	*v*	commit; make (a mistake)	L 11
饭	飯	fàn	*n*	meal; cooked rice	L 2
饭菜	飯菜	fàncài	*n*	meal; food	L 9
饭馆	飯館	fànguǎn	*n*	small restaurant	L 6
方面		fāngmiàn	*n*	aspect	L 16
方式		fāngshì	*n*	way; mode	L 12
房子		fángzi	*n*	house; building	L 6
放下		fàngxia	*vc*	lay/put down	L 2
飞	飛	fēi	*v*	fly	L 3
非常		fēicháng	*adv*	very; extremely	L 10

风俗	風俗	fēngsú	*n*	custom	L 10
封		fēng	*m*	(for sth enveloped)	L 16
逢年过节	逢年過節	féngnián-guòjié	*idiom*	on New Year's Day and other festivals	L 12
缝	縫	fèng	*n*	a narrow opening; crack; fissure	L 5
否则	否則	fǒuzé	*conj*	otherwise	L 14
服务员	服務員	fúwùyuán	*n*	attendant; waiter/waitress	L 9
附近		fùjìn	*n/adj*	vicinity; nearby; neighboring	L 5
父亲节	父親節	Fùqīnjié	*pn*	Father's Day	L 16
复姓	複姓	fùxìng	*n*	compound surname	L 9

G

干杯	乾杯	gānbēi	*vo*	drink a toast; cheers	L 12
感恩节	感恩節	Gǎn'ēnjié	*pn*	Thanksgiving Day	L 10
感情		gǎnqíng	*n*	feeling; emotion; affection	L 12
赶快	趕快	gǎnkuài	*adv*	quickly; hastily	L 3
赶上	趕上	gǎnshàng	*v*	be in time for; overtake	L 11
刚	剛	gāng	*adv*	just; just now	L 2
高		gāo	*adj*	tall; high	L 2
高兴	高興	gāoxìng	*adj*	glad; happy; cheerful	L 5
高中		gāozhōng	*n*	high school	L 8
告诉	告訴	gàosu	*v*	tell (someone); inform	L 3
哥哥		gēge	*n*	elder brother	L 2
个	個	gè	*m*	(a generic measure word)	L 1
个子	個子	gèzi	*n*	height; stature	L 2
各		gè	*n*	each; every; all	L 9
各个	各個	gègè	*pron*	each; every; all	L 16
给	給	gěi	*v/prep*	give; by; with; to	L 3
跟		gēn	*prep*	with	L 2
更		gèng	*adv*	more; even more	L 4
恭喜		gōngxǐ	*v*	congratulate	L 13
恭喜发财	恭喜發財	gōngxǐ-fācái	*idiom*	May you be prosperous!	L 13
公元		gōngyuán	*n*	AD (Christian era)	L 7
公园	公園	gōngyuán	*n*	park	L 7

工作		gōngzuò	*n*	work; job	L 12
狗		gǒu	*n*	dog	L 11
够	夠	gòu	*v*	be enough; reach (a standard)	L 15
谷歌		Gǔgē	*pn*	Google	L 16
故事		gùshi	*n*	story; tale	L 3
观念	觀念	guānniàn	*n*	concept; idea	L 16
关心	關心	guānxīn	*v*	be concerned about	L 13
管		guǎn	*v*	control; discipline	L 4
广州	廣州	Guǎngzhōu	*pn*	Guangzhou, the capital of Guangdong Province	L 11
国家	國家	guójiā	*n*	country; nation	L 6
过	過	guò	*v*	spend (time); cross; pass	L 1
过道	過道	guòdào	*n*	passageway; corridor	L 11
过奖	過獎	guòjiǎng	*v*	overpraise; flatter	L 15
过来	過來	guòlai	*v*	come here	L 8
过去	過去	guòqu	*v*	pass (by); go over; (used after a verb to indicate motion away from the speaker)	L 13
过生日	過生日	guò shēngrì		celebrate one's birthday	L 12

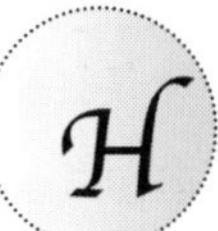

哈尔滨	哈爾濱	Hā'ěrbīn	*pn*	Harbin (city)	L 16
汉	漢	Hàn	*pn*	Han Dynasty (206 BC—220 AD)	L 7
汉字	漢字	hànzì	*n*	Chinese character	L 8
汉族	漢族	Hànzú	*n*	Han ethnic group	L 10
好		hǎo	*adj*	good; fine; nice; (used to express approval, conclusion, discontent, etc.)	L 1
			v	so as to; so that	L 3
好吃的		hǎo chī de		delicious food	L 3
好看		hǎokàn	*adj*	good-looking	L 15
号	號	hào	*n*	date; number in a series	L 11
喝		hē	*v*	drink	L 7
和		hé	*conj*	and	L 2
很		hěn	*adv*	very; quite	L 1
红白喜事	紅白喜事	hóng-bái xǐshì	*idiom*	weddings and funerals	L 12

互相		hùxiāng	*adv*	each other; mutually	L 13
花		huā	*v/n*	spend; flower	L 4
话	話	huà	*n*	talk; word; what somebody says	L 2
欢迎	歡迎	huānyíng	*v*	welcome	L 15
还	還	hái	*adv*	still	L 1
还是	還是	háishi	*conj*	or	L 6
黄河		Huánghé	*pn*	Yellow River	L 7
晃		huàng	*v*	shake; sway	L 13
回答		huídá	*n/v*	reply; answer; response	L 9
回到		huídào	*vc*	return; go back	L 2
回家		huíjiā	*vo*	come/return home	L 3
回来	回來	huílai	*vc*	return; come back	L 2
回族		Huízú	*pn*	Hui ethnic group	L 10
会	會	huì	*aux*	be likely to; can; be able to; be good at	L 6
活动	活動	huódòng	*n*	activity	L 13
火车	火車	huǒchē	*n*	train	L 11
或者		huòzhě	*adv/conj*	perhaps; or; either...or...	L 11
获	獲	huò	*v*	obtain; win	L 16

J

机会	機會	jīhuì	*n*	opportunity	L 12
几	幾	jǐ	*nu*	several	L 8
几十	幾十	jǐ shí		tens; dozens	L 10
挤	擠	jǐ	*v*	crowd; cram	L 11
计算	計算	jìsuàn	*v*	count; calculate	L 6
记	記	jì	*v*	commit to memory; remember	L 8
记得	記得	jìde	*vc*	remember	L 3
既然		jìrán	*conj*	since; now that	L 12
寄		jì	*v*	send; mail; post	L 10
加		jiā	*v*	add	L 14
夹	夾	jiā	*v*	place in between	L 10
家		jiā	*n*	family; home	L 2
家人		jiārén	*n*	family member	L 3

家庭		jiātíng	*n*	family	L 16
减价	減價	jiǎnjià	*vo*	reduce the price; mark down	L 15
简	簡	Jiǎn	*pn*	(a surname)	L 14
简介	簡介	jiǎnjiè	*n*	brief introduction; synopsis	L 10
见	見	jiàn	*v*	meet; see; meet with	L 3
建立		jiànlì	*v*	build; establish; found	L 7
健在		jiànzài	*v*	(of a person of advanced age) be still living and in good health	L 3
江		Jiāng	*pn*	(a surname)	L 14
将	將	jiāng	*adv*	about to	L 16
讲	講	jiǎng	*v*	say; speak; tell	L 3
讲话	講話	jiǎnghuà	*vo*	speak; talk	L 15
交		jiāo	*v*	associate with; be friend	L 4
交流		jiāoliú	*v*	exchange	L 12
脚		jiǎo	*n*	foot; feet	L 11
叫		jiào	*v*	ask; order	L 1
叫做		jiàozuò	*v*	be known as; be called	L 10
教授		jiàoshòu	*n*	professor	L 14
教养	教養	jiàoyǎng	*n*	education; upbringing	L 14
接		jiē	*v*	receive	L 2
接风	接風	jiēfēng	*vo*	give a dinner of welcome (to a visitor from afar)	L 5
接受		jiēshòu	*v*	accept	L 15
街		jiē	*n*	street	L 15
结婚	結婚	jiéhūn	*vo*	marry; get married	L 2
结束	結束	jiéshù	*v*	end; finish; conclude	L 7
姐姐		jiějie	*n*	elder sister	L 14
借		jiè	*v*	borrow; lend; make use of	L 12
今天		jīntiān	*n*	today	L 1
今晚		jīn wǎn		this evening; tonight	L 12
金牌		jīnpái	*n*	gold medal	L 16
经济	經濟	jīngjì	*n*	economy	L 16
经济大国	經濟大國	jīngjì dàguó		economic power	L 16
经理	經理	jīnglǐ	*n*	manager	L 9
经历	經歷	jīnglì	*v/n*	go through; undergo; experience	L 7

惊叹不已	驚嘆不已	jīngtàn bùyǐ	*idom*	wonder at sth greatly	L 16
纠正	糾正	jiūzhèng	*v*	correct; rectify	L 5
九百		jiǔbǎi	*nu*	nine hundred	L 6
酒		jiǔ	*n*	wine; liquor	L 12
酒吧		jiǔbā	*n*	(wine) bar	L 15
就		jiù	*adv*	as early as; already; at once; in a moment	L 1
就要		jiùyào	*adv*	about to; going to	L 1
举	舉	jǔ	*v*	raise; lift	L 13
据说	據說	jùshuō	*v*	it is said; allegedly	L 8
聚		jù	*v*	get together; gather	L 12
觉得	覺得	juéde	*v*	think; feel	L 1

K

开口	開口	kāikǒu	*vo*	open one's mouth; start to talk	L 9
开始	開始	kāishǐ	*v*	begin; start	L 7
开玩笑	開玩笑	kāi wánxiào		joke; make a joke	L 15
开心	開心	kāixīn	*adj*	happy	L 4
看		kàn	*v*	think; look at; read	L 2
看见	看見	kànjiàn	*vc*	catch sight of; see	L 8
可		kě	*adv*	indeed; very (used in a declarative sentence for emphasis)	L 7
可是		kěshì	*conj*	but; however	L 6
可以		kěyǐ	*v*	can; may; be able to	L 13
客厅	客廳	kètīng	*n*	living room	L 6
课	課	kè	*n*	L	L 1
孔子		Kǒngzǐ	*pn*	Confucius	L 15
口		kǒu	*m*	(for mouthfuls, persons, etc.)	L 7
夸	誇	kuā	*v*	praise; boast	L 15
跨国公司	跨國公司	kuàguó gōngsī	*n*	multinational corporation	L 16
快		kuài	*adj/adv*	quick; fast	L 4
筷子		kuàizi	*n*	chopsticks	L 2

L

拉		lā	*v*	pull; draw; shake (hands)	L 4
来	來	lái	*v*	come; arrive	L 1
唠叨	嘮叨	láodao	*v*	be garrulous; nag; chatter	L 4
老		lǎo	*adv/adj*	always; old; aged	L 1
老板	老闆	lǎobǎn	*n*	boss	L 14
老奶奶		lǎonǎinai	*n*	granny; great grandmother; (used by children in addressing an old woman)	L 14
老师	老師	lǎoshī	*n*	teacher	L 5
老爷爷	老爺爺	lǎoyéye	*n*	grandpa; great grandfather; (used by children in addressing an old man)	L 14
老远	老遠	lǎoyuǎn	*adv*	far away	L 13
姥姥		lǎolao	*n*	maternal grandma	L 3
姥爷	姥爺	lǎoye	*n*	maternal grandpa	L 3
乐	樂	lè	*adj*	happy	L 12
乐园	樂園	lèyuán	*n*	amusement park	L 16
离	離	lí	*v/prep*	leave; part from; be at a distance from	L 4
离不开	離不開	lí bu kāi		can't do without	L 12
礼貌	禮貌	lǐmào	*n*	politeness; manners	L 14
礼物	禮物	lǐwù	*n*	gift; present	L 15
李		Lǐ	*pn*	(a surname)	L 9
里	裏	lǐ	*n*	inside; inner	L 4
里边	裏邊	lǐbian	*n*	interior; inside	L 6
理由		lǐyóu	*n*	reason; excuse	L 12
历史	歷史	lìshǐ	*n*	history	L 7
两岸	兩岸	liǎng'àn	*n*	both banks (of the river)	L 7
聊天儿	聊天兒	liáotiānr	*vo*	chat	L 6
了		le	*particle*	(often used to indicate change of situation)	L 1
了不起		liǎobuqǐ	*idiom*	amazing; terrific; wonderful	L 15
另		lìng	*pron*	another; other	L 9
另外		lìngwài	*pron* *conj*	other; another in addition; besides	L 11 L 15
刘	劉	Liú	*pn*	(a surname)	L 14
六十		liùshí	*nu*	sixty	L 6

喽	嘍	lou	*particle*	(used to indicate certainty)	L 7
路上		lùshang	*n*	road; way	L 13
律师	律師	lǜshī	*n*	lawyer	L 14

M

妈妈	媽媽	māma	*n*	mom; ma	L 1
马	馬	Mǎ	*pn*	(a surname)	L 13
吗	嗎	ma	*particle*	(interrogative particle at the end of a sentence)	L 2
嘛		ma	*particle*	(used to indicate that something is obvious)	L 4
买	買	mǎi	*v*	buy	L 12
满	滿	mǎn	*adj*	full (of)	L 11
满意	滿意	mǎnyì	*adj*	be satisfied; be pleased	L 9
慢		màn	*adj*	slow	L 9
忙来忙去	忙來忙去	mánglái-mángqù	*idiom*	be busy doing this and that	L 9
毛笔	毛筆	máobǐ	*n*	Chinese writing brush	L 8
毛笔字	毛筆字	máobǐzì	*n*	characters written with a writing brush	L 8
没		méi	*adv*	not have; be without	L 1
枚		méi	*m*	(used in connection with coins, stamps, bombs, etc.)	L 16
每		měi	*pron*	each; every	L 3
每天		měitiān	*adv*	every day	L 4
美德		měidé	*n*	virtue	L 15
美国	美國	Měiguó	*pn*	United States of America (USA)	L 1
美国人	美國人	Měiguórén	*pn*	American	L 1
妹妹		mèimei	*n*	younger sister	L 14
蒙古族		Ménggǔzú	*pn*	Mongolian ethnic group	L 10
眯		mī	*v*	narrow one's eyes	L 5
免不了		miǎnbuliǎo	*idiom*	be unavoidable; be bound to be	L 15
面积	面積	miànjī	*n*	surface area	L 6
民族		mínzú	*n*	ethnic group	L 10
名不正，则言不顺	名不正，則言不順	míng bù zhèng, zé yán bù shùn	*idiom*	If names be not correct, language is not in accordance with the truth of things.	L 14

名字		míngzi	*n*	name or given name	L 8
明		Míng	*pn*	Ming Dynasty (1368–1644)	L 7
明白		míngbai	*v/adj*	know; understand; realize; clear	L 10
明天		míngtiān	*n*	tomorrow	L 14
母亲节	母親節	Mǔqīnjié	*pn*	Mother's Day	L 16

N

拿		ná	*v*	present; show; hold; take	L 15
哪里	哪裏	nǎli	*pron*	(a polite response to a compliment)	L 15
那		nà	*conj/ pron*	in that case; that	L 2
那些		nàxiē	*pron*	those	L 1
奶奶		nǎinai	*n*	paternal grandma	L 1
难	難	nán	*adj*	difficult; hard; troublesome	L 8
难上难	難上難	nánshàngnán	*idiom*	be extremely difficult	L 11
呢		ne	*particle*	(used at the end of interrogative sentences to indicate special, altemative or rhetorical question)	L 4
能		néng	*aux*	can; be able to	L 2
你		nǐ	*pron*	you	L 1
年		nián	*n*	year	L 3
年长	年長	niánzhǎng	*adj*	senior; older in age	L 14
年轻	年輕	niánqīng	*adj*	young	L 14
念		niàn	*v*	read aloud; study; attend school	L 5
您		nín	*pron*	you (polite singular)	L 1
农村	農村	nóngcūn	*n*	rural area; the countryside	L 16

O

噢		ō	*int*	oh (indicating realization)	L 4

P

爬		pá	*v*	climb	L 14

排		pái	*v*	put in order	L 9
盼		pàn	*v*	long for; look forward to	L 3
跑		pǎo	*v*	run; run away; escape	L 4
陪		péi	*v*	keep (someone) company; accompany	L 7
朋		péng	*n*	friend	L 12
朋友		péngyou	*n*	friend	L 1
批评	批評	pīpíng	*v/n*	criticize; criticism	L 15
漂亮		piàoliang	*adj*	beautiful	L 15
平辈	平輩	píngbèi	*n*	person of the same generation	L 14
平方公里		píngfāng gōnglǐ		square kilometer	L 6
平平		Píngping	*pn*	(a given name)	L 2
平时	平時	píngshí	*adv*	ordinarily; normally	L 2
瓶		píng	*n/m*	bottle	L 12
普通列车	普通列車	pǔtōng lièchē		local train	L 11

其实	其實	qíshí	*adv*	actually; in fact; as a matter of fact	L 6
其他		qítā	*pron*	others; else	L 10
其中		qízhōng	*n*	within; among them	L 8
起		qǐ	*v*	rise; get up; start (used before a noun of time or place preceded by 从 or 由)	L 1
起床		qǐchuáng	*vo*	get up; get out of bed	L 1
起来	起來	qǐlai	*v*	(used after a verb or an adjective to indicate the beginning and continuation of an action)	L 6
千		qiān	*n*	thousand	L 7
千万	千萬	qiānwàn	*adv/nu*	be sure to; must; ten million	L 14
谦虚	謙虛	qiānxū	*n*	modesty	L 15
前边	前邊	qiánbian	*n*	front	L 14
钱	錢	qián	*n*	money	L 4
强调	强調	qiángdiào	*v*	stress; emphasize	L 13
敲门	敲門	qiāomén	*vo*	knock the door	L 13
亲朋好友	親朋好友	qīnpéng-hǎoyǒu	*idiom*	relatives and friends	L 12

亲戚	親戚	qīnqi	*n*	relative	L 12
亲属	親屬	qīnshǔ	*n*	relatives	L 14
秦朝		Qíncháo	*pn*	Qin Dynasty (221 BC—206 BC)	L 7
秦始皇		Qín Shǐhuáng	*pn*	the first emperor of Qin Dynasty	L 7
清		Qīng	*pn*	Qing Dynasty (1616—1911)	L 7
清楚		qīngchu	*v*	know; be aware of	L 1
情人节	情人節	Qíngrénjié	*n*	Valentine's Day	L 13
请	請	qǐng	*v*	request; ask (a favor); please	L 5
请教	請教	qǐngjiào	*v*	consult; seek advice (from someone)	L 8
请问	請問	qǐngwèn	*v*	excuse me; it may be asked	L 9
庆祝	慶祝	qìngzhù	*v*	celebrate	L 12
求人		qiúrén	*vo*	ask for help	L 12
去		qù	*v*	go to; leave for	L 2
去世		qùshì	*v*	die; pass away	L 3
全		quán	*n*	whole; entire	L 3
全国	全國	quán guó		whole nation/country	L 10
全球		quán qiú		whole world; globe	L 16
却		què	*adv*	but; yet	L 6

R

然后	然後	ránhòu	*conj*	then; afterwards; after that	L 5
让	讓	ràng	*v*	allow; let	L 4
人口		rénkǒu	*n*	human population	L 6
人们	人們	rénmen	*n*	people	L 11
人山人海		rénshān-rénhǎi	*idiom*	hordes of people; huge crowds of people	L 11
人数	人數	rénshù	*n*	number of people	L 10
认识	認識	rènshi	*v*	know; recognize; be acquainted with	L 8
认为	認爲	rènwéi	*v*	think; consider; deem	L 14
任		rèn	*v*	assume; take up	L 7
容易		róngyì	*adj*	easy; likely; liable	L 8
如		rú	*v*	such as; for example	L 13
如果		rúguǒ	*conj*	if; in case; in the event of	L 8
入境		rùjìng	*vo*	enter a country	L 11

S

三代同堂		sān dài tóng táng	*idiom*	three generations living under the same roof	L 16
三国	三國	Sānguó	*pn*	Three Kingdoms (220—280): Wei (220—265), Shu (221—263), and Wu (222—280)	L 7
三人行，必有我师	三人行，必有我師	sān rén xíng, bì yǒu wǒ shī	*idiom*	Where there are three people walking together, one of them must be qualified to be my teacher.	L 15
三十		sānshí	*nu*	thirty	L 6
散步		sànbù	*vo*	take a walk; go for a walk/stroll	L 7
商业	商業	shāngyè	*n*	business; commerce	L 13
上		shàng	*adj/v*	preceding; previous; go to; leave for	L 3
上班		shàngbān	*vo*	go to work	L 2
上海		Shànghǎi	*pn*	Shanghai	L 3
上级	上級	shàngjí	*n*	higher level; higher authority	L 13
少		shǎo	*adj*	few; little; less	L 10
少不了		shǎobuliǎo	*idiom*	can't do without; be indispensable	L 12
少数民族	少數民族	shǎoshù mínzú	*n*	minority ethnic group	L 10
社会	社會	shèhuì	*n*	society	L 16
社交		shèjiāo	*n*	social exchanges	L 14
甚至		shènzhì	*conj*	even; so much so that	L 12
升级	陞級	shēngjí	*vo*	go up one grade; promote to a higher grade	L 12
生孩子		shēng háizi		give birth to a baby	L 12
生活		shēnghuó	*n/v*	life; livelihood; live	L 4
生人		shēngrén	*n*	stranger	L 14
声	聲	shēng	*n/m*	sound; (used for sounds)	L 13
圣诞节	聖誕節	Shèngdànjié	*pn*	Christmas	L 10
剩下		shèngxia	*vc*	be left (over); remain	L 7
十		shí	*nu*	ten	L 3
十八九		shíbā-jiǔ	*nu*	eighteen or nineteen	L 6
十三		shísān	*nu*	thirteen	L 6
什么	什麼	shénme	*pron*	what	L 2
什么的	什麼的	shénmede	*pron*	and so on; thing like that	L 12

时代广场	時代廣場	Shídài Guǎngchǎng	*n*	Times Square	L 11
时候	時候	shíhou	*n*	time; moment	L 2
时间	時間	shíjiān	*n*	(concept of) time; (duration of) time	L 3
实习	實習	shíxí	*v*	practice; do fieldwork	L 10
史		Shǐ	*pn*	(a surname)	L 14
使用		shǐyòng	*v*	use; make use of	L 13
世界		shìjiè	*n*	world	L 6
世界贸易组织	世界貿易組織	Shìjiè Màoyì Zǔzhī	*pn*	World Trade Organization	L 16
式		shì	*n*	form; style	L 13
事		shì	*n*	matter; affair; thing	L 4
事后	事後	shìhòu	*n*	after the event; afterwards	L 12
事情		shìqing	*n*	thing; affair; matter	L 4
是		shì	*v*	be	L 1
收		shōu	*v*	receive; accept	L 10
手		shǒu	*n*	hand	L 4
守		shǒu	*v*	stay with	L 2
首先		shǒuxiān	*adv/conj*	first; first of all	L 5
受		shòu	*v*	receive	L 15
叔叔		shūshu	*n*	uncle; father's younger brother; (used as a form of address for a man of one's father's generation but younger than one's father)	L 14
舒服		shūfu	*adj*	comfortable	L 11
熟人		shúrén	*n*	acquaintance	L 13
竖	豎	shù	*v*	set upright; erect	L 5
双方	雙方	shuāngfāng	*n*	both sides	L 13
谁	誰	shéi	*pron*	who; someone; anyone	L 12
水		shuǐ	*n*	water	L 7
睡		shuì	*v*	sleep	L 1
睡觉	睡覺	shuìjiào	*v*	sleep	L 4
说	説	shuō	*v*	speak; say	L 1
说话	説話	shuōhuà	*vo*	speak; talk	L 2
司马	司馬	Sīmǎ	*pn*	(a compound surname)	L 9
思想家		sīxiǎngjiā	*n*	thinker	L 15

宋		Sòng	*pn*	Song Dynasty (960—1279)	L 7
送礼	送禮	sònglǐ	*vo*	give as a present	L 15
算是		suànshì	*v*	count as; be considered as	L 13
隋		Suí	*pn*	Sui Dynasty (581—618)	L 7
孙中山	孫中山	Sūn Zhōngshān	*pn*	Sun Yat-sen, the founder of the Republic of China	L 7
所见所闻	所見所聞	suǒjiàn-suǒwén	*idiom*	what one sees and hears	L 16
所以		suǒyǐ	*conj*	so; therefore; as a result	L 11
所有		suǒyǒu	*adj*	all	L 12

T

他		tā	*pron*	he; him	L 2
她		tā	*pron*	she; her	L 3
他们	他們	tāmen	*pron*	they	L 3
他人		tārén	*pron*	other people	L 14
它们	它們	tāmen	*pron*	they; them	L 5
台北	臺北	Táiběi	*pn*	Taipei	L 3
唐		Táng	*pn*	Tang Dynasty (618—907)	L 7
特别		tèbié	*adj/adv*	special; especially; particularly	L 2
提前		tíqián	*v*	do sth in advance	L 11
天		tiān	*n*	day	L 2
条	條	tiáo	*m*	(used for something long, narrow or thin)	L 5
贴	貼	tiē	*v*	keep close to; paste	L 11
听	聽	tīng	*v*	listen to; hear	L 3
听说	聽說	tīngshuō	*v*	hear about	L 6
停		tíng	*v*	stop; halt; pause	L 5
停下		tíngxia	*vc*	stop; pause	L 8
通常		tōngcháng	*adv*	generally	L 13
同事		tóngshì	*n*	colleague; fellow worker	L 14
同学	同學	tóngxué	*n*	schoolmate	L 8
统一	統一	tǒngyī	*v*	unify; unite	L 7
头衔	頭銜	tóuxián	*n*	title	L 13

图片	圖片	túpiàn	*n*	picture; photograph	L 10
推		tuī	*v*	push	L 9
退休		tuìxiū	*v*	retire	L 3

哇		wa	*int*	ah; oh (used to express surprise)	L 10
外国	外國	wàiguó	*n*	foreign country	L 16
完		wán	*v*	run out; use up (used at the end of a verb as a resultative complement); finish; complete	L 4
晚辈	晚輩	wǎnbèi	*n*	younger generation; one's junior	L 13
晚上		wǎnshang	*n*	evening; night	L 1
万	萬	wàn	*nu*	ten thousand	L 6
万事如意	萬事如意	wànshì-rúyì	*idiom*	everything is as one wishes	L 11
网上	網上	wǎngshàng		online; on the internet	L 9
忘		wàng	*v*	forget	L 7
微笑		wēixiào	*v/n*	smile	L 13
为了	爲了	wèile	*conj*	for; for the sake of; in order to	L 5
维吾尔族	維吾爾族	Wéiwú'ěrzú	*pn*	Uygur ethnic group	L 10
位		wèi	*m*	(used to refer to people)	L 9
喂		wèi	*int*	hello	L 2
文化		wénhuà	*n*	culture	L 12
文化课	文化課	wénhuàkè	*n*	culture course	L 13
文字		wénzì	*n*	character; writing; written language	L 10
问	問	wèn	*v*	ask; inquire	L 2
问长问短	問長問短	wèncháng-wènduǎn	*idiom*	take the trouble to make detailed enquiries	L 4
问路	問路	wènlù	*vo*	ask the way	L 14
问题	問題	wèntí	*n*	question; problem	L 15
我		wǒ	*pron*	I; me	L 1
我们	我們	wǒmen	*pron*	we; us	L 2
无论	無論	wúlùn	*conj*	whatever; however	L 13
无论如何	無論如何	wúlùn-rúhé	*idiom*	in any case; anyway	L 12
午饭	午飯	wǔfàn	*n*	lunch	L 8

X

西安		Xī'ān	*pn*	Xi'an, the capital of Shaanxi Province	L 11
希望		xīwàng	*v/n*	hope; wish	L 3
习惯	習慣	xíguàn	*n*	habit	L 10
喜欢	喜歡	xǐhuan	*v*	like; be fond of	L 5
下级	下級	xiàjí	*n*	subordinate	L 13
下课	下課	xiàkè	*vo*	dismiss a class; finish a class	L 3
下来	下來	xiàlai	*vc*	come down; (used after a verb to indicate the completion or result of an action)	L 5
下面		xiàmian	*n*	next	L 16
先		xiān	*adv*	first	L 11
先生		xiānsheng	*n*	Mr.; sir; one's husband	L 7
现在	現在	xiànzài	*n*	now; at present	L 3
相反		xiāngfǎn	*adj/adv*	opposite; contrary; on the contrary	L 15
相聚		xiāngjù	*v*	meet; gather	L 12
相遇		xiāngyù	*v*	meet	L 13
香港		Xiānggǎng	*pn*	Hong Kong	L 3
享受		xiǎngshòu	*v*	enjoy	L 12
响	響	xiǎng	*v/adj*	sound; ring; noisy	L 2
想		xiǎng	*v*	want/wish (to do sth); would like (to do sth); think	L 2
想法		xiǎngfǎ	*n*	idea; opinion	L 14
向		xiàng	*prep*	to; towards	L 9
像		xiàng	*v*	resemble; be like; such as	L 4
消费	消費	xiāofèi	*v*	consume	L 16
小		xiǎo	*adj*	small; little; young	L 3
小车	小車	xiǎochē	*n*	small cart	L 9
小妹		xiǎomèi	*n*	little sister; younger sister	L 5
小名		xiǎomíng	*n*	pet name for child	L 14
小三口		xiǎo sān kǒu	*idiom*	small family with two parents and one child	L 16
小声	小聲	xiǎoshēng	*n*	low voice	L 9
小时	小時	xiǎoshí	*n*	hour	L 7
小时候	小時候	xiǎoshíhou	*n*	childhood	L 3

小意思		xiǎoyìsi	*n*	small gift; keepsake	L 15
笑		xiào	*v*	smile; laugh	L 5
写	寫	xiě	*v*	write; compose; depict	L 8
心理		xīnlǐ	*n*	mentality; psychology	L 16
新		xīn	*adj*	new	L 4
新年		xīnnián	*pn*	New Year	L 10
信息		xìnxī	*n*	information	L 12
星期		xīngqī	*n*	week	L 1
星期天		xīngqītiān	*n*	Sunday	L 1
星期五		xīngqīwǔ	*n*	Friday	L 3
姓		xìng	*n/v*	surname; be surnamed	L 9
姓名		xìngmíng	*n*	name	L 14
休息		xiūxi	*v*	rest	L 14
许多	許多	xǔduō	*adj*	many; a lot of; much	L 10
选	選	xuǎn	*v*	choose; select; elect	L 4
学	學	xué	*v*	imitate; learn; study	L 1
学期	學期	xuéqī	*n*	school term; semester	L 10
学习	學習	xuéxí	*v*	study	L 4
学校	學校	xuéxiào	*n*	school; educational institution	L 4

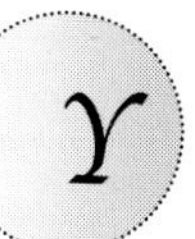

呀		ya	*particle*	(used at the end of a sentence to express agreement, defensiveness, urge, etc.)	L 4
雅虎		Yǎhǔ	*pn*	Yahoo	L 16
亚洲	亞洲	Yàzhōu	*pn*	Asia; Asian	L 6
研究		yánjiū	*v/n*	research	L 15
眼睛		yǎnjing	*n*	eye(s)	L 5
宴会	宴會	yànhuì	*n*	banquet; dinner party	L 12
洋节	洋節	yáng jié		foreign festival/holiday	L 16
样子	樣子	yàngzi	*n*	appearance; manner; shape	L 5
要		yào	*v/aux*	want; wish; be about; going to	L 1
要是		yàoshi	*conj*	if; suppose; in case	L 6
爷爷	爺爺	yéye	*n*	paternal grandpa	L 1
也		yě	*adv*	also; too	L 4

夜		yè	*n*	night; evening	L 11
一		yī	*nu*	one	L 1
一百		yībǎi	*nu*	one hundred	L 7
一边	一邊	yībiān	*conj*	while; as	L 7
一定		yīdìng	*adv*	surely; certainly; necessarily	L 8
一共		yīgòng	*adv*	altogether; in all	L 8
一连	一連	yīlián	*adv*	in a row; in succession	L 12
一路上		yílùshàng	*adv*	all the way; throughout the journey	L 11
一下		yīxià	*m*	one time; once; in a short while	L 7
一向		yīxiàng	*adv*	always	L 9
一些		yīxiē	*m*	a few; some	L 13
一样	一樣	yīyàng	*adj*	the same; equal; alike	L 4
一直到		yīzhí dào		until; up to	L 5
衣服		yīfu	*n*	clothing; clothes	L 15
已经	已經	yǐjing	*adv*	already	L 1
以后	以後	yǐhòu	*n*	after; afterwards	L 3
以前		yǐqián	*n*	earlier times	L 3
以上		yǐshàng	*n*	more than; over; above	L 10
以为	以爲	yǐwéi	*v*	consider; think	L 15
亿	億	yì	*nu*	a hundred million	L 6
异口同声	异口同聲	yìkǒu-tóngshēng	*idiom*	with one voice; in unison	L 9
意思		yìsi	*n*	meaning	L 11
因为	因爲	yīnwèi	*conj*	because	L 11
饮茶	飲茶	yǐnchá	*vo*	eat dim sum (literally, “drink tea”)	L 9
印象		yìnxiàng	*n*	impression	L 11
应该	應該	yīnggāi	*aux*	should; ought to	L 2
用		yòng	*v*	use	L 2
邮包	郵包	yóubāo	*n*	postal parcel	L 10
有		yǒu	*v*	have; possess; there is	L 3
有时候	有時候	yǒushíhou	*adv*	sometimes	L 4
又		yòu	*adv*	again; both...and	L 4
愉快		yúkuài	*adj*	happy; joyful	L 13
语言	語言	yǔyán	*n*	language	L 10
遇		yù	*v*	meet; encounter	L 12

元		Yuán	*pn*	Yuan Dynasty (1206—1368)	L 7
原来	原來	yuánlái	*adv/adj*	as it turns out; originally; original	L 4
远	遠	yuǎn	*adj*	far; distant; remote	L 4
远方	遠方	yuǎnfāng	*n*	distant place	L 12
月		yuè	*n*	month	L 1
月底		yuèdǐ	*n*	end of a month	L 4
越来越	越來越	yuèláiyuè	*idiom*	more and more	L 16

Z

再		zài	*adv*	once more; again	L 1
再见	再見	zàijiàn	*v*	goodbye; see you again	L 2
在		zài	*v/prep*	be (in a place); in; on; at	L 1
赞美	贊美	zànměi	*v*	praise	L 15
早点儿	早點兒	zǎodiǎnr	*adv*	earlier	L 3
早饭	早飯	zǎofàn	*n*	breakfast	L 7
早上		zǎoshang	*n*	morning	L 1
藏族		Zàngzú	*pn*	Tibetan ethnic group; the Tibetans	L 10
怎么	怎麼	zěnme	*pron*	how; what; why	L 9
怎么样	怎麼樣	zěnmeyàng	*pron*	how about; what about	L 4
占		zhàn	*v*	constitute; make up; account for	L 10
战国时期	戰國時期	Zhànguó Shíqī	*pn*	the Warring States Period (475 BC—221 BC)	L 7
站		zhàn	*v*	stand	L 11
张	張	zhāng	*m*	(measure word for tables, paper)	L 9
长辈	長輩	zhǎngbèi	*n*	elder generation; one's senior	L 13
长大	長大	zhǎng dà		grow up	L 1
招呼		zhāohu	*v*	greet; say hello to	L 13
招手		zhāoshǒu	*vo*	beckon; wave one's hand	L 13
找		zhǎo	*vc*	look for; try to find	L 12
这	這	zhè	*pron*	this	L 5
这儿	這兒	zhèr	*n*	here	L 11
这就是说	這就是說	zhè jiù shì shuō	*idiom*	this is to say...	L 6
这么	這麼	zhème	*adv*	so; such; like this	L 6
这么说吧	這麼說吧	zhìme shuō ba	*idiom*	put it this way	L 11
这些	這些	zhèxiē	*pron*	these	L 7

这样	這樣	zhèyàng	*pron*	so; such; like this; this way	L 7
着		zhe	*particle*	(indicating the continuation of an action or a situation)	L 2
真		zhēn	*adv/adj*	really; truly; indeed; real	L 1
真的		zhēnde	*adv*	truly	L 11
真是的		zhēnshìde	*idiom*	(expressing gentle displeasure or annoyance)	L 15
争论	爭論	zhēnglùn	*v*	dispute; argue; debate	L 6
整整		zhěngzhěng	*adv*	wholly; fully	L 11
正好		zhènghǎo	*adv*	just right; coincidentally	L 11
正在		zhèngzài	*adv*	in the process of; in the course of	L 8
政治		zhèngzhì	*n*	politics	L 16
之		zhī	*particle*	(used between an attribute and the word it modifies)	L 11
之间	之間	zhījiān	*n*	among; between	L 7
知道		zhīdào	*v*	know; be aware of	L 2
只		zhǐ	*adv*	only; just; merely	L 10
只是		zhǐshì	*adv*	only; just; merely	L 5
只要		zhǐyào	*conj*	if only; as long as	L 13
指		zhǐ	*v*	point at; point to	L 8
至少		zhìshǎo	*adv*	at (the) least	L 6
中		zhōng	*n*	inside	L 10
中餐馆	中餐館	zhōngcānguǎn	*n*	Chinese restaurant	L 5
中国	中國	Zhōngguó	*pn*	China	L 1
中国城	中國城	Zhōngguó-chéng	*n*	Chinatown	L 7
中国人	中國人	Zhōngguórén	*pn*	Chinese	L 1
中华民国	中華民國	Zhōnghuá Mínguó	*pn*	Republic of China (1912–1949)	L 7
中华人民共和国	中華人民共和國	Zhōnghuá Rénmín Gònghéguó	*pn*	People's Republic of China	L 7
中文		Zhōngwén	*pn*	Chinese language	L 1
中文角		Zhōngwénjiǎo	*n*	Chinese Corner	L 6
中午		zhōngwǔ	*n*	noon	L 9
种	種	zhǒng	*n*	type; kind	L 13

重要		zhòngyào	*adj*	important; significant	L 12
周末		zhōumò	*n*	weekend	L 3
主动	主動	zhǔdòng	*adj*	on one's own initiative	L 13
住		zhù	*v*	live; reside	L 3
祝		zhù	*v*	wish; express good wishes	L 11
祝愿	祝願	zhùyuàn	*n/v*	wish	L 13
转眼	轉眼	zhuǎnyǎn	*adv*	in the twinkling of an eye; in an instant	L 10
装	裝	zhuāng	*v*	load; hold; pack	L 10
壮族	壯族	Zhuàngzú	*pn*	Zhuang (Chuang) ethnic group	L 10
桌子		zhuōzi	*n*	table; desk	L 9
自		zì	*prep*	from	L 12
自高自大		zìgāo-zìdà	*idiom*	arrogant	L 15
自己		zìjǐ	*pron*	self; oneself	L 1
自由		zìyóu	*n/adj*	freedom; liberty; free	L 4
总	總	zǒng	*n*	chief; president (of a company)	L 14
总是	總是	zǒngshì	*adv*	always	L 3
总统	總統	zǒngtǒng	*n*	president	L 7
总之	總之	zǒngzhī	*conj*	in short	L 12
走		zǒu	*v*	walk; go; leave	L 7
祖父母		zǔfùmǔ	*n*	paternal grandparents	L 3
祖先		zǔxiān	*n*	ancestor	L 7
最		zuì	*adv*	most	L 4
最后	最後	zuìhòu	*adv*	finally; eventually	L 5
尊敬		zūnjìng	*v*	respect; honor	L 15
左右		zuǒyòu	*n*	about; or so; the left and right sides	L 10
作业	作業	zuòyè	*n*	homework	L 4
坐		zuò	*v*	sit; take a seat	L 6
座位		zuòwèi	*n*	seat	L 5
做		zuò	*v*	make; do; write	L 3
做梦	做夢	zuòmèng	*vo*	dream; have a dream	L 4
做主		zuòzhǔ	*vo*	decide; make the decision; have the final say	L 4